Developing Mental Toughness

Improving performance, wellbeing and positive behaviour in others

Peter Clough
Doug Strycharczyk

D1341517

KoganPage

LONDON PHILADELPHIA NEW DELHI

First published in Great Britain and the United States in 2012 by Kogan Page Limited.

Reprinted 2012 (twice), 2014

2nd Floor, 45 Gee Street
London EC1V 3RS
United Kingdom
www.koganpage.com

1518 Walnut Street, Suite 1100
Philadelphia PA 19102
USA

4737/23 Ansari Road
Daryaganj
New Delhi 110002
India

© Peter Clough and Doug Strycharczyk, 2012

The right of Peter Clough and Doug Strycharczyk to be identified as the authors of this work has been asserted by them in accordance with the Copyright, Designs and Patents Act 1988.

ISBN   978 0 7494 6377 9
E-ISBN   978 0 7494 6378 6

British Library Cataloguing-in-Publication Data

A CIP record for this book is available from the British Library.

Library of Congress Cataloging-in-Publication Data

Clough, Peter, 1949-
   Developing mental toughness : improving performance, wellbeing and positive behaviour in others / Peter Clough, Doug Strycharczyk.
      p. cm.
   Includes bibliographical references.
   ISBN 978-0-7494-6377-9 -- ISBN 978-0-7494-6378-6 1. Performance--Psychological aspects.
2. Stress (Psychology) 3. Toughness (Personality trait) I. Strycharczyk, Doug. II. Title.
   BF481.C57 2011
   155.2'4--dc23

                                                        2011027131

Typeset by Cenveo Publisher Services
Print production managed by Jellyfish
Printed and bound by Ashford Colour Press Ltd.

CONTENTS

PRAISE FOR
DEVELOPING
MENTAL TOUGHNESS

Mental toughness has emerged as an important concept which can be used to help individuals understand their own capacity, strengths and weakness and helps coaches, managers and leaders understand the problems individuals and organizations may face when dealing with change. This timely book is very welcome – it describes in a very practical way an idea which appears to have almost unlimited application.

David Eva is North West England Regional Manager of unionlearn (the TUC's learning and skills arm) and Chairman of CWP (an NHS Foundation Trust providing mental health, learning disability, addiction and community services).

ABOUT THE CONTRIBUTORS

Editors and key authors

Dr Peter Clough is a Chartered Sport and Exercise Psychologist and a Chartered Occupational Psychologist. He is a senior lecturer at the University of Hull. His main research interests are in performance in high-pressure environments. He is co-developer, with Keith Earle, of the mental toughness model and the MTQ48 mental toughness questionnaire.

Working with AQR, Peter is supervising the ongoing development of the world's first integrated psychometric measure for leadership style and behaviour, the ILM72, which maps to all major leadership models. Supported by the Institute of Leadership & Management, it was published in January 2008.

Peter's consultancy experience in the world of work embraces a wide variety of projects with major organizations in the UK and elsewhere including the design and implementation of assessment and development centres, workplace counselling, employee and culture surveys, leadership development and psychometric testing and training.

Peter's first degree is in Psychology and his master's degree (awarded by Sheffield University) is in Occupational Psychology. Peter earned his PhD at Aberdeen University. He can be contacted at P.J.Clough@hull.ac.uk.

Doug Strycharczyk has more than 30 years' experience in a variety of line, HR and consultancy roles with a number of global blue-chip businesses. In 1989 he founded AQR (as TCA Consultants) and he is the CEO of AQR Ltd – now recognized as one of the most innovative (and fast growing) test publishers in the world.

Doug's areas of expertise include development of psychometric tests and programmes, playing a key role in developing MTQ48 and ILM72, organizational development, senior management/leadership development and top team assessment. More recently, this role has led to work within the education sector. He is working at SE, FE and HE levels to develop programmes and approaches that attend to student wellbeing/satisfaction, employability, performance and transition.

Doug has co-authored with Dr Peter Clough chapters in the following leading books: *Psychometrics in Coaching* (2009; Kogan Page and Association for Coaching), *Leadership Coaching* (2010; Kogan Page and Association for Coaching) and *Coaching in Education* (2011).

Doug holds a first-class honours degree in Economics. He is a Fellow of the Chartered Institute of Personnel and Development and a member of the Institute of Leadership & Management. E-mail Doug at doug@aqr.co.uk.

About the contributors

Damian Allen is Executive Director of Children and Family Services for Knowsley Council. Damian led the first educational application of mental toughness in secondary schools and is a strong advocate of innovation in public services. He is the UK representative on the Cisco Global Education Leaders' Program (GELP), to which he has introduced MTQ48. Contact Damian via damian.allen@knowsley.gov.uk.

David Ayre is an Advisory Officer to the Children & Family Services Leadership Team in Knowsley. He has a BSc in Politics with Law (Aston), at which time he worked as a research assistant to a member of the UK Parliament, and an MA in Political Thought (Durham). He can be contacted at David.Ayre@knowsley.gov.uk.

Angela Clough is a Chartered Physiotherapist. She is a Senior Lecturer at the University of Hull. Her main applied work is in orthopaedic medicine and sports injuries. Her research focus is on the psycho-social aspects of injury. She has extensive experience as a practitioner and manager in the UK National Health Service. E-mail: A.Clough@hull.ac.uk.

Dr Lee Crust is a senior lecturer and researcher at the University of Lincoln. Lee is a BPS Chartered Sport and Exercise Psychologist, a Health Professions Council Practitioner Psychologist, and a Science Council Chartered Scientist. The majority of Lee's published research has concerned understanding what mental toughness is and how it develops in athletes.

Adrian Eagleson is a Director with TOWARD, a company that aims to build resilience through behavioural change. He has a background in organizational behaviour and occupational psychology. His interests lie in how resilience and psychological capital impact upon performance. He works with elite sports, senior leaders and executive boards to offset crisis and build sustainable leadership behaviours. Adrian can be contacted at adrian@towardconsulting.com.

Dr Fiona Earle is a Chartered Occupational Psychologist and Psychology Lecturer at the University of Hull working in the field of work and wellbeing. Fiona specializes in stress, workload and fatigue. With significant consultancy experience, she has expertise in the design of assessment centres, development of bespoke psychometric instruments and management development. E-mail Fiona at F.Earle@hull.ac.uk.

Dr Keith Earle is a Chartered Sport and Exercise Psychologist working as a senior lecturer at the University of Hull. He is both an active researcher and an applied sport psychologist, working with athletes from a wide range of sports. Keith is the co-developer with Dr Peter Clough of the mental toughness model. Contact Keith at K.Earle@hull.ac.uk.

Kieran Gordon is the Chief Executive of Greater Merseyside Connexions Partnership Limited. He has 30 years' experience of working with young people as a professionally trained careers adviser and in various management and leadership roles. He has worked closely with government at national, regional and local levels to raise the standard and profile of careers and related support services aimed at increasing aspirations, attainment and progression for individuals as they make the transition from school into and through working life. Kieran is also a Past President of the Institute of Career Guidance (ICG), which is a UK-wide body representing the interests of career guidance professionals. Contact Kieran at Kieran.Gordon@connexionslive.com.

Dr David Marchant is Senior Lecturer in Sport and Exercise Psychology at Edge Hill University. Before joining the Department of Sport and Physical Activity, David lectured in Sport, Exercise and Health Psychology at the University of Hull, where he worked closely with Peter Clough on a number of projects on mental toughness. David continues to carry out and publish research that embraces mental toughness, and can be contacted on David. Marchant@edgehill.ac.uk.

Dr Christian van Nieuwerburgh works as a Senior Lecturer in Coaching Psychology at UEL, where he specializes in coaching in education. He is currently involved in a number of research projects in schools and colleges and the impact of mental toughness training in schools leading to the formation of the International Centre for Coaching in Education. Christian can be contacted at christian@aqr.co.uk.

Johnny Parks is a Director with TOWARD, a company that aims to build resilience through behavioural change. His interests lie in how culture and individuals contribute to crisis and the role of the leader in building resilience. Johnny delivers the executive coaching programme within the University of Ulster MSc in Executive Leadership (Resiliency Programme). E-mail: johnny@towardconsulting.com.

Dr Craig Thomson has been Principal of Adam Smith College since it was created in August 2005. Prior to this, he was Principal of Glenrothes College, having taken up that post in 1999. Craig has worked variously in schools, further and higher education as teacher, manager, teacher trainer and researcher in Scotland, England and internationally. Contact Craig at CraigThomson@adamsmith.ac.uk.

ACKNOWLEDGEMENTS

The development of the mental toughness model with its universal application and the MTQ48 has been a long and often complex piece of work. We could not have done it without the support of an awful lot of people, many of whom have given their ideas, their time and their resources freely to enable us to explore new areas and fresh applications.

It has often seemed to us that we have learnt far more from our supporters than they have ever learnt from us. Many of these are identifiable as contributors to this book. There is a risk that there are others whom we don't formally mention but who have also played an important role. We thank them too and hope that they are not offended that we haven't singled them out for special mention.

We will single out one or two people who have encouraged and supported us in spreading the message as we develop globally: Stephen Fischer from Ecole Hoteliere de Lausanne, Dr Howard Reed, Director, Dubai Women's College (HCT), Bob Lillicrapp, Hult International Business School, and Dr Jim Knight, University of Kansas. Special thanks have to go to Dr Jonathan Passmore. Jonathan's experience and expertise in authorship have been invaluable, as has his support for our concept in general.

Internally at AQR, the whole team has provided support 'above and beyond the call of duty'. Helen Murray has done a sterling job in pulling together the book on our behalf. We are especially grateful to Doug's co-director Claudine Rowlands – for many years she really has been the hidden cornerstone in all of this work. If you want to see what mental toughness means in practice, look no further.

Finally, Peter offers his dedication to Angela, his wife, and Emily, his daughter – both are tough and sensitive.

Doug offers his to his wife Pauline and to his grandsons Jay and Charlie. They have helped him to find his sensitive side.

Introduction to the concept of MT

Success is not final, failure is not fatal: it is the courage to continue that counts. **WINSTON CHURCHILL**

The mental toughness (MT) concept has provided both of us with a truly remarkable journey and experience. What started as a small-scale academic adventure has blossomed into a truly global phenomenon – more about that a little later in this chapter.

Most applications for mental toughness in most sectors have proved to be valuable and worthwhile. What has emerged is the identification of a personality trait that appears to be extremely important in considering individual and organizational performance, wellbeing and the development of positive behaviours. All are crucially important in enabling people to deal with the pressures and challenge of modern life.

The first question to answer is, 'What is mental toughness?'

The 4 Cs model

Our work is based on a scientific investigation of mental toughness. Science is all about data and evidence. Reassuringly, the vast majority of the data is supportive, some might appear less so. This is the nature of applied psychology; individuals are complex and no model can encapsulate everything.

We define mental toughness as:

> The quality which determines in large part how people deal effectively with challenge, stressors and pressure ... irrespective of prevailing circumstances.

In the 4 Cs model the overall mental toughness is a product of four pillars:

1 *Challenge:* seeing challenge as an opportunity.
2 *Confidence:* having high levels of self-belief.
3 *Commitment:* being able to stick to tasks.
4 *Control:* believing that you control your destiny.

The model is described in great detail later in this book. Figure 1.1 provides an overview.

It's useful to understand how we arrived at this model. We adopted what researchers should recognize as a four-step science modelling process: read, create, test and develop, and evaluate.

1. Read, read and read some more

Initial work, mostly carried out with Dr Keith Earle, identified a major gap in the literature on mental toughness. Mental toughness was often referred to but rarely operationalized. It became a rather meaningless and empty truism. This type of 'need analysis' is the starting point of most research and development activity. This earlier work was useful in that it provided an insight into what others had imagined mental toughness and similar notions to be. The phrase 'standing on the shoulders of giants' is very apt: you learn from others and then develop their ideas based on your own knowledge and views. This is what happened here.

FIGURE 1.1 Mental toughness by Emily Clough, aged 9

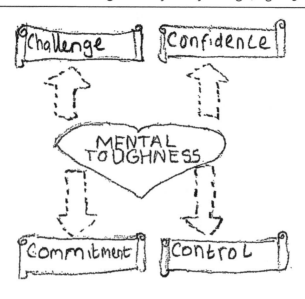

2. Create

This is the real joy of science. Creativity has two main strands:

a Convergent thinking – the structured approach
   Will it work?
   Can we do it?
   Have we got the resources?
   Is the timing right?
b Divergent thinking – the intuitive and paradigm shifting approach
   What if?
   Why not?
   What assumptions are at work?

Through these two strands a coherent and testable model emerges from the chaos.

3. Test and develop

This is at the heart of scientific research. If something is not directly testable then it does not sit well in the world of science. It should be possible to develop clear and testable hypotheses. These are then actioned and the model developed according to the answers that emerge.

4. Evaluate

When a final model is developed it needs to be evaluated. The key question here is, 'Does it really work?'

The next chapters of this book, substantially written by Dr Keith Earle, put flesh on the bones of this process. They show the time and care that went into the development of the model. It's neither a whim nor an existing concept. It is distinct and built upon sound psychological principles.

Once we had a concept we could present with confidence to others – practitioners and academics – we found that we would consistently be asked the same four key questions. In a way they are the obvious questions to ask and we learnt to call them 'the four big questions'. Providing an answer to these largely determines the structure of this book. The four big questions are:

1 Does mental toughness really exist?
2 Can it be measured?
3 Is it useful?
4 Can mental toughness be developed?

1 and 2. Does mental toughness exist and can it be measured?

The early part of the book is devoted to these vital questions. The short answer is – we believe mental toughness exists and we have solid evidence to back up that view. Moreover, we have developed the capability to measure mental toughness in a useful way. A longer and more thoughtful answer to these questions is provided in the early chapters in this book.

Too much popular psychology is merely predicated on an individual's subjective point of view – the person often emerging as some sort of 'guru'. There is a great deal of 'cod psychology' out there. Much of it faith-based: practitioners adopt these 'models' and 'approaches' on the basis of the flimsiest of evidence – and sometimes no evidence at all. Whilst our views have certainly created many of the hypotheses central to our work and have directed the research, it is important that they have been intertwined with the views and research findings of many others. We are committed to an evidence-based approach.

Chapters 2, 3, 4 and 5 of this book deal with the work's fundamental theoretical beginnings and the design and development of the MTQ48 measure. The following four chapters go into more detail about the 4 Cs, relating them to relevant psychological models. The 4 Cs model does not in any way negate these: it simply builds upon them.

3. Is it useful?

Doug trained as an economist and found his calling in the world of business, and Peter as an applied psychologist. What binds their philosophies together is the belief that things we do can and should impact on performance. It is therefore a driving mission that we show that knowing about and measuring mental toughness is more than simply an academic exercise. When answering the question of whether or not it works there are two main approaches.

First there are the technical aspects. Is it reliable, valid, and robust? Information about these is included in the first two chapters. Another way of looking at this question is to think about how the measure and model have been used and whether or not this has helped us understand why some people perform better than others. Secondly and an equally important consideration has been whether using the instrument has been effective in applied settings.

A number of diverse case studies have been included in the book to provide an answer to some of these points. We hope you find them interesting and useful. They include a review of research findings in peer-reviewed journals. The peer review process is the bedrock of true research: accepted papers are published solely on their merits, not by grace and favour. Other case studies focus on education and learning. They raise an important point. Our offering of mental toughness is a developmental concept: it is there to help people progress. The evidence overwhelmingly suggests that it does just that.

4. Can mental toughness be developed?

We believe it can. A good deal of practice in the sports world suggests that this is the case.

Is it nature or nurture? Evidence in this book shows that there is a clear genetic link in mental toughness. As everybody suspects, some people are born tough. This nature element is supported by recent findings relating to brain structure. Again this cutting-edge research is described here. Nevertheless, mental toughness levels can be changed. In the occupational section of this book there is an organizational case study that demonstrates that formal mental toughness training can work.

Most of the final part of the book is given over to techniques that can aid in mental toughness development. They are drawn from many areas of applied psychology and we have asked experts in areas such as relaxation, attention control and fatigue to provide chapters that help explain the processes involved.

Four fallacies about MT

In our many contacts we are regularly asked many other questions than the big four addressed above. These too are all good questions and must have an answer if the questioner is to be confident about mental toughness. While we can't answer every question that has ever been raised, or will be raised, in this book, we will attempt to address some of the more popular directly in this chapter. They all relate to what seem to us to be emerging fallacies.

We have sought to provide enough information throughout this book for readers to make their own informed choice. When teaching first-year undergraduate psychology students at the University of Hull, Peter continually stresses the importance of a questioning approach to psychological models. Just because someone says something with conviction it does not mean it is true. They need to provide evidence that is verifiable. We are confident we can do this for this concept.

Fallacy 1: Implicit in the model is the suggestion that everyone should be mentally tough

It is obvious that some people are tougher than others. We would argue that mentally tough individuals are better able to deal with high-pressure environments. Consequently they tend to do better at school, at work, at competitive sports, etc and are likely to excel in work assessment systems. However, it should be clearly noted that the opposite of mental toughness is mental sensitivity *not* mental weakness.

A mentally tough person will deal with stress, pressure and challenge by not letting it 'get to them'. Colloquially it is 'water off a duck's back'. A mentally sensitive person will feel the impact of stress, pressure and challenge and it will 'get to them' and they will feel some consequent response. They will be uncomfortable in some way.

A balanced society needs a mix of the sensitive and the tough. It is quite difficult to identify a highly successful yet sensitive elite sports person just as it can be equally hard to identify a tough-minded artist.

Please note that this does not mean that the mentally tough are not emotionally intelligent, whatever that may mean. Emotional intelligence (EI) describes a different kind of sensitivity – EI people are sensitive to what is happening around them and how others are responding to what they do. Emerging evidence suggests that mental toughness and emotional intelligence can, and often do, go hand in hand.

Whereas it might be generally true that the mentally tough seem to get a better deal in life – for instance they often earn more, they are more likely to get promoted, they are more likely to be materially successful – all we are saying here is that sensitive people find it harder to cope with the stressors and pressures of life. They are more likely to show some of the negative consequences of not being able to deal with life's changes and will often suffer from conditions such as depression and anxiety.

It is also clear to us that the techniques in this book can be helpful for everyone – the mentally sensitive as well as the mentally tough – in dealing with the world as they find it. Some people want to be tough. Others want to stay as they are, but they would also like to have a toolkit of skills to deal with some situations that prove difficult for them. There are many people who are successful in life on their own terms but who are mentally sensitive and not mentally tough.

In education mental toughness does provide an advantage – but it's certainly not the only, or even necessarily the most important thing for everyone. Measuring mental toughness allows teaching staff to provide the appropriate support for different types of individuals.

You may have noticed that Figure 1.1 was produced by Peter's daughter, Emily. She has always been interested in our work and the figure formed part of her presentation to her classmates entitled, 'What is wrong with being sensitive anyway?' Our short answer is, 'Nothing at all' but being mentally sensitive does make life a bit harder.

At the same time we know that mentally tough people are far from perfect – there are potential downsides to being mentally tough too, and these are covered in the chapters describing the 4 Cs. Everyone has development needs. A mentally tough individual may accidently bruise others by not fully recognizing the needs of a more sensitive individual and, through that, may adversely affect his or her own performance if that relies in part on the co-operation of others. Knowledge of what you are will always allow you to make better choices.

As ever, there are many ways of looking at this issue. In economics there is an interesting approach that sometimes enables us to ask the same question and get two different but helpful answers. Economists will talk about macroeconomics (the big picture) and microeconomics (the specific). So we can ask a global question – 'Should we have a more mentally tough society?' We might conclude that, as stated above, we would prefer a balanced society but we might argue for a small shift generally in one direction or another to secure a desirable benefit. A more specific question might be about our children or our work colleagues: would I like them to be more mentally tough? We might because we know they are likely to get a better deal in life and they are likely to achieve more. However, we also know that they can lead a satisfactory and fulfilling life whilst remaining comparatively mentally sensitive and we know that we can support them in this.

Fallacy 2: We are only interested in success at work or in sports

We are both drawn to performance enhancement and it can be easy to believe this is only related to things like output, sales, promotions, salaries and qualifications. In many situations these are very important but we are concerned with a much broader understanding of performance. When economists talk about creating wealth and distributing it, they generally talk about wealth in its widest sense. Wealth is the sum of everything that adds up to wellbeing and contentment.

In our mental toughness training programmes one emphasis is on the importance of goal setting. This could relate equally well to being the best parent or the happiest person in your town. Mental toughness does, of course, relate to achievement orientation, meaning that many mentally tough people are driven to rise to the top of their careers. However, this is not for everyone. As an example, Peter once worked with an elite swimmer on the fringes of international success. They worked together to develop her mental toughness with a good deal of success. The outcome? She decided to stop swimming and do something she wanted to do more instead! Just because you are good at something does not mean you want to do it. Through developing her mental toughness she was able to make better life choices for herself.

Fallacy 3: Mental toughness is a macho, male-dominated concept

At first sight this might appear to be true. However, when you consider this statement in the light of fallacy 2, it seems less true. Mental toughness is about being all you can be. Whilst competitive by nature, mentally tough individuals are often simply competitive with themselves. They are internally referenced.

There is very clear evidence from the many studies we have carried out that men and women are equally tough. There may be some differences in the coping systems adopted and the willingness to express their feelings but the underlying core toughness emerges from study after study as being identical.

Fallacy 4: Mentally tough people are uncaring and individualistic

This obviously relates to some extent to fallacy 3. Mentally tough individuals can function well in teams. Many elite sport people play in very cohesive team settings and they are undoubtedly mentally tough.

The idea that tough individuals are always domineering and unsupportive is simply not the case. Much bullying behaviour and petty sniping is a result of low self-esteem and insecurity. If you are tough, secure in your own skin, there is little need to prove your superiority by 'proving' the inferiority of others.

Defining and describing mental toughness

The first step is to begin the process of defining and describing mental toughness.

In our work we now run hundreds of workshops on mental toughness and, between us, we make at least 80 major presentations each year at conferences around the world. Quite often we will open a discussion about mental toughness without explaining to anyone precisely what we mean by the term. This is deliberate. We do it to make a point.

What we consistently find is that you can have a sensible discussion about mental toughness without a pre-agreed definition. The term is reasonably accessible and self-explanatory. Most people guess correctly that it is to do with mindset and on that basis they can usefully contribute to a discussion. However, there will nearly always come a point when the participants recognize that they may also be describing slightly different ideas. It will emerge that some will in fact be speaking about resilience; others will be talking about commitment and tenacity; yet others will be describing confidence in some form.

It is important to have a clear definition of mental toughness so that everyone can examine the concept from their own standpoint. One of the earliest steps in the development of the model and presenting it to the outside world was creating a clear, accessible and sensible definition of mental toughness. From that solid base most of the rest can follow.

Incidentally, there are still some who do not like the term 'mental toughness' although as it becomes better understood and used more frequently this is beginning to diminish. For better or for worse, for the present time, psychologists and practitioners in the various fields in which we work have accepted that 'mental toughness' is the correct and proper term for what we are about to describe.

The remainder of this chapter provides another perspective to the mental toughness story. It explains how we came to work on the concept and what provoked our interest. If you are impatient to get into the meat of the matter, skip these sections and move straight on to Chapter 2. You can return to this later.

This book explains and brings up to date everything that has emerged through research and application of the model and the measure. It is written with two audiences in mind. One consists of students of psychology who want to know about the concept, how it works, the evidence and how it relates to the rest of psychological thinking. The other consists of practitioners who are concerned with understanding it well enough to be able to use it effectively in their work. As far as we can we have written the book to be accessible to both audiences.

The beginnings

Here we describe how and why we became engaged with mental toughness – the 'penicillin of the people development business'.

In September 1996 we were running, at a hotel in Newport in South Wales, the first of a series of development centres designed for Her Majesty's Customs & Excise which would eventually embrace over 700 senior managers. In the evening when relaxing before reflecting on their day's work, Peter began to describe enthusiastically some work he had been carrying out in sports psychology. It revolved around a concept he called 'mental toughness' and it seemed to provide an explanation for a number of interesting things.

For instance, he suggested that this is why very talented athletes, sports people and teams can lose out to less able but apparently more successful opponents. This is not that uncommon. It is one of the elements that make sporting contests so interesting – it's not always the favourite who wins. There seemed to be factors involved in success and performance other than talent and raw ability. Peter spoke about confidence, challenge, emotional control and commitment and how these too play a part in sports success. He and a colleague, Keith Earle, had developed a simple 18-item questionnaire to measure some of this, which had delivered some promising results.

Later that evening they got down to the business of the day and began to analyse what they had observed with the dozen or so managers who had participated in the development centre exercises. Amongst those observations were things like:

- Some of the managers were clearly very able and exceptionally well qualified but didn't achieve as much as others.
- Some who were less knowledgeable were able to be surprisingly effective.
- Some appeared happy to be on the programme and were using every minute for their own benefit. Others were reluctant attendees.
- Some approached the events in the programme with real determination to achieve something. Other seemed to be fearful about their attendance.

As the review proceeded, both of us experienced a sense of déjà vu. A great deal of the observations about managerial behaviour echoed what had been described for the behaviour of athletes earlier, and they appeared to have similar implications. One immediate consequence was that Doug approached the organizers of the development centre programme with an idea. They agreed that we could introduce, into the battery of tests already being used in the centre, a short 'mental toughness' questionnaire purely for research purposes. Thus began a remarkable journey which has since taken a concept that was 'trapped' in one domain and steadily developed it into a concept that has universal application and has real significance for the performance, wellbeing and behaviour of most people in all walks of life.

By 2002 research had enabled Peter and Keith to pin down a robust definition of mental toughness and in 2003 Doug and AQR took it to the occupational market. In 2008 it was being used in the educational sector at secondary, further and higher education levels in Switzerland and the UK, and by 2011 it was being used in more than 40 countries worldwide. In 2010 the first pilots in health and social applications had begun. And of course the sports sector had consistently shown an interest – mostly supportive, sometimes challenging.

Doug has described it as the 'penicillin of the people development business'. Like Fleming's work, the discovery was almost accidental, the impact enormous. We have both found ourselves 'making a genuine difference' for a lot of people and organizations. We now work regularly in areas that we would never have guessed we would, or could. This includes working with the disadvantaged and the underprivileged as well as the more usual applications in the worlds of work, education and sport.

The mental toughness model we have developed, and its associated measure (the MTQ48), are nowadays discussed globally and hardly a week passes without us receiving comments and ideas about our work from around the world. We have had the genuine privilege of being involved with outstanding researchers, business people, educators, sports people and many others. This constant interaction has both consolidated and developed the model.

We have welcomed enquiry, comment and criticism – it has helped us to develop a better concept. We are especially interested to hear from readers who are interested in using the concept and the measure in some way.

Mental toughness provides an answer and solutions to many issues, but obviously not all. It is simply another tool to help enhance our understanding of behaviour and performance.

The importance of stress

02

DR KEITH EARLE

To fully understand the concept of mental toughness some background of the broader theoretical underpinnings of the stress literature is required, as these are closely related constructs. One could argue that a central component of mental toughness is how effectively one deals with potentially stressful situations. Within modern psychology the concept of stress remains a major focus of interest, with significant research efforts across a range of disciplines including work psychology, sports psychology, clinical psychology and health psychology.

The concept first emerged in the 18th century when the French physiologist Claude Bernard proposed that life was dependent on an organism maintaining an internal environment in a constant state during changes in the external environment. Bernard's recognition of the physiological need for balance between the internal state and the range of external variables formed the foundation of stress research. However, there was little conceptual advancement over the following century until the seminal work of Harvard physician Walter Cannon in the early 20th century.

Cannon continued to expand on the physiological perspective with his research on the roles of adrenalin and the autonomic nervous system in regulating and maintaining physiological balance. This research by Cannon (1929) led to the introduction of the key stress-related term 'homeostasis', which described the balance of physiological systems. Following on from this initial theorizing, Selye (1936, 1950) proposed what he called the 'general adaptation syndrome' (GAS), which has its foundation in the activation of the adrenal cortex in response to stress. Where Selye furthered the stress literature was in his proposition that changes in homeostasis were not just a response to alterations in the environment, but that an animal's physiological systems could be trained to maintain adaptive defences against potential exposure to stress. He suggested that 'conditioning factors', such as previous exposure and controllability of a stressor, could alter the GAS.

Furthermore, Selye proposed that stressors, including physical exercise, could possibly lead to cross-stressor adaptations that would develop resistance to psychosomatic and neurotic diseases.

Selye's recognition of the impact of previous exposure to stressors and the proposition of conditioning factors represented a significant advancement in the field of stress. These themes are central to our thesis and will be developed further later on in the chapter.

Since the 1950s, research interest in stress has continued to grow. While it has long been recognized that stressful situations have both psychological and physiological implications, developing a broadly accepted definition of stress has been difficult (Lazarus and Launier, 1978). However, there has been some broad agreement about the physiological and psychological correlates that indicate stress. Typical physiological changes include increased blood pressure, sweating, increased heart rate and a dry mouth, and psychological behaviours may range from aggression to social withdrawal (Tenenbaum, 1984). These symptoms and behaviours can either occur independently or together with stress emotions, which are the subjective responses, both physiological and behavioural, that the individual experiences. These may include responses such as happiness, fear and anxiety among many others (Holahan and Moos, 1990). Therefore, it is generally accepted that the condition of stress is associated with physiological changes, a range of psychological behaviours and changes at the subjective/emotional level.

Research strands

In addition to the ongoing and considerable research that has attempted to investigate fully the 'stress state' from physiological and psychological perspectives, three further and closely related strands of research have developed. Essentially, researchers have taken a range of contrasting perspectives and considered stress as either a response to certain conditions that can broadly be considered to be 'stress inducing', or as a causal factor in a range of performance-related variables. Therefore, the strands of research have included:

1 the situational factors that generate stress;
2 the consequences of the stress state for performance;
3 individual differences.

The third strand of research is focused on the existence and nature of any individual differences that may moderate the stress response – and it is this issue that relates most closely to the work reported in this book, as mental toughness should be considered to be a key individual difference which, in individuals, can significantly moderate the stress process.

Situational moderators of stress

As with all areas of research, the situational moderators of stress have been considered from a number of different perspectives, first with regard to the context, eg occupational settings or sporting settings, and secondly with a focus on the physiological changes associated with certain situational (or task-related) variables or the subjective experience.

From a physiological perspective, research carried out by Frankenhaeuser (1971) was particularly significant in exploring the physiological responses to a range of task-related variables. She found that responses in the adrenal glands were at their greatest when individuals were required to carry out tasks that are multifaceted, require quick decisions and when the individual has little control over the event in question. This highlighted three of the most widely considered stress-inducing factors in the occupational setting – aspects of workload, time pressure and control.

With regard to workload, Wickens (1986) has provided a framework for considering those tasks that are more likely to be stressful when combined. He based his model on the principle that we have a series of 'pools' of resources upon which we can draw to carry out information-processing tasks. Essentially, the model proposes that we will be less able to cope effectively with multiple tasks that draw on the same resources, eg two tasks that require auditory processing will clearly be more demanding (and therefore potentially stressful) than tasks that combine aspects of verbal and auditory processing.

Time pressure is a further factor that has been broadly accepted as an occupational stressor (Hackman and Oldham, 1976). This is clearly intuitive, as it is not difficult to imagine the increased subjective pressure associated with having too many things to do in not enough time.

With regard to the factor of control, this construct is a fundamental aspect of the occupational stress literature. The influential job design model of Hackman and Oldham (1976) and the demands-control model of Karasek (1979) both highlight the importance of control as a moderator of the work-stress relationship. However, the construct of control is a fuzzy one used in many different ways within psychology theory. For example, it is proposed as a personal need or drive, within motivational theory (eg Bandura, 1977) or as an individual difference in the need to exert control (Burger and Cooper, 1979). In the context of the Karasek, and Hackman and Oldham models, control refers primarily to employees having a high degree of decision latitude or autonomy over the way work tasks are managed.

While the issue of control will be returned to throughout this book, as this construct is an important component of mental toughness, the meaning of control here will refer more closely to control as an individual difference. This will be discussed in more detail later.

Stress and performance

A good deal of the research in stress and performance looks at situational moderators and considers stress from the response perspective – as an outcome of environmental conditions. Our work on mental toughness looks at the individual's perspective of stress as a causal factor. Stressors exist but they don't always give rise to stressed people. There is something in the way we each deal with stressors and pressure that moderates these.

Within this body of research, the concepts of stress, arousal and anxiety are closely linked and it is not unusual to find these terms used interchangeably. Nonetheless, the impact of these closely related constructs on performance is important from both practical and theoretical perspectives and in a wide range of contexts – sports, occupational, educational, health, social, etc.

It is therefore not surprising that this has been a major area of research that has led to the development of numerous theories that have been used, with varying degrees of success, to explain differential performance and suggest potential interventions to aid the functioning of certain tasks. The following section aims to highlight a number of important theoretical explanations regarding the impact of stress on performance.

Drive Theory

Early researchers in the field of performance psychology suggested that there was a direct and linear relationship between arousal and performance. This view was embodied in the work of Hull (1943, 1951). Hull proposed Drive Theory, a multifaceted stimulus-response theory of motivation and learning, which predicted that as drive (arousal) increased it brought about the elicitation of the 'dominant response'. In simple terms, as an individual's arousal level increases, so does the performance of that individual.

This somewhat simplistic explanation of the relationship between arousal and performance clearly does not fully explain the complex nature of the relationship. However, Drive Theory did highlight the important role of physiological arousal in performance and the theory obviously has implications for training and learning environments.

Inverted-U Theory

Further influential work in this field was undertaken by Yerkes and Dodson (1908) who developed the basic premise of Drive Theory and further examined the relationship between arousal and task difficulty and their effect on performance.

Initial findings were formulated into the Yerkes-Dodson law, which, in its simplest terms, proposed that as the complexity of a skill required to carry out an action increases, the amount of arousal required for peak performance decreases. We see this in all walks of life.

Irrespective of the type of skill involved, it is argued that performance always conforms to the inverted-U principle. There is a plethora of research documenting the inverted-U relationship between performance and arousal.

Building on the work of Yerkes and Dodson, Easterbrook (1959) attempted to explain this stress–performance relationship and theorized that, as arousal increases, attention narrows and it is a consequence of attentional narrowing that information (cues) are missed. It is argued that, at first, the cues missed are irrelevant ones, but as arousal increases, relevant cues are likely to be missed. Therefore, when arousal is low the presence of irrelevant cues is a distracting element and causes performance to diminish. At the optimal level of arousal only the irrelevant cues are removed and performance is subsequently high. When arousal is too high, attentional focus is narrow, and this results in both relevant and irrelevant cues being discarded. It is not difficult to see how this could lead to reduction in performance, as proposed by the inverted-U theory, and this clearly provides some explanation to the process that may underlie the stress–performance relationship.

It is interesting therefore to wonder why, given this early understanding, attentional control which may be an effective source of interventions for stress management and for mental toughness development should, until now, be generally so underdeveloped (except perhaps in the sports world where it is much valued).

Catastrophe Theory

Since the development of the inverted-U theory, a number of researchers and practitioners have criticized this simplistic explanation of the relationship between strain-related variables (stress, arousal and anxiety) and performance.

The basic tenets of the theory propose that relatively small increases in arousal have a proportionate effect on performance, either negatively or positively, and that optimal performance is obtained when arousal is moderate. However, the Catastrophe Theory, proposed by Fazey and Hardy (1988) brought a new perspective to bear and challenged both of these assumptions.

Fazey and Hardy proposed that when athletes are faced with debilitating stress, they encounter more dramatic decrements in performance (hence catastrophic in nature). They further suggest that small reductions in arousal do not bring the athletes back to their previous level of performance when under a similar amount of stress. This model clearly proposes a more complex relationship between stress and performance than accounted for in earlier models. A significant number of studies in the 1990s provided some support for this theory (eg, Hardy and Parfitt, 1991).

Individualized Zones of Optimal Functioning (IZOF)

Yuri Hanin (1980, 1986, 1997), again working with athletes, proposed that individual athletes have their own zone of optimal state anxiety within which they perform at their peak.

This theory differs in two ways from the inverted-U theory in that the optimal level of state anxiety differs from individual to individual and does not always occur on the midpoint of the continuum, and the optimal level of state anxiety is considered to be a bandwidth rather than a single point. With regard to the individual differences issues, this has real relevance in the field of applied psychology. If this optimum level of anxiety (stress level) can be determined it is then possible to manipulate, through psychological interventions, the athlete's level of anxiety that has been shown to correlate with optimal performance.

Flow Theory

This theory proposed by Csikszentmihalyi (1990) is closely related to the IZOF model in that it attempts to identify the optimal performance state for an individual (known as the 'flow' state). This state is one in which the performance of the task undertaken is done in an effortless and almost mystical manner. This theory supports anecdotal evidence from athletes and has been subject to research scrutiny for the past 15 years.

In particular, Jackson has produced a body of research examining the concept of flow in relation to sport and exercise (1992, 1995, 1996). She defines flow as 'a state of optimal experiencing involving total absorption in a task, and creating a state of consciousness where optimal levels of functioning often occur' (1995: 138). A further definition proposed by Csikszentmihalyi himself includes a loss of self-awareness (becoming one with the activity) and a loss of time awareness. While these models clearly have value in the way they describe an important subjective state, they fall short of providing an explanation of the broader stress process.

Individual moderators of the stress process

The latter models above do provide some recognition of the importance of individual differences in the stress process, rather than attempting to outline a 'stimulus response' model that suggests the individual is a passive respondent to the situation, and responds in a uniform manner to given stressors. More recent models of stress have placed the individual at the centre of the process, providing an active interaction with the situation (see Lazarus, 1993). In light of the importance such researchers place on the individual, a major goal within this field has been the identification of potential individual differences that can moderate the stress process.

Many factors have been considered including high trait anxiety and low self-esteem. Trait anxiety is a personality factor that predisposes an individual to view certain situations as more or less anxiety-provoking (Spielberger, 1983). Individuals with high trait anxiety will perceive events as being more threatening than individuals with lower trait anxiety. Mental toughness is potentially the most important individual difference in the stressor–strain relationship.

An applied perspective on mental toughness, stress management and peak performance

At the time we were beginning to work on applications of mental toughness in the occupational market there was a significant amount of interest and debate in stress management. This interest was largely due to the work of the Health and Safety Executive in the UK in developing a set of management standards for stress management. These standards are useful and welcome but they have a significant limitation as they focus solely on the role of the employer.

The employer is encouraged and required to minimize or eliminate stressors in the workplace. Of course, any good employer should seek to achieve this in order to have employees who don't become stressed in a way that affects their wellbeing or prevents their normal functioning. The inherent problem with this is that, as we have already noted, there is no definition of stress that is objectively measurable. A person is stressed if he or she says they are stressed. What we do know is that we can put two people of equal ability, knowledge, skill and experience into the same situation and they can respond differently. One will thrive and use the stressors as a motivator – the challenge acts as a stimulant and that person may perform exceptionally well. The other will perceive the situation in a completely different way. They may see only threat in the challenge in front of them and find themselves adversely stressed by that. They will probably underperform and may well attract a number of unwanted consequences.

Moreover, it is not always possible to significantly influence the situation. Many roles are inherently hazardous and potentially stressful. You can't tell a nurse that no patient will ever die or a police officer that criminals won't work at night or a fire officer that fires only break out on weekdays or a manager that no competitor will try to take their business, and so on. Life is stressful. From the moment we wake until we go to sleep we meet with a succession of stressors. Rather poetically we often describe people as 'swimming in a sea of stressors'. What matters is how we deal with stressors. We all do this differently and most of us have the capability to develop this. This is where the mental toughness concept is especially useful. It explains in large part how we deal with stressors.

Stress is a complex phenomenon that has a number of definitions. We have adopted the following:

> Stress is an adaptive response, mediated by individual characteristics and/or a psychological process, that is a consequence of any external action, situation or event that places special physical and/or psychological demands on a person.

The main themes encompassed by this definition are that:

- stress is not necessarily bad and is unavoidable;
- individuals react differently to the same stressors;
- stress can be physically and psychologically damaging.

There is a bewildering array of stress models but we find the work of Karasek (1979) provides the best understanding of organizational stress. This model concentrates on two components: 1) job demands (these cause stress), psychological stressors such as the requirement to work fast, having lots to do, working to targets, conflicting demands; and 2) job decision latitude (these help individuals deal with stress), workers' authority to make decisions, the variety of skills they use. An ideal job for most people will therefore involve high demands but will also give employees high degrees of operational freedom and a wide variety of activities that will allow them to use all their skills.

However, it is also the case that, as already noted, in many occupations stress is unavoidable – and is a feature of a culture or of the environment in which the organization operates. The challenge here is to identify stressors and to enable the organization and its staff to develop and implement coping strategies and mechanisms that help them handle their work without damage.

The stress definition and the following model developed by AQR provide the starting point for much of our work in this area.

The AQR stress model

Stress is most often a result of the combination of the impact of some stressor and the way that the individual responds to that stressor. It is how we respond that leads us either to feeling stressed or to achieving peak performance.

Stressors exist. They come from many sources. We will be the source of many in our own right. Some will arise from the close relationships we have in our work groups, family groups, social groups, etc. Other will come from the environment in which we work, learn, play, etc. Stressors can also arise from the general world in which we live and operate.

It is important to note here that one important group of stressors that can be self-imposed or imposed by others is the requirement to do well at something. It can be work performance (hitting a challenging sales target), academic performance (a piece of coursework), sports (achieving a personal best), etc. If we succeed in dealing with that particular stressor we find that we achieve peak performance.

Key factors that influence how we respond to stressors are shown in Figure 2.1 and include:

- Personality.
- Age – it seems there is a U-shaped curve here. The young and the old are better at dealing with stressors than the middle-aged.

FIGURE 2.1 AQR Stress Model

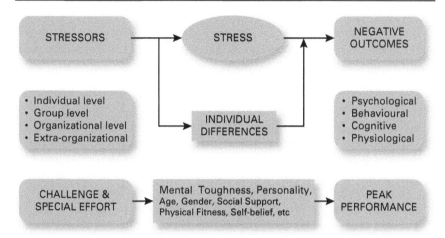

- Gender – females appear better able to deal with stressors: they are more likely to talk about them and this helps.
- Social support – family, friends, carers, etc all help you to deal with stressors.
- Fitness – fitness and exercise are effective moderators.
- Mental toughness.

Examples of sources of stress include:

- *Individual (from within)*. Conflict with others – especially role conflict; uncertainty and ambiguity – not knowing what is expected from you; your role overlaps with another's role; the extent to which you have control over your situation and you can make decisions; boredom and repetitive tasks; goals and targets – performance measures; your relationships with key people.
- *Group*. The behaviour of the group leader; the extent to which there is team cohesion; conflict and dissent within the group.
- *Organizational*. The prevailing culture; structure and processes – the extent to which these exist and the manner in which they are enforced; technology and the pace at which it is introduced; change; commercial and competitive pressures; values.
- *Extra-organizational*. The interface between life-work-family-leisure, etc; the state of the economy – one of the key influences on wellbeing; travel – time spent travelling especially to and from work; what is happening in society generally – crime, unemployment, etc.

Whether we are talking about education, the world of work, health, etc, all of these areas will have sources of stressors that emerge from those four broad headings.

If we are less effective at dealing with those stressors then there is potential for unwanted consequences of varying severity and impact. Broadly these can be grouped as follows:

- *Psychological:* low satisfaction and contentment; poor self-esteem; burnout; depression, etc.
- *Behavioural:* these are important – they commonly translate into measurable unwanted consequences that are damaging to the individual and to those around them. They can include absenteeism – poor attendance at work and study; staff turnover and programme dropout; poor performance; increased propensity for accidents; increased incidence of alcohol and substance abuse.
- *Cognitive:* these can be very observable and include poor decision making; poor concentration; increased forgetfulness; development of mental health problems, etc.
- *Physiological:* these include deterioration of the immune system; high blood pressure; serious illness, etc.

However, if you are effective at dealing with and in coping with stressors then you may achieve an entirely different outcome – optimizing your performance. Sometimes this is referred to as achieving peak performance.

Principles of peak performance

Evidence shows that high-performing individuals and teams demonstrate the same key characteristics time and time again (note that many correspond closely with the mental toughness scales). These are shown in Table 2.1.

Peak performance is the ability to function efficiently at your best, enabling you to express your full potential. And as we see from the above, peak performance is the flip side of effective stress management. The two are inextricably linked. Optimizing performance generally means responding positively to challenges and to pressures to achieve significant goals and targets. It will also usually involve dealing with some form of adversity or difficulty that would deter a lesser motivated individual. Developing mental toughness is an important ingredient in enabling us to perform to the best of our abilities.

Why does your performance vary?

Our performance does vary. Sometimes we can be highly productive, at other times we can be remarkably ineffective. Research shows that variations in our performance can be attributed as shown in Table 2.2.

TABLE 2.1 Key characteristics of high-performing individuals and teams

Passion	A high level of interest in their job, task, etc
High self-confidence	A high level of confidence in their own abilities and their ability to deal with others
Controlling the things you can	And not worrying unnecessarily about that which cannot be controlled
Resilience – dealing with setbacks	The ability to bounce back
Seeing the challenge not the threat	Finding opportunities for self-development within each new challenge
Focus	The ability to clear the mind of unnecessary thoughts and clutter
The ability to relax	And can recognize when they need to relax

TABLE 2.2 Attributes affecting performance

Your abilities	What you bring to the task?
Your approach	How you approach the task – your motivation and your interests?
Your reward	What you will get if you get involved?
Your colleagues	How you interact with those around you?
Your state of mind	What is happening inside your head. Are you in a state to rise to the challenge?

It has been variously estimated that state of mind accounts for at least 50 per cent of the variation in an individual's performance but on average we often only spend around 5 per cent of time on optimizing our performance through mental training.

It is within this notion of stress management that the concepts of performance and wellbeing are connected. When we are more consistent at performing to our optimum we also tend to feel better. When we are more content we perform better. The two notions can connect to give rise to a virtuous cycle of development and growth. Developing mental toughness has an important role in this. Of course, the absence of mental training can lead to the opposite – a vicious cycle of stress and unwanted consequences.

A brief history of mental toughness

03

DR KEITH EARLE

The term 'mental toughness' was first coined by Loehr, who was a sports psychologist working with athletes with the principal goal of improving sporting performance. Since the pioneering work of Loehr in the mid-1980s, 'mental toughness' has become synonymous with sporting greatness. Following his regular interactions with elite US athletes, Loehr identified a highly relevant concept that has become a frequently used layperson's term for individual tolerance to stress and performance maximization. Whilst what Loehr did was important for bringing the term 'mental toughness' into modern-day parlance, the work he and his associates did was limited in its development of that construct and it could be argued that the anecdotally-based work generally lacked the rigours of a scientific approach.

Over the next 15 years, interest in mental toughness was limited to that of sporting practitioners and journalists and the term became increasingly mentioned on television, radio broadcasts and the sports pages of newspapers and magazines. However, since the publication of a book chapter entitled 'Mental toughness: the concept and its measurement' (Clough *et al*, 2002) academic interest has flourished. In the past five years a number of research groups in Britain, and more recently Australia, have started to contribute to a growing body of literature and begun to address the fundamental issues surrounding the construct of mental toughness.

Before going on to detail the current status of the mental toughness literature, some background into the broader theoretical underpinnings of the stress literature is required, as these are closely related constructs. It can be argued that a central component of mental toughness is how effectively an individual deals with potentially stressful situations. Furthermore, the development of scientific rigour in the field of mental toughness requires researchers to draw upon pre-existing and scientifically sound psychological frameworks.

Constructs relating to mental toughness

What is mental toughness?

The term 'mental toughness' is commonly used in all manner of sporting contexts, whether it is when Michael Atherton bats for 10 hours saving a test match, or when the German football team win another trophy with an apparently 'untalented' side. Vincent Lombardi, the former and legendary Green Bay Packers coach stated:

> Mental toughness is many things and rather difficult to explain. Its qualities are sacrifice and self-denial. In addition, most importantly, it is combined with a perfectly disciplined will that refuses to give in. It's a state of mind – you could call it character in action. (Curtis Management Group, 1998: 20)

There are obviously shared elements to this range of ideas and concepts and, in essence, what this commonly means is an individual's ability to resist the stressors that would normally cause a reduction in performance levels. Within the context of applied experience, one description of mental toughness emerged:

> It's the ability to handle situations. It's somebody who doesn't choke, doesn't go into shock, and who can stand up for what he believes. It's what someone has who handles pressures, distractions, and people trying to break their concentration. It involves focusing, discipline, self-confidence, patience, persistence, accepting responsibility without whining or excuses, visualizing, tolerating pain, and a positive approach. (Brennan, 1998: 2)

Therefore, mental toughness would appear to incorporate aspects of both commonly recognized sports psychology interventions, such as focusing and visualization, and a number of personality characteristics, which include persistence, resilience, confidence and discipline. The importance of both these elements needs to be considered to formulate a definitive explanation of what mental toughness is. The concept as it currently stands could be argued to contain both the theoretical underpinnings of personality constructs as well as the practical implications involved with sports psychology interventions. This mixture of application and theory provides the key to the comprehensive development of the construct.

From a theoretical perspective, the conceptual development of mental toughness benefits from considering related constructs. Existing relevant constructs include hardiness (Kobasa, 1979), physiological toughness (Dienstbier, 1989) and resilience (Dyer and McGuinness, 1996). The majority of the aforementioned terms have their roots firmly in the area of health psychology. However, the underlying principles of these terms have significant relevance in the fields of sports, occupational, educational and social psychology.

Resilience

In layperson's terms, resilience can be described as the process by which people are able to bounce back from adversity. This ability to bounce back (reboundability) is an essential tool for humans in everyday life, and this is intensified in the sporting arena, in business and in education. As mentioned previously, most of the research in this area examined resilience in the context of general health, and indeed it has been defined as the way in which a person acts to modify their responses to situations incorporating elements of psycho-social risk (Rutter, 1985).

Resilience is described as a dynamic process in which a number of elements, known as protective factors, are either available or unavailable for a particular person to utilize. These factors consist of specific competencies, or abilities, that an individual can access. These factors obviously have relevance to mental toughness as the resulting effects of the act of resilience lead to psychological toughening of the individual. This 'stickability' represents the amount of effort and perseverance that an individual is prepared to expend in completing a particular task or reaching a specific goal.

It can be said that a resilient person is not afraid of dealing with the adversities that are commonplace both in everyday and sporting life. Extreme cases that highlight resilience can be taken from any sport; for example, an athlete who undergoes career-threatening surgery and may be out of the sport for over a year, must show this quality to regain fitness and form despite the pain and the psychological effects (eg depression) of non-competition.

Recent research in the field of occupational psychology has been undertaken examining the concept of resilience, its impact on performance at work and the development of resilience within individuals (Jackson and Watkin, 2004). Their research suggested that the following items were key in the way individuals deal with difficult situations:

- the accuracy of analysing events;
- the number of alternative scenarios envisaged;
- flexibility;
- internal drive to face new challenges.

Jackson and Watkin posited that our internal thinking processes can both moderate the impact of these adversities and provide a valuable resource in moving forward from them, focusing on the things we can control rather than those we cannot. They further proposed that the key to resilience is the ability to recognize one's own thoughts and structures of belief and harness the power of flexibility of thinking to manage the emotional and behavioural consequences more effectively. Most interestingly they stated that this ability can be measured, taught and improved and they further proposed a resilience development programme that is outlined below (taken from Jackson and Watkin, 2004):

Emotion regulation – the ability to manage our internal world in order to stay effective under pressure. Resilient people use a well-developed set of skills that help them to control their emotions, attention and behaviour.

Impulse control – the ability to manage the behavioural expression of thoughts and emotional impulses, including the ability to delay gratification explored in Daniel Goleman's (1996) work on emotional intelligence. Impulse control is correlated with emotion regulation.

Causal analysis – the ability to identify accurately the causes of adversity. Resilient people are able to get outside their habitual thinking styles to identify more possible causes and thus more potential solutions.

Self-efficacy – the sense that we are effective in the world – the belief that we can solve problems and succeed. Resilient people believe in themselves and, as a result, build others' confidence in them – placing them in line for more success and more opportunity.

Realistic optimism – the ability to stay positive about the future yet be realistic in our planning for it. It is linked to self-esteem but a more causal relationship exists with self-efficacy and involves accuracy and realism – not Pollyanna-style optimism.

Empathy – the ability to read others' behavioural cues to understand their psychological and emotional states and thus build better relationships. Resilient people are able to read others' non-verbal cues to help build deeper relationships with them, and tend to be more in tune with their own emotional states.

Reaching out – the ability to enhance the positive aspects of life and take on new challenge and opportunity. Reaching out behaviours are hampered by embarrassment, perfectionism and self-handicapping.

Clearly this work has strong links to mental toughness and the elements of resilience outlined above will be closely considered when attempting to develop further the construct of mental toughness from this broader base of existing research.

Hardiness

Another concept, similar to resilience, is that of hardiness (Kobasa, 1979). This important construct also has its roots in health psychology, and more particularly in the stress–illness relationship. There has been a plethora of research investigating the concept of hardiness or 'hardy personality' (Funk, 1992).

Kobasa proposed that hardiness consists of three interrelated concepts: control, challenge and commitment. This concept of hardiness is considered to have a buffering effect between stressful life events and illness. Earlier work by Lazarus (1966) suggested that this buffering effect is influenced by the type of coping strategies used by the individual, which are in turn dependent on the personality dispositions of that individual. Kobasa considered that hardiness is an important factor in the way individuals perceive situations and the way in which they decide to undertake an appropriate set of actions. This can best be done by transforming the event so it can be perceived as less threatening, helping to avoid 'illness-provoking' biological states such as adaptational exhaustion (Selye, 1976) or depressed immunological surveillance (Schwarz, 1975; Kobasa *et al*, 1982).

It was suggested that the qualities possessed by 'hardy' individuals activated the transformation process so that the event, no matter how stress-inducing, became congruous with the individual's self-view. If this is correct, it leads us to a number of implications, one of which is the identification of the less 'hardy' individuals and providing them with appropriate psychological interventions or coping strategies. As mentioned earlier, Kobasa proposed three components of hardiness (control, challenge and commitment). These components are briefly summarized below.

Control is 'expressed as a tendency to feel and act as if one is influential (rather than helpful) in the face of the varied contingencies of life' (Averill, 1973; Seligman, 1975; Kobasa *et al*, 1982). As discussed above, this is a complex concept that operates on a number of levels. Within this context it is argued that control gives the cognitive ability to incorporate stressful events into 'an ongoing life plan' (Kobasa, 1979), using knowledge, skill and choice, thus influencing how situations are appraised. Control is further said to allow an individual to choose the most appropriate course of action when facing a potentially stressful situation. This in turns is likely to transform the situation into something more congruous for that individual.

Challenge is expressed as the belief that change rather than stability is normal in life and that the anticipation of change provides incentives to grow rather than threats to security (Kobasa *et al*, 1982). Seeing potentially stressful occurrences as challenging has the effect of mitigating the stressfulness of the situation. In relation to the coping strategies used, the challenge disposition empowers the individual to develop and grow instead of protecting what the individual has already.

Commitment is the 'tendency to involve oneself in (rather than experience alienation from) whatever one is doing or encounters' (Maddi *et al*, 1982). Commitment is relevant to cognitive appraisal as it helps identify and give meaning to new situations in the individual's environment. At the action level it makes the person take the initiative in the environment rather than passively accept it. Moss (1973) proposed that failure to feel involved in an environment that provides accurate and congruent information can leave an individual vulnerable to disease.

Further research into hardiness has found that the concept appears to be more effective at buffering stressors than either social support or physical exercise (Kobasa *et al*, 1985). Studies have also found that hardy individuals are more likely to cope with stressors by transforming them mentally into something less threatening (eg Rhodewalt and Aguostsdottir, 1984; Maddi, 1991).

Furthermore, physiological responses have also been related to the hardy personality. For example, Contrada *et al* (1991) found associations with heart rate and blood pressure patterns in the resting state and in response to stressful situations. However, while little research has been carried out in the area of hardiness and performance effectiveness, Westman (1990) found that trainees entering the Israeli Military Officer Training School had more chance of performance success if they scored highly on the hardiness scale.

Physiological toughness

The researcher most associated with the concept of physiological toughening is Dienstbier. He has produced some interesting and influential work on the process by which individuals can actually develop their physiological toughness.

Dienstbier (1989, 1991) primarily investigated the relationship between arousal and physiological toughness by examining individuals' confrontations with stress that evoke both central and peripheral physiological arousal. The physiological reactions to stress have been frequently explored, and the work of researchers such as Frankenhaeuser and colleagues has consistently shown relationships between psychological stressors and changes at the physiological level in markers such as cortisol and adrenalin.

However, in addition to investigating the response to stressors in general, Dienstbier (1991) observed a within-person change over time, when repeatedly exposed to physiological stressors. His conceptualization of stress is consistent with theorists such as Lazarus (1993), and he describes a 'stressor' as a situation which an individual appraises either as threatening or harmful. This organism–situation interaction would result in an appraisal of either challenge (positive emotion) or stress (negative emotion). Dienstbier examined the work carried out in the area of reactions to stressors and found that in non-human experiments subjects were, in fact, able to be 'toughened up' by means of exposure to intermittent stressors.

Therefore, it is implicit in his work that the conceptualization of physiological toughness is the response to stressful situations as an appraisal of challenge. Based on his observations, Dienstbier proposed that there are four toughening manipulations that influence the physiological mediators, which in turn are the cause of the performance and temperament characteristics. Brief descriptions of these manipulations are:

1 *Early experience* – the ways in which children have faced extreme stress in early life and its relationship to differences in their resilience.

2 *Passive toughening* – Weiss *et al* (1975) highlighted the impact of repeated exposure to cold water and electric shocks and an increase in stress tolerance.

3 *Active toughening* – by (aerobic) exercising self-regulated toughening can occur.

4 *Ageing* – effects for ageing are generally opposite to those of the three other manipulations. It seems that at a certain point, as you grow older, you are likely to become more mentally sensitive.

Interestingly, Dienstbier's model has important and counter-intuitive implications for the use of techniques that are currently utilized for long-term coping. These techniques (including relaxation-based interventions, eg biofeedback, autogenic training, meditation, tranquillizers) may provide short-term relief, but could possibly be removing the very situations that would lead to physiological toughening.

Dienstbier went further than this and suggested that toughening also operates at the psychological level, elicited by exposure to mental challenges. However, very little research has been carried out in this particular area because of the practicalities of such research. Manipulating the amount of challenge that individuals have in their life is obviously extremely difficult, therefore real-life research in this area may actually prove unfeasible.

Dienstbier's work clearly had relevance to the concept of mental toughness. His concepts provide a further basis for the development of the mental toughness concept. Just as important, it provided some support for the proposition that mental toughness can be developed within individuals.

Mental toughness itself

The beginnings of mental toughness research

As stated earlier in this chapter, the term 'mental toughness' has become increasingly common across a number of domains, including sporting and occupational contexts. Within the psychology literature, the usage of this term can be traced back to the work of Loehr (1982). In this capacity he found that athletes and coaches were beginning to use 'mental toughness' to describe a desired trait. This led Loehr to investigate the construct and attempt to identify what this 'mental toughness' actually is.

In his book, *The New Toughness Training for Sports* (1995), Loehr defined mental toughness as 'the ability to consistently perform toward the upper range of your talent and skill regardless of competitive circumstances' and from his interactions with athletes, Loehr expanded upon this definition by identifying four key markers in respect of toughness:

1 *Emotional flexibility* – 'the ability to absorb unexpected emotional turns and remain supple, non-defensive, and balanced, able to

summon a wide range of positive emotions to the competitive battle. Inflexible athletes are rigid and defensive in emotional crisis and therefore are easily broken'.

2 *Emotional responsiveness* – 'the ability to remain emotionally alive, engaged, and connected under pressure. Responsive competitiveness is not calloused, withdrawn, or lifeless as the battle rages'.

3 *Emotional strength* – 'the ability to exert and resist great force emotionally under pressure, to sustain a powerful fighting spirit against impossible odds'.

4 *Emotional resilience* – 'the ability to take a punch emotionally and bounce back quickly to recover from disappointments, mistakes, and missed opportunities and jump back into battle fully ready to resume the fight'.

On the basis of this model, he prepared a 42-item questionnaire consisting of seven scales, which he called the Psychological Performance Inventory (PPI). This questionnaire has been used in a number of studies and will be discussed in detail later in this chapter. It should be noted that Loehr's model of mental toughness and the resulting questionnaire were both generated from informal interactions with athletes and Loehr made no attempt to scientifically test the model or develop his questionnaire into a psychometric instrument.

Following the work of Loehr, a number of researchers have offered alternative conceptualizations of the mental toughness concept. For example, in their review, Williams and Krane (1993) suggested that mentally tough athletes possess a greater ability to concentrate, higher levels of self-confidence, less anxiety before and during competition, and the ability to rebound from mistakes. However, they also recognized that the majority of recent research in sports psychology has focused on the psychological skills and strategies that are used by successful athletes rather than profiling their personality characteristics. This clearly highlights the practical importance of sports psychology interventions; however, if one of the goals of applied sports psychologists is to enhance mental toughness, then the concept must be soundly developed first.

Once there is some agreement about what mental toughness is, attention can be turned to considering if this is something that can be developed, and what should constitute effective training programmes. The following two sections outline the qualitative and quantitative work that has been carried out up to the present time.

The qualitative approach

As can be seen from the previous section, Loehr uses very emotive language when describing the key markers of mental toughness. These have no doubt been obtained from his many years' experience working with elite athletes. However, no matter how valid this approach is in providing grounded preliminary work, it only represents the beginnings of scientific conceptual development.

In more recent years, research into the concept of mental toughness has become more scientifically rigorous (eg Jones *et al*, 2002; Golby *et al*, 2003; Golby and Sheard, 2004; Middleton *et al*, 2004). This body of research has mostly used a qualitative approach to examine a range of issues, using mainly interviews and focus group techniques. It is also true that much of this work has remained focused on the world of sport. This introduces, as we have learnt, limitations to that work. It has been extremely valuable to widen our attention to other fields and applications.

This work nevertheless has further contributed to the wide variety of mental toughness definitions, and the research of Jones *et al* reiterates the fact that the concept is well used in applied sports psychology and in the wider arena of professional sport. However, the wide-ranging definitions of mental toughness have served to confuse the area and inhibited the development of an operational concept.

It would seem that many, if not all, positive psychological characteristics have at some time been linked with the attributes of a mentally tough performer. This work was summarized by Jones *et al* (2002), who stated that this range of characteristics implies that a mentally tough athlete is generally someone who has an 'ability to cope with stress and resultant anxiety associated with high pressure competitive situations' (p 206).

The most notable qualitative study is arguably that of Jones *et al*, who actively aimed to provide some degree of rigour in their investigation of the mental toughness concept that was previously lacking. Their aim was to define and identify key attributes in the concept of mental toughness and they selected qualitative methods because they, among others, argued that this would provide the opportunity to probe people's responses and establish detailed information, especially with regard to new research questions.

The study incorporated both interviews and focus groups, and focused on the view of elite athletes in order to generate data for a profile of a mentally tough athlete. This approach, described in more detail below, can be considered to have bypassed the 'pop' sports psychology approaches that 'emphasize macro-components such as confidence and coping with adversity as underpinning the construct and to identify the micro-components of mental toughness' (Jones *et al*, 2002: 207).

Conversely, Jones *et al* were able to elicit from the athletes their complex construction of what constitutes a mentally tough performer, a process that has been effectively undertaken in a number of specific athletic areas such as athletics, cycling, rowing and modern pentathlon, among others (Butler, 1989; Butler and Hardy, 1992; Jones, 1993; Dale and Wrisberg, 1996). Their resulting definition of mental toughness was:

> Mental toughness is having the natural or developed psychological edge that enables you to: generally, cope better than your opponents with the many demands (competition, training, and lifestyle) that sport places on a performer;

specifically, be more consistent and better than your opponents in remaining determined, focused, confident, and in control under pressure.

The attributes developed by Jones *et al* were as follows (ranked in order of importance):

- Having an unshakeable self-belief in your ability to achieve your competition goals.
- Bouncing back from performance setbacks as a result of increased determination to succeed.
- Having an unshakeable self-belief that you possess unique qualities and abilities that make you better than your opponents.
- Having an insatiable desire and internalized motives to succeed.
- Remaining fully focused on the task at hand in the face of competition-specific distractions.
- Regaining psychological control following unexpected, uncontrollable events.
- Pushing back the boundaries of physical and emotional pain, while still maintaining technique and effort under distress in training and competition.
- Accepting that competition anxiety is inevitable and knowing that you can cope with it.
- Not being adversely affected by others' good and bad performances.
- Thriving on the pressure of competition.
- Remaining fully focused in the face of personal life distractions.
- Switching a sports focus on and off as required.

This is clearly a broad conceptualization with a focus on the key characteristics to be found within the mentally tough athlete; however this research does potentially provide fertile ground for further investigation.

An interesting point is made within this definition of mental toughness in that it is considered both to be a natural phenomenon as well as a trait that can be developed with the appropriate psychological interventions. A further point of interest is the fact that the participants acknowledged the complex interaction of the life/sports domains: the importance of dealing with life situations outside of the sporting context, and that this aspect plays an important part in the development of mental toughness. Situations considered include time management skills, social and personal demands, and balancing their training regime.

The psychometric approach

The use of psychometric instruments in research is commonplace. For example, psychometric methods can be used with the aim of developing psychometric instruments that are capable of reliably and validly assessing a given construct; questionnaires can be devised with the different but obviously closely related aim of examining the underlying structure of a construct, by assessing the nature of relationships between different items.

Also, psychometric instruments can be used to address research questions relating to the extent different populations possess given traits. Such approaches are obviously common in psychology and, within the field of mental toughness, there are a number of existing studies that can provide some further insight and support the development of the construct.

Golby *et al* (2003) used psychometric methods to compare mental toughness across a number of cultures and across different playing standards (ie, first division, second division). The driving force for this research was the apparent performance gulf between northern and southern hemisphere rugby league teams. Previous research had not found any significant differences in the tactical or physical attributes of the players (Brewer and Davis, 1995), which has led to questions about the psychological profiles of the athletes as an explanation for performance differences.

In brief, Golby and his colleagues examined the potential cultural differences in both mental toughness and hardiness between rugby nations (Wales, France, Ireland and England) competing in the World Cup of 2000. This work utilized two measures. One was Loehr's PPI, 'designed' in 1986, which claims to assess the mental toughness of an athlete by asking questions in the following categories: self-confidence, negative emotion, attention control, visualization and imagery control, motivation, positive energy, and attitude control. In addition to the PPI, the second instrument used in this study was the Personal Views Survey III-R (Maddi and Khoshaba, 2001). This instrument aims to measure hardiness, and possesses three subscales of control, commitment and challenge. The psychometric properties of this instrument have been soundly validated with acceptable internal consistency of between .60 and .84 for the subscales and .88 for total hardiness.

In summary, the results showed that the Welsh team reported higher levels of commitment and control (hardiness scale) in comparison with the French team. These results were interpreted as the Welsh team demonstrating a more active involvement in progressing in the tournament, as well as feeling that their efforts on the pitch would influence the outcome of a match.

Further analysis indicated a strong relationship between the PPI and the PVS III-R. It was suggested by Golby *et al* that both of the inventories used in the study were probably measuring related but distinct attributes of psychological skills. However, no firm conclusions could be reached from the analysis undertaken, although one interesting issue highlighted in the study was the fact that the majority of athletes scored well above the average scores for both mental toughness and hardiness. This was explained by the fact that there is a 'natural filtering' that takes place whereby only athletes who possess high levels of both hardiness and mental toughness would reach a position where they could be selected to represent their country.

Two explanations for this are given by Golby *et al*. First, different psychological factors have a highly significant (and maybe undervalued) impact on performance, and secondly, the measures used possess insufficient discriminative power. Finally, it was highlighted that significant differences were only found with the hardiness scale, therefore giving support to the robust psychometrics properties of the PVS III-R.

A similar study was undertaken by Golby and Sheard (2004), which again aimed to compare athletes' measures of mental toughness and hardiness across differing standards of rugby league (international, super league and division one). The results again showed a highly significant difference of both mental toughness (PPI) and hardiness (PVS III-R) across playing standards.

In respect of the hardiness measure, it was found that the international players scored significantly higher in the areas of commitment and challenge compared to both super league and division one players, as well as scoring significantly higher than division one players in the control scale. On the other hand, in regard to the measure of mental toughness, the international players scored significantly higher on the areas of negative energy control and attentional control compared to super league and division one players. There were found to be no significant differences between super league and division one players.

The findings of Golby *et al* have been replicated outside the sporting environment with studies highlighting the effectiveness of hardiness in numerous settings, eg health care professionals (Topf, 1989), business executives (Kobasa *et al*, 1982), student teachers (Thompson and Wendt, 1995), public sector employees (Rush *et al*, 1995) and military personnel (Westman, 1990).

The development of the MTQ48 and the 4 Cs model

In this chapter we have tried to provide a brief overview of the state of mental toughness research at the time the MTQ48 was developed. It was apparent that:

- mental toughness was an important factor;
- it was usually very fuzzily defined;
- there was arguably no credible measure of mental toughness.

A number of the models briefly described here – especially the work on hardiness and physiological toughening – offered an ideal starting point for developing an applied model and measure that could be used in a wide variety of settings. Dr Keith Earle and Dr Peter Clough took up the challenge with enthusiasm. They identified a clear need for the development of the mental toughness concept. As with all research, it is clear that the work described in this book is built upon a foundation laid by others. All research is predicated on the 'building on the shoulders of giants' mantra. Other impressive groups have continued to research in this area and have developed other views of mental toughness. We feel these are complementary to ours. There is never a right answer – just right answers. The focus of this book from now on is on our work and ideas. They appear to work very well wherever they are applied. We hope you find them helpful.

Developing the model and the MTQ48

04

DR KEITH EARLE

Early in our work there emerged the need to develop the mental toughness construct in the sense that there was a need to pull together what had been developed by others and add what we had identified. There have been countless attempts to identify the different facets of mental toughness, including: 'the ability to perform toward the upper range of your talent' (Loehr, 1995); the 'ability to cope with intense pressure' (Williams, 1988); and the 'ability to cope better than your opponents with the demands of competitive sport' (Jones *et al,* 2002). You could say that we 'made sense out of the chaos' that was mental toughness thinking until that point.

Although there are clearly some common elements to these ideas and models, our presentation of mental toughness seeks to clarify this milieu of definitions and offer a model of the construct based on scientific research. This research-based approach has not always been adopted by others who delve into this field. Many users appear to have relatively little interest in the research context and pedigree of tools and techniques, preferring to take a far more pragmatic approach.

Given that our joint interest in mental toughness was, initially at least, very much in the application of mental toughness in the workplace and in sport, it is important that anything that emerged was practical and accessible. It also had to make sense in terms of what the potential practitioners already knew and used. Pragmatism was important to us too. However, there is already too much practice in people development and organization development that is 'faith' based and has little real evidence to support it. It was important to all those involved in developing this concept and the measure that we adopt an evidence-based approach. Although this approach has its critics and carries risk, not least that you cannot find evidence to support what you are doing, we are happy that we took this course of action. We now have something we can explain, we can develop and, if needed, defend.

Once we had a sound and research-based definition of mental toughness, it became possible to develop an accurate measure. This involves a basis of theory, followed by item and reliability analysis, factor analysis, tests of convergent and divergent validity, validation in relation to external criteria, and application in research and practice. It is this process that will be briefly described in this chapter.

Preliminary field research

The previous research into mental toughness and related constructs clearly provided a significant volume of information on which to base a further investigation into the nature and breadth of mental toughness. However, past research and existing questionnaires had been beset with inconsistencies and psychometric anomalies.

Considering this, it was decided that a grounded approach should be used (Glaser and Strauss, 1967). This method focuses on the emergence of theory from unstructured data collection, rather than relying wholly on pre-existing theory with its inherent problem of restriction of data collection. It was intended that this approach would ensure that the new model of mental toughness was developed from the bottom up, rather than potentially perpetuating a limited framework.

To this end, an exploratory study was undertaken that investigated the extensive range of personal experiences of situations with relevance to mental toughness. This also allowed the researcher to consider the way individuals utilized the terms relating to the different aspects of this construct.

Twelve in-depth interviews were carried out with sports people. These were three rugby coaches, one rugby chief executive, two rugby players, two golfers, two footballers and two squash players. The interviews lasted for an average of 45 minutes, with the shortest being 25 minutes with one of the rugby coaches and the longest lasting 90 minutes, which was held with one of the squash players. All interviewees were either professional or playing at an elite level. The aim of the process was twofold: to identify notions of mental toughness and to identify circumstances and events that necessitated mental toughness.

Although the interviews raised many questions they also met their broad goal, which was to provide a grounded basis for the development of the construct. The most striking aspect of the interviews was the importance all interviewees placed on having a high level of mental toughness. All interviewees stated that they thought this was a vital ingredient in the profile of a successful athlete. When asked to state what they thought this 'mental toughness' was, however, all interviewees found it difficult to define. Some of the descriptions offered in these interviews are shown in Table 4.1.

Interestingly, what emerged were two recurrent themes covering new aspects of mental toughness. First, most of the interviewees considered

TABLE 4.1 Interviewees' descriptions of mental toughness

1	The ability to carry on when the world seems to have turned against you, and keep your 'troubles' in proper perspective.
2	The capacity to face all pressures and deal with them internally, delivering the same level of performance outwardly, regardless of what pressures one feels internally.
3	The ability to keep going when the world seems to be against you and keep a true sense of perspective on your situation.
4	Resistance under pressure (including when working in new areas).
5	To maintain effective personal control over your own stress levels and effective working relationships whilst handling a whole range of complex and sensitive issues/problems.
6	The ability to change when necessary, to be flexible when necessary and to resist when necessary in order to get the job done.
7	The ability to maintain effective control over the environment by displaying commitment to deliver, confidence in their ability, resilience to negative pressures, ability to see change as a positive opportunity and a recognition of their own limits to handle stress.
8	The ability to be reliable, in control, effective and composed under pressure.
9	The ability to handle events, planned and unplanned, and any conflict, emotional or otherwise, which arises from those events.
10	The ability to remain emotionally stable and make rational decisions under pressure.
11	The ability to appear calm and in control when everything is going wrong.
12	Ability to withstand the unexpected diverse challenges of (i) management, (ii) the pressures of legal work and (iii) personal and professional disappointments in a pressured working environment.
13	The ability to be able to continue to focus on long-term outcomes and deliver an effective performance in the face of real or potential obstacles, maintaining perspective and a balanced, objective view.

TABLE 4.1 Continued

14	Resilient – not easily baulked in the face of opposition/adversity.
15	Ability to think clearly under pressure together with determination to achieve a solution.
16	Intellectual resilience, ability to deal with difficult situations, taking forward ideas which may be subject to resistance. Flexibility and adaptability responding to changing circumstances are competencies (stubbornness to be actively discouraged).
17	Being able to remain objective and complete the task irrespective of impact on feelings and emotions.
18	To do what hurts because you know it to be right.
19	Ability to cope and perform under a variety of situations and circumstances.
20	Ability to accept change, resist unacceptable change, be flexible enough to get the job done.
21	Ability to defend arguments and reason situations intellectually.
22	Being resilient to pressures, changes and feedback.
23	A person who is able to stay focused on important issues when change is rampant and is able to make difficult decisions affecting others, even when they don't like it themselves.
24	The ability to produce quality work, remaining evenly tempered, without changing own attitudes and standards.
25	Ability to absorb pressure without impacting upon performance.
26	The ability to react positively to setbacks whether personal or physical that affects your thought processes. Not to have fear of failure.
27	Determination to see tasks through in all circumstances whether under internal or external pressure.
28	Resistance to pressure, forcefulness, ability to deal with problems.
29	Ability to deal effectively with stressful situations.

confidence as playing a large part in dealing successfully with the immense problems and setbacks that are faced by professional athletes. Secondly, the ability to suppress emotions during play was also considered to be a key factor for athletes to perform at the top of their ability range.

Development of the four-factor model

Two sources of data now existed on which to begin to develop a model of mental toughness. First, there was the existing published research on mental toughness and related constructs, and secondly, the interviews with 12 sports people. Broadly speaking, all the data pointed to a four-factor model. The model of hardiness put forward by Kobasa seems to incorporate most of the elements generated by the literature. Most of the elements can be summarized under the broad headings of control, commitment and challenge.

Secondly, the interviews provided support for all of these elements and support for a fourth element of confidence. At that point, none of the research in this field had incorporated this aspect of personality in mental toughness. However, confidence was mentioned by half of the interviewees and it is an intuitively comfortable aspect of mental toughness.

Ultimately, therefore, these two sources of data enabled the emergence of a four-factor model of mental toughness. There was more: the interviews provided evidence to support the subdivision of two of these factors into four further subscales.

Two distinct aspects of confidence were generated, ie, interpersonal confidence and confidence in one's ability, and two distinct aspects of control were also proposed, ie, emotional control in addition to the well-recognized element of locus of control. This work led on to a comprehensive definition of the concept of mental toughness:

> Mentally tough individuals tend to be sociable and outgoing as they are able to remain calm and relaxed, they are competitive in many situations and have lower anxiety levels than others. With a high sense of self-belief and an unshakeable faith that they control their own destiny, these individuals can remain relatively unaffected by competition or adversity. (Clough *et al*, 2002: 38)

Preliminary scale development

On the basis of this model, a broad range of items were generated (via a panel of experts). The aim was to develop items that could encapsulate each of the four components of the model (challenge, commitment, confidence and control). Data from the interviews and existing questionnaires were considered in an attempt to sample the full breadth of the construct and different aspects of each factor were incorporated in an attempt to be as comprehensive as possible. Each item consisted of a statement followed by a five-point Likert scale with verbal anchors ranging from (1) strongly disagree to (5) strongly agree.

The initial questionnaire consisted of 66 items. They were written to ensure that all items are understandable, unequivocal and specific. The items were piloted with 20 participants who examined every item to ensure each was unambiguous and clear. All the items examined were thought to be suitable to be understood by the general population.

Questionnaires were then completed. The sample of 215 participants consisted of students, professional athletes and administration/managerial staff. The data were analysed using complex statistical techniques such as factor analysis.

A six-factor mental toughness model had emerged on the basis of the following related theoretical perspectives: existing questionnaires relating to mental toughness; qualitative data from the interviews and the analysis of the various factor solutions of the questionnaire.

To investigate further the factor structure, a second development sample was obtained and subjected to analysis. In total, 963 questionnaires were completed. The sample consisted of students, administrators/managers, engineers and athletes.

A preliminary analysis of the gender data revealed statistically significant differences in total mental toughness as well as all the subscales. However, to ascertain the practical significance of these findings, effect calculations were carried out using the guidelines provided by Cohen (1988). Even the largest differences produced small effect sizes, eg MT: eta squared = 0.001. Expressed as a percentage only 0.1 per cent of the variance of mental toughness is explained by gender. It should be noted that when the MTQ48 is used for non-research purposes the scores produced for the scales are converted to stens. These stens are clustered into three broad groupings (low = 1, 2, 3; medium = 4, 5, 6, 7; high = 8, 9, 10). None of the gender differences noted would impact in any significant way on the reported score. This sample was subjected to the same approach as the first sample. The same model emerged from the forest of data.

How can you judge the quality of a test? There are two main benchmarks to judging the quality of tests: reliability and validity.

Reliability

Reliability is basically concerned with consistency. It relates to the test's ability to measure in the same way. If a test reported that you were mentally tough one week and then the next week it reported you were very sensitive it would raise concerns, particularly if there had been no events or interventions that might explain such a shift.

Obviously mental toughness could change. Much of this book is given over to mental toughness development using targeted interventions – so it can change. However, for most people, most of the time, it won't change on its own. Reliability is usually estimated using two methods: internal consistency and test-retest.

TABLE 4.2 Scale reliability of the Mental Toughness Questionnaire 48 (MTQ48)

MTQ48 Subscales	No. of Items	Cronbach's Alpha
Challenge	8	.71
Commitment	11	.80
Control	14	.74
Emotional control	7	.70
Life control	7	.72
Confidence	15	.81
Confidence in abilities	9	.75
Interpersonal confidence	6	.76
Whole scale	48	.91

Internal consistency looks at the way the items cluster. So, for example, items written to measure confidence should covary together. Score high on one item and you would normally score highly on the others in that category. Cronbach's alpha was calculated for each subscale as a measure of internal consistency; see Table 4.2. All subscales reached the minimum acceptable level. This supports the homogeneity of each subscale and the MTQ48 as a whole.

Test-retest reliability is basically doing the questionnaire twice, after a suitable gap. The relationship will never be perfect, but it should be substantial. The test-retest reliability measured by Pearson's correlation coefficient was high for all scales, with a range from .80 for challenge to .87 for emotional control. The sample consisted of 108 psychology undergraduates tested at a six-week interval.

Validity

Basically validity answers the question: does it work? There are many types of validity. We will focus on four of them here:

1 face;
2 content;
3 construct; and
4 criterion-related.

Face validity refers to how the instrument is accepted by its target population. Too simple or too complex questions quickly lead to non-acceptance of the questionnaires. Likewise if questions appear odd or inappropriate people will not answer them. For example, you might find that a question about toilet habits relates to anxiety. From a technical point of view this would probably work – there is a relationship – but it would create a degree of defensiveness and suspicion on behalf of the respondent! The MTQ48 is acceptable to a wide range of people and there are seldom any issues about its applicability.

Content validity refers to the instrument's ability to cover the full domain of the underlying concept. So, for example, if you wanted to test somebody's geographical knowledge you ask them to name the capitals of various countries. You would get very different results if you restricted this to only Western Europe or opened it up to the rest of the world. The former would in fact be a very poor measure as it clearly lacks content validity.

Construct validity can be a very complex thing indeed. However, at its simplest it is very easy to describe. Basically, it signifies the test's relationship with other similar tests. For the MTQ48 to be said to be valid in this domain it has relate to other closely related constructs. Much work has been done on this and the results are both supportive and encouraging. An example of this type of approach is shown below and in Table 4.3.

An example of construct validation

A sample of 106 individuals completed both the MTQ48 and a variety of personality measures. The sample consisted entirely of undergraduate students, who completed the battery of measures during a research methods lecture.

Significant correlations were found with the MTQ48 and all of the five scales investigated. Interestingly, the highest correlations were found with the self-efficacy scale. This is an expected finding as the concept of self-efficacy has strong associations with that of the confidence that is a subscale of the MTQ48; indeed the correlation with the subscale 'confidence in abilities' was even higher. Another relevant finding was the correlation with the State Trait Anxiety Indicator (STAI), with the strongest correlation of the subscales being control. Again, this finding was expected as the control subscale does include the element involving the ability to control oneself in stressful experiences.

Finally there is *criterion-related validity*. We feel this is both the core and the key to the MTQ48. It is a measure of whether or not a score on the MTQ48 is associated with an external measure. For many this is the acid test for a psychometric measure – 'can it predict what it claims to predict?' Much of our work has concentrated on performance measures. Many of these studies are liberally sprinkled throughout this text but an illustrative example is included here.

TABLE 4.3 Correlations table for MTQ48 and various personality scales

	Life Orientation Test	Satisfaction with Life Scale	Self-esteem Scale	Self-efficacy Scale	State Trait Anxiety Inventory
Overall MT	0.48**	0.56**	0.42*	0.68**	−0.57**
Challenge	0.39*	0.59**	0.45*	0.66**	−0.54**
Commitment	0.45*	0.52**	0.40*	0.69**	−0.59**
Control	0.49**	0.55**	0.41*	0.64**	−0.61**
Control: life	0.53**	0.59**	0.49**	0.66**	−0.63**
Control: emotions	0.46*	0.56**	0.34*	0.59**	−0.61**
Confidence	0.47*	0.50**	0.39*	0.70**	−0.58**
Confidence: in abilities	0.49**	0.49**	0.45*	0.74**	−0.60**
Confidence: interpersonal	0.41*	0.56**	0.37*	0.69**	−0.61**

CRITERION STUDY Mental toughness and reaction to a test environment – Appraisal and physiological response

This study aimed to investigate individuals' responses to and appraisal of taking a test in a stressful environment. Participants' subjective ratings of the test were measured as well as their heart rate response to the environment. These measures were then correlated with MTQ48 scores. The study involved 29 participants who were all university students and were participating to gain experience of the graduate recruitment process. As such, it is argued that they were motivated to perform well on the test.

Task and measures

Each participant carried out a standardized psychometric test of verbal and numerical abilities under formal test conditions. To ensure participant involvement in the test environment, they were informed that they would receive feedback on their performance later and that the time limits would be strictly adhered to. The test was split into two halves of 30 minutes; the first was for verbal ability, the second for numerical ability. Participants' heart rates were measured throughout the test, measures of state anxiety were taken before and after the test, and measures of subjective experiences were taken post-test. This bespoke subjective measure consisted of three questions:

1   How stressful was it?

2   How much effort did the test require?

3   How much time pressure did you feel?

As hoped and expected, the MTQ48 provided evidence of the negative relationship with anxiety in respect of both pre- and post-measures. The strongest relationships found within the study were those surrounding the subscale of control, which once more highlights the importance of the ability to control nerves when faced with pressurized environments.

Summary

We believe we now have a reliable and valid test of a substantial and well-formulated construct. This means that competent users (ie, after some suitable training in the use of psychometrics and the mental toughness model) should be able to use the measure with confidence as a useful and valuable tool in a wide range of applications including assessment, development and evaluation. Since the original studies, ongoing studies both carried out by us and independently by others, overwhelmingly confirm the reliability and validity of the MTQ48 measure.

The rest of the book is devoted to examples of using the test in the 'real world' and tools and techniques for developing this vital trait.

Mental toughness and the MTQ48

05

The MTQ48 was originally created to meet a very tangible need in the occupational world. It sought to respond to four questions increasingly at the front of the minds of most managers:

- Why do some people handle stressors, pressure and challenge well and others don't?
- Can we measure where people have strengths and weaknesses in these matters?
- Can we do something to improve 'mental toughness' in people to improve their performance?
- Can we evaluate the effectiveness of interventions that are all claimed to be effective?

In 2002, more than eight years of careful and innovative research enabled Drs Peter Clough and Keith Earle to emerge with a tool that allowed these questions, and others, to be answered positively and effectively.

Initially, the concept and the measure were applied mainly in the occupational world, looking at developing employees and managers to perform effectively, especially in challenging environments (eg emergency services) and in adverse circumstances (eg the 2008/9 economic downturn). These are obvious applications for mental toughness and MTQ48. In recent years additional versions of the MTQ48 measure have emerged where the items and the expert report text database use language more appropriate to the needs of young people and sports persons. They are all based on the original.

The MTQ48 is a 48-item questionnaire that takes about 10 minutes to complete. It is most commonly completed in online format. It features the ability to generate expert reports for each individual's scores almost instantly on completion of the measure. There is a 'paper and pencil' version that uses the online facility to process data and create reports.

There are two basic versions: the Standard Version, which generates up to five different reports (described below) which meets the needs of most users; and the Young Person's Version, which produces a reduced range of reports. The latter version is most widely used with young people where it is much more appropriate to provide feedback in oral rather than written form.

Mental toughness is a concept with a universal application, enabling MTQ48 now to be used in a much wider range of applications. There are major applications in education, health, social work, sports and care as well as in occupational settings. As of 2011 the model and measure is in use in more than 40 countries and is available in more than 10 major languages.

A great deal of thought has been put into the development of the measure to enable it to be used properly and with confidence by the widest range of users. It is rarely described as a psychometric measure although this is, at heart, what it is. The MTQ48 is more commonly described as a people development tool. It is:

- Extremely easy to administer. The questionnaire uses a five-point Likert scale to capture responses. The test is available in online or paper and pencil format. Online instructions are intuitive and easy to follow.

- Accessible. The reading age for the item databank in the original UK English version is 9+ years. Language in the reports is such that the reports can be read and understood by those who are not trained psychologists. This principle is applied to all versions including versions in other languages.

- Quick. Test results are processed immediately online and expert reports are available within seconds of test completion.

- User friendly in the reports it generates. Several expert reports are available to the test user; see below.

- Reliable. A technical term to indicate whether MTQ48 measures mental toughness consistently. The reliability score for MTQ48 overall is 0.90, which is generally acknowledged as a high or acceptable score.

- Valid. Another key technical term that indicates whether it measures what it claims to measure. The concurrent validity score for MTQ48 overall and its scales ranges from 0.25 to 0.42, which again is generally acknowledged as a high or acceptable score. The MTQ48 measure is generally recognized as a valid and reliable one. It is increasingly used by independent researchers, and academic journals accept studies for publication that are based on the use of MTQ48.

- Normative. This means that test results for an individual are compared to test results for a relevant norm group that represents the population at large. It is designed to operate in a normative sense.

This provides significant additional value for the user. This means that the measure can be used for:

– diagnosis: identifying the factors at play for individuals and groups in each situation;
– evaluation: measuring progress consistently;
– research: assessing which interventions are most effective and with which people.

The MTQ48 technical manual provides a significant amount of information about the technical characteristics of the MTQ48 measure, particularly in terms of reliability, validity and the norm group composition. The manual is downloadable from the AQR website: www.aqr.co.uk/.

MTQ48 report types

The standard version

MTQ48 will generate up to five different reports from the candidate data using an expert report system. Users and candidates should read the introduction to each report carefully to ensure that they use the report properly.

Development report

This provides the individual's scores and an explanation of what they mean, together with an indication of possible implications. With each of the four component scales, generic development suggestions are offered to enable the candidate to think about modifying behaviour should the situation require this.

Assessment report

This report provides an interpretation of the individual's scores and identifies some potential implications for the workplace. The narrative is provided for the overall measure and for each of the four component scales.

With each narrative, a list of six to 10 suggested questions is provided to enable a user to probe the score. The questions are designed to be open and to be behaviourally oriented to generate the fullest responses. They need adjustment by the manager to ensure that they are appropriate to their specific situation.

Coaching report

This report provides an interpretation of the individual's scores and identifies some of the potential implications for the workplace. With each narrative comes a list of suggested coaching or development actions that the user (including manager or coach) can consider for application with the candidate. It is important that the candidate accepts and agrees with any action to be taken.

Distance travelled report

This is a comparison report based on a current and a previous assessment for an individual. This will identify areas in which an individual's sten scores have changed or remained the same after a period of time and/or a period of training and development.

This report is widely used in training, development and coaching programmes to assess differences arising from the intervention. Hence it is very valuable in ROI (return on investment) studies.

Organization development report

This report is created from data gathered from individuals who form a particular group. The report takes the form of histograms of the patterns of scores for individuals who form the selected group.

For example, that group can be a specific team, or it could be the entire management cohort of an organization or a year group in a school or college. It shows the pattern of results for each scale as a histogram of the total number of people who achieve a particular sten score within that group.

This report is useful in identifying trends and patterns within a group and may be an indicator of cultural issues within an organization.

The young person's version

The version normally used within secondary education and FE generates:

- A Coaching Report – reporting the scores, what they mean, and offering general coaching suggestions and suggested interview questions to explore.
- A Development Report – reporting the scores, what they mean, and offering general development suggestions, which can be used in conjunction with the coaching report to encourage the candidate to think about modifying behaviour where required.
- A Group Analysis report – which creates histograms of the patterns of scores for selected groups.

It is generally not recommended to provide copies of reports to young people. It is more effective to provide oral feedback that is correlated to other information and data.

The future

Technology enables data to be stored and analysed almost endlessly. Equivalency studies are continually carried out to ensure the technical properties of the measure wherever it is applied.

Control

06

Destiny is as destiny does. If you believe you have no control, then you have no control. **WESS ROBERTS**

The more that individuals feel that they can shape and influence what is happening around them the more likely they are to feel that they can make a difference and achieve what is necessary. This is a reasonably well understood concept, particularly when it comes to stress management and peak performance. Studies consistently show that the less people feel they are in control, the more likely they are to feel more stressed in a way that leads to negative consequences. Early work on developing the mental toughness model showed that there were two components to the control scale: life control and emotional control.

Life control represented what many understand to be meant by control generally. This captures the idea that individuals believe that they have sufficient control over the factors that influence their behaviour and their performances for them to believe that they are capable of achieving what they set out to achieve.

Those with a high level of life control will have a sense that success is down to them and their own attitude towards the task and they won't be prevented from achieving. They will generally not need validation or encouragement or support from others. Their own inner belief is enough. Those with a low level of life control will not possess that inner belief and are much more likely to seek support and encouragement from others, which may mean that they are dependent upon others, whether they are individuals or groups.

It's not difficult to see examples of both ends of the scale in all walks of life. Those with a strong sense of life control often emerge as better managers of their own time. They are more effective at prioritizing tasks and at planning and organizing these tasks. As a result they are usually effective at handling more than one task at a time. If asked to take on additional tasks, they are likely to do so in the knowledge that they can do it. Unsurprisingly therefore they will typically emerge as more positive than the norm – tending to see the solution and not the problem. They are also more likely to 'do what it takes' to complete the task. They are hard working.

Those with a low sense of life control tend to be less well organized and can be messy. They are often only effective when handling one thing at a time. If asked to take on additional tasks, they will feel anxiety and be more prepared to fail. They are much less positive and are more likely to find blame for failure in their environment – something will have prevented them from succeeding. They will often see the problem and not the solution, readily identifying reasons why they might not succeed. Again this is a mindset. They may be the equal in every other respect to the individual with a high sense of life control.

It is not difficult to see examples of all points on the scale in work, in education, in sports and in society. Current attention on worklessness where unemployment is institutionalized into several generations of a family or community provides a good example. The inability to get a job will be substantially down to the belief that they are flotsam on the oceans of life.

The second component is *emotional control*. This describes the extent to which individuals are in control of their emotions and the extent to which they will reveal their emotional state to others. This does not mean they do not experience emotions or that there are not emotionally sensitive (intelligent). This is about their ability to control those emotions.

Those with a strong sense of emotional control can choose how much of their emotional state they will reveal to others. This can be relevant and valuable in a number of interpersonal situations. Handling complex negotiations will be one obvious example; operating in a leadership role where you need to portray a sense of calm in difficult circumstances will be another.

Less obvious examples might be bullying or harassment. Quite often the modus operandi for the bully is to provoke the victim. However, if the victim does not appear to respond to that provocation, the bully is often left unsure as to his or her impact and may well cease that activity because it is not producing the desired effect. This is described in more detail elsewhere in the book.

Those with low levels of emotional control will find it difficult not to reveal their emotional states to others. They will respond more readily to provocation or annoyance. They are typically more likely to show their emotions in the sense they will exhibit anger, embarrassment, frustration, etc. As a result they will often deal poorly with criticism, feedback (especially negative feedback) and setbacks. Another response can be to sulk if things don't go their way.

Studies show that they are more likely to report bullying. They may see bullying behaviours in others (teachers, managers, coaches, etc) when others in their group with better emotional control simply shrug them off and see the behaviour as the other person's problem.

Control – defined and applied

Defined: control is the extent to which a person feels they are in control of their life. Some individuals believe that they can exert considerable influence over their working environment, that they can make a difference and change things. In contrast, others feel that the outcome of events is outside their personal control and they are unable to exert any influence over themselves or others.

Applied: this means for example that, at one end of the scale, individuals feel their input really matters and are motivated to make a full contribution. At the other end, they may feel that their contribution is of little importance and hence may not play as full a part as they could. An implication may be that one can handle lots of things at the same time and the other cannot.

Ongoing development has enabled the identification of two subscales to this scale:

1 Control (Emotion) – Individuals scoring highly on this scale are better able to control their emotions. They are able to keep anxieties in check and are less likely to reveal their emotional state to other people.
2 Control (Life) – Those scoring highly on this scale are more likely to believe they control their lives. They feel that their plans will not be thwarted and that they can make a difference.

Emotional control

This measures the extent to which we control our anxieties and our emotions and reveal our emotional states to others; see Table 6.1.

Life control

This is a measure of self-worth. It indicates the extent to which we believe we shape what happens to us... or the other way round; see Table 6.2.

Key psychological perspectives related to control

These are:

- learned helplessness;
- attributions;
- luck;
- superstitions; and
- neuroticism.

TABLE 6.1 Emotional control scores

Lower Scores	Higher Scores
Feel things happen to them	Feel they shape what happens
See issues as 'my problem'	See issues as 'someone else's problem'
See things in terms of guilt and blame	Good at controlling emotions
Internalize problems and the feelings that arise from them	Understand other people's emotions/feelings and know how to manage these
Show emotions when provoked or challenged	Difficult to provoke or annoy
Anxious	Do not appear anxious
Show a reaction when criticized	Impassive when others make comments which could upset or annoy
Show anger or annoyance when things don't go their way	Can be insensitive to others remarks
Show discomfort when others 'have a go at them'	Stay calm in a crisis
Deal poorly with provocation	Keep a broader perspective on things
Respond poorly to poor marks or the prospect of poor performance.	Believe they make their own luck
Can create a sense of fear and avoidance in others	Better able to articulate their emotions
Will cry or show histrionics and may try to get others to behave in the same way.	Use active language
Sulk when things don't go their way	Direct their energy to their choices
Adopt a fatalist approach	High level of self-awareness
Use negative language a great deal	Better at helping others to manage their emotions
Use passive language	Have a sense of 'I have earned this' or 'I deserve this'
Feel 'I don't deserve this...'	

A look at learned helplessness

The control dimension of mental toughness is closely related to that of learnt helplessness. This important idea was proposed by Seligman in 1975. At its most basic, when people have learnt helplessness they have the generalized perception that things are outside their control. Whilst it is obviously the case that some things are outside an individual's control, in a learnt helplessness scenario even things that should be controllable become uncontrollable.

When under pressure learnt helplessness individuals tend to underperform. For example, Peterson and Barrett (1987) reported that college students with helplessness beliefs obtained lower marks. They tended to be more passive learners, for example seeking out less help from their academic advisers. Similarly work at Hull University showed that undergraduates

TABLE 6.2 Life control scores

Lower Scores	Higher Scores
Believe things happen to them	Believe they can make a difference
Often believe 'I can't do this because of my... beliefs/religion/upbringing, etc'	Generally believe 'they can'
	Comfortable when asked to do several things at a time
Will readily find excuses for not getting things done	Good at planning and time management
Tend to wait for things to happen rather than take an initiative	Good at prioritizing
	Prepared to work hard to clear blockages
Live in chaos which provides a ready excuse	Happy to take on multiple commitments and know how to deal with them.
Find it hard to do more than one thing at a time	
Prone to depression	Tend to see others as problems ... which can be handled
Will tend to respond to the last person who pressures them	Will feel they have more choices in life 'If this doesn't work I'll do something else'
Freezes when overloaded	
Can feel stretched with modest workloads – poor at time management	Happy to reorganize as they go along – aren't unsettled by errors and mistakes
Will tend to blame outside factors for preventing success	Believe they can define what needs to be done
May panic when given assignments	
Tend to be 'staid or stuck in the sand'	Break down tasks into manageable chunks
Comparatively unresourceful	
Won't see the opportunities within their own skill set	Able to say 'no' when needed: 'I can do that for you but I can't do it now'
Have a limiting belief system: 'I can't do this because ...'	See the solution rather than the problem

with lower control scores were more likely to drop out of the course, and those who stuck to it tended to obtain lower marks. Again these students tended to have much less contact with their home departments and were often described as 'invisible'.

Do not let what you cannot do interfere with what you can do. (John Wooden)

Learnt helplessness refers to the expectation, based on previous experience, that one's actions cannot possibly lead to success. Much of the early work in helplessness focused on animal studies and was really an accidental finding. Seligman was investigating classical conditioning when he made an interesting discovery. Most people are aware of the work of Pavlov, who paired sound with food, resulting in the finding that in the end the sound on its own would produce the desired response from the animal.

Seligman paired the auditory tone with a mild shock to a dog suspended in a hammock. The idea was that the tone itself would induce a fear response. This element worked as predicted. The 'trained' dogs were then put into a box which was split into two areas, separated by small barrier. The researchers expected that the dogs would jump the barrier when they sounded the tone – to avoid the shock. However, they just sat there! They had learnt (falsely) that there was no point in trying to avoid the pain.

This early animal work has been extended to human behaviour. It is argued that some individuals' life experience has shown them that there is no point in trying – no matter what they do they cannot change their life experience. So, for example, a small child who constantly finds that when he cries he is ignored will in the end simply stop trying to influence the world in this way. This can have both positive and negative consequences. Some childcare experts suggest that it is important not to run to the baby every time he cries and in the end this leads to more independent children (and better sleep for all). At the opposite end of the 'care continuum' a small number of children experience parental neglect. This often results in serious mental health and adjustment issues in later life.

It has been argued that it is not simply exposure to uncontrollable events that produces helplessness. Peterson and Barrett (1987) argue that individuals must attribute the lack of controllability to their own inadequacies. Other authors have suggested that it is not simply a disconnect between actions and outcomes, rather it is repeated failures that are the vital ingredient. The evidence is far from clear.

THE IMPACT OF FAILURE ON PERFORMANCE
A case study

The criterion-related validity of the MTQ48 was investigated by a study that examined the moderating effects that mental toughness has on performance. The study explored the ability of individuals to compartmentalize or show resilience when faced with 'failure'.

The study involved 79 participants (42 males, M age = 22.74 years, SD = 3.43; 37 females, M age = 22.43, SD = 3.85) who were given either positive or negative feedback after completing a number of motor tasks. They then carried out a cognitive task (planning exercise) as an objective measure of performance. The motor tasks and cognitive tasks should have been completed independently, involving very different skills.

Feedback tasks

Task 1

The shooting task entailed shooting a 'laser' gun at targets. The task was initially and successfully demonstrated by the experimenter. For each of the 30 trials, the experimenter switched on the appropriate light bulb for the target and the participants were asked to shoot. Depending on the feedback categories, the participants either scored less than estimated (negative feedback group) or higher than estimated (positive feedback group). The success rate was manipulated by the experimenter. When all 30 trials have been completed the participants were fed back their 'actual' results.

Task 2

Immediately after the first task the participants were asked to complete a snooker shot task. After rating their snooker ability on a 1–10 scale, participants were asked to complete five practice shots. Participants were then directed to carry out five pre-set shots and each shot was rated as to its success. At the end of this task the participants were given either negative or positive feedback in accordance with their allocated group. Again this feedback did not relate to actual performance.

Planning task

Straight after the snooker task the participants undertook a planning exercise. The exercise required various details and information to be organized into a timetable of sessions for a series of training classes. The main subtasks involved arranging appropriate dates for trainers, candidates and availability to hold the training sessions. More than one answer could be found for each subtask to fit in the appropriate slots on the timetable. However, only one totally correct answer could be found in which all details would fit into the timetable. Participants were provided with all subtask information at the beginning of the exercise and were able to work through the information in any order they chose. All participants were given 30 minutes to complete the exercise. The scores are shown in Tables 6.3 and 6.4.

The extreme scores of mental toughness (high and low 25 per cent) were examined and they showed that the participants with high mental toughness scored significantly higher on the planning exercise than the low mental toughness group (M = 2.71, SD = 1.10, M = 2.05, SD = .97; t = 2.08, df40, p = .044).

TABLE 6.3 Population scores of mental toughness

	N	Minimum	Maximum	Mean	Std Deviation
Challenge	79	2.50	4.75	3.75	.44
Commitment	79	2.00	4.36	3.47	.44
Control	79	2.36	4.07	3.30	.38
Confidence	79	2.27	4.60	3.47	.47
Mental toughness	79	2.48	4.17	3.46	.34

TABLE 6.4 Performance scores on planning exercise for participants receiving positive and negative feedback

Mental toughness group	N	Negative Feedback		Positive Feedback	
		Mean	Std Deviation	Mean	Std Deviation
Low	9	1.56	.882	2.42	.90
High	12	2.25	1.055	3.33	.87

The group that were given negative feedback scored significantly lower than the group that received positive feedback (M = 2.86, SD = .96, M = 2.29, SD = 1.14; t = 2.02, df77, p = .047).

The results

These results clearly illustrate how failure can loom over individuals, impacting on other aspects of their lives. However, the performance level of high mental toughness participants was not adversely affect by negative feedback. In other words they had not *learnt to fail.*

> I am not judged by the number of times I fail, but by the number of times I succeed; and the number of times I succeed is in direct proportion to the number of times I can fail and keep on trying. (Tom Hopkins)

The power of attributions

However, one repeated and validated finding is that attributions are central to feelings of control. Two seminal pieces of work have tackled this: Rotter's (1966) work on internal and external locus of control and Heider's (1944) work on attributions.

People with an internal locus of control believe they make things happen. This is obviously reflected closely in high scores on the MTQ48 control dimension. This clear dichotomy between internal and external loci is also reflected in the work of deCharms and Carpenter (1968). They too believed that there are two types of people: *origins* – these people love to be in control and originate their own behaviours; and *pawns* – these people often feel powerless and disenfranchised, being swept along by external pressures.

Cox (1998: 218), writing about locus of control, states, 'Research suggests that an internal orientation is more mature than an external orientation.' He then goes on to argue that childhood attributions should shift

TABLE 6.5 Attributions

	Internal	External
Stable	Ability	Task difficulty
Unstable	Effort	Luck

towards the internal and that perhaps involvement in sports and exercise may facilitate this shift. It is perhaps one of the most powerful ideas in psychology: that it's not what is happening that is important, rather it is what a person thinks is happening that is the key.

It can be claimed that it was Fritz Heider who first developed a coherent and useable theory of attributions. He again emphasized the importance of internal and external factors but further subdivided these. Within the internal category he identified ability and effort. In the external category he describes task difficulty and luck. So when an activity is performed the success or otherwise of it can be attributed to ability, hard work, its difficulty or chance. However, it was Weiner (1972), building on this work, who produced the model that is most widely used today; see Table 6.5.

In this model ability and effort are within the person. It is assumed that ability is relatively fixed in nature, but effort is very malleable. Individuals who believe they control their destiny will attribute success *and* failure to the internal factors. In other words they will succeed because they have talent and work hard. They fail because they do not have the skills or they simply do not try enough.

One of the core philosophies of mental toughness is just that. Success and failure are down to the individual. We are an intensely blame-ridden society at the moment – but that blame is usually focused on everything but ourselves. The mentally tough individual is willing to accept the consequences of his or her actions: both good and bad.

Later Weiner added a third dimension: controllability. This dimension related to individuals' belief that something was under their control or not. It is quite hard to identify an external factor that is also controllable. One candidate here is perhaps luck.

What of luck?

Luck and superstition give people a feeling of control over a very unpredictable world. It is clear that some people believe themselves to be unlucky: many fewer think that in fact they are blessed with good luck. It is very clear that perceptions of luck are based on faulty thinking.

Whilst by definition there has to be the world's unluckiest person – it's a statistical certainty – most people have about the same amount of ups and downs in life. However, their perceptions and attributions are very different. Some people dwell on the good; others on the bad. Individuals low in control tend to wait for something to come along, whereas the high controllers believe they will make it come along.

Professor Wiseman of the University of Hertfordshire is one of the few researchers who have seriously investigated luck. He identified four key principles (Wiseman, 2003):

1 *Maximize chance opportunities:* lucky people are skilled at creating, noticing and acting upon chance opportunities and experiences.

2 *Listen to lucky hunches:* lucky people make effective decisions by listening to their intuition and gut feelings.

3 *Expect good fortune:* lucky people are certain that the future is going to be full of good fortune. These expectations become self-fulfilling prophecies by helping lucky people persist in the face of failure, and shape their interactions with others in a positive way.

4 *Turn bad luck to good:* lucky people employ various psychological techniques to cope with, and often even thrive upon, the ill fortune that comes their way.

Superstition certainly gives a sense of control, but it is basically faulty thinking. The great behavioural scientist B F Skinner demonstrated that you could produce superstitious behaviour in pigeons. He fed the birds randomly. Obviously at the time of feeding the birds were carrying out some form of behaviour. Although these were completely irrelevant they tended to repeat them consistently in the mistaken 'belief' that their actions would produce reward – lo and behold a new superstition was born!

Mentally tough individuals clearly have a grasp on reality and also a need to be in charge of their own destiny.

Emotional control

Whilst the clear focus of the control component is on individuals controlling their own lives and development, an important subcomponent is the control of emotions. It has long been recognized that some individuals are more emotionally reactive than others. This particular personality dimension, usually described as neuroticism, is often seen as one of the 'big five' personality factors that are used to describe humans. These are:

1 *Openness* – inventive/curious vs consistent/cautious.

2 *Conscientiousness* – efficient/organized vs easy-going/careless.

3 *Extraversion* – outgoing/energetic vs shy/reserved.

4 *Agreeableness* – friendly/compassionate vs cold/unkind.

5 *Neuroticism* – sensitive/nervous vs secure/confident.

Research at Hull University has shown that scores on the emotional control subscales correlate negatively with both neuroticism and trait anxiety. Individuals with greater emotional control have lower levels of neuroticism. Lower scores on neuroticism are also related to emotional stability and the ability to bounce back quickly from setbacks.

Eysenck, who carried out the initial work on neuroticism, felt that these traits were closely linked to the operating of the central nervous system and also that personality is highly heritable. This 'biological basis' of personality has echoes in the latest work at Hull University involving brain scanning. This has shown a number of interesting findings. Control of emotion showed a correlation with the precuneus and with the inferior parietal lobule. The inferior parietal lobule has been shown to have a number of links to emotion, for instance it is involved with perspective-taking of social emotions and it has been shown to be involved in the processing of happiness-specific information. These links to the regulation of emotion and recognition of the emotion of happiness, again combined with the feeling of agency provided by the precuneus, could explain why people with these attributes would feel that they have good control over their emotions.

Commitment

07

> *Courage and perseverance have a magical talisman, before which difficulties disappear and obstacles vanish into air.*
> **JOHN QUINCY ADAMS**

Commitment is a measure of how and why we set goals and also how we respond to them. This component reflects the extent to which we make promises, particularly those which are tangible and measurable, and the extent to which we commit to keeping those promises. Those promises can be promises we make to others and/or they can be promises we make to ourselves.

We tend commonly to make promises to others in the workplace. This underpins many appraisal or personal development processes. But it can also include working towards sales or delivery targets, completing projects on time, dealing with a rush job, etc. We are often pressed to make similar promises to others in many other ways, for example promising to visit ailing relatives, to help someone achieve something, to train to be a fit or competent member of a team, to do well in exams, to get a job, etc.

We also make many promises to ourselves. New Year resolutions are one obvious example. Giving up smoking, trying to lose weight, passing an exam, staying in touch with friends are other examples.

Fall seven times, stand up eight. (Japanese proverb)

Making and keeping promises are an important aspect of the way people deal with each other. We can sometimes be judged in terms of our reliability: 'I can trust him or her to do that.' It can be an important aspect of the way that others see us. This can have a big impact on performance, particularly in groups or teams. If you are viewed as unlikely to be committed to something then others with whom you need to cooperate may take the view it's not worth the effort of supporting you and will avoid doing so, negatively affecting your ability to succeed.

Our approach to goals and targets (and indeed the same goal or target) can vary. For some of us the very notion of a target is motivating. In our mind we can see that goal or target as helping to define what success looks like. Provided it is reasonably achievable we will go for it and do whatever it takes to hit the target. Even if obstacles arise this won't necessarily dampen our enthusiasm for the target, the driver is there – we want to hit most or the entire target. It equates broadly to notions of tenacity, persistent determination, perseverance, doggedness, resolve, diligence, application and purpose.

Quite often, for some people all that is needed to get them going is the goal or target. It is sufficiently motivating to them to work out how that target can be achieved. For others, goals and targets are intimidating and will induce fear, anxiety and even mental paralysis. For them, goals and targets are to be avoided or ignored. The notion is one that doesn't just describe success – it also indicates what failure might look like. The object of our commitment can appear overwhelming: 'When I fail to achieve this, and it doesn't look achievable, then I and everyone else will know I am a failure.' Indeed the more they think this way the more they believe the goal is not achievable.

Again, two people of equal ability, experience and skill can look at the same goals or targets and one will view them in one way and the other will view them differently. This translates into differences in performance, well-being, behaviour, etc.

As with all the components of mental toughness, an exceptionally high level of commitment can have its downside. Highly committed people can be obstinate, intransigent and stubborn. They can persevere with a task past the point where it makes any sense to continue. If in a managerial position or a position of authority this can mean they will drive others with the same level of will. At times this may mean that the individual is being driven out of his or her comfort zone with all the attendant consequences.

Similarly, they will often 'manage by numbers'. Because knowing the goal or target is sufficient for their own need to get going they may not appreciate that others (who may not be as committed) will need a degree of support or guidance in order to deliver to a task. Most people need to know not only 'what' is to be achieved but something about the 'how'. Without that, delegation or tasking others can become a stressful exercise.

Commitment – defined and applied

Defined: this subscale measures the extent to which an individual is likely to persist with a goal or work task. Individuals differ in the degree to which they remain focused on their goals. Some may be easily distracted, bored or divert their attention to competing goals, whereas others may be more likely to persist.

Applied: an individual who scores at the high end of the scale will be able to handle and achieve things when faced with tough and unyielding deadlines.

An individual at the other end will need to be free from those types of demands to handle work.

Sample descriptors and behaviours that are often associated with extreme positions on the commitment scale are shown in Table 7.1. This is not an exclusive or comprehensive list.

> Nothing in this world can take the place of persistence. Talent will not; nothing is more common than unsuccessful people with talent. Genius will not; unrewarded genius is almost a proverb. Education will not; the world is full of educated derelicts. Persistence and determination alone are omnipotent. (Calvin Coolidge)

The psychological context

Procrastination

Putting things off, or procrastination, is one of the most common forms of self-handicapping amongst a wide range of people.

> Self-handicaps are anticipatory excuses that are presented to obscure the link between performance and ability. Self-handicaps protect people's images of self-competence in the event of poor performances. (Galluci, 2008: 217)

There have been a number of explanations given to why people put things off when they know they shouldn't. It can be seen as a coping mechanism to reduce stress. However, whilst it can certainly help in the short term, in the longer term it makes the situation much worse. At best it's an effective passive coping strategy. It has been suggested that trait procrastination comes into being as a result of childhood experiences. It can be suggested that it might be a passive aggressive way for a child to express his or her anger at having to achieve all the time. This links closely to learnt helplessness. Ferrari and Tice (2000) showed in an experimental study that procrastinators sometime find it better to risk failure than to look foolish. Galluci (2008: 240) writes:

> procrastinators protect their self-esteem at the cost of underachievement, unrealized goals, and wasted potential. Perhaps ruminations about 'what might have been' sustain hope in abilities, but again this comes at the considerable cost of regret regarding lost and squandered opportunities.

The trait of conscientiousness

Another way of looking at the problem of procrastination is to adopt a trait approach. It has been suggested that human beings only have five predominant personality traits; see for example, McCrae and Costa (1987). These are often described as the 'big five' personality traits and are:

1 *Extraversion:* this trait includes characteristics such as excitability, sociability, talkativeness, assertiveness and high amounts of emotional expressiveness.

TABLE 7.1 Commitment scores

Lower Scores	Higher Scores
Intimidated by goals and measures – they induce paralysis	Like goals and measures – these describe what success looks like
May feel inadequate or 'stupid' when asked to do something	Goals are translated into something which is achievable
May lack a sense of purpose – they can think 'win-lose'	Tend to be more objective about things
Goals become something which appears overpowering	Will break things down into manageable chunks
May resent the imposition of goals and targets	Prepared to do what it takes - Will work long and hard if needed
Unwilling to make an effort or give up something less important	Maintain focus
May respond emotionally when given tasks	Like the repeated opportunity to measure and prove themselves
Allow themselves to be easily distracted	Diligent about projects – deliver on time
Adopt a minimalist approach – will do the absolute minimum	Will prioritize effort and activities
Will avoid targets	Will attend meetings/classes even if they don't like the people/topic
Will skip meetings or classes	(hyper-) Active
More likely to be late for things	Accept responsibility
May sleep in at times	Set high standards for self and others
Find reasons to miss the target	May overdo a task (may overwork too)
'I can't do... Maths'	Like being judged or assessed
May try self-sabotage to get out of doing something	Won't let others down
Will default to a life experience which provides an excuse to blame someone else for failure – 'I couldn't do this because my parents...'	May deliver too quickly at times
	Can inconvenience others with their focus on KPIs
Unlikely to volunteer for things, especially extreme tasks	Have a sense of purpose – will often think 'win-win'
Prepared to let others down	Like ownership, acceptance and responsibility
Can be seen as irresponsible	
Easily bored – won't commit time and effort	
Can feel unlucky – it's not my day	
Not happy about being judged	

2 *Agreeableness:* this personality dimension includes attributes such as trust, altruism, kindness, affection and other pro-social behaviours.

3 *Conscientiousness:* common features of this dimension include high levels of thoughtfulness, with good impulse control and goal-directed behaviours. Those high in conscientiousness tend to be organized and mindful of details.

4 *Neuroticism:* individuals high in this trait tend to experience emotional instability, anxiety, moodiness, irritability and sadness.

5 *Openness:* this trait features characteristics such as imagination and insight, and those high in this trait tend to have a broad range of interests.

Conscientiousness reflects an individual's degree of self-discipline. High scorers make plans and are organized, avoiding distractions. Conscientiousness has been clearly linked to academic and business success. Intriguingly, people who are more conscientious – or have a tendency to be self-disciplined, careful and purposeful – appear less likely to develop physical and psychological diseases.

That conscientiousness seems to promote longevity is not surprising. People with this trait tend to practise a number of healthy behaviours such as not smoking, drinking in moderation, exercising regularly and adhering to medical recommendations. They also tend to get better jobs and earn higher salaries.

It has been shown that out of the big five personality traits only conscientiousness predicts success across *all* categories of work. The other four have specific advantages in particular jobs but conscientiousness has a generally powerful impact across the board. Although it is the case that this trait has a generally positive impact on people, it can have its dark side. Individuals who are high on conscientiousness or commitment can suffer if they are prevented from reaching their goals by outside factors.

For example, Boyce *et al* (2010) carried out a four-year longitudinal study of 9,570 individuals. They found that that the drop in an individual's life satisfaction following unemployment was moderated by his or her conscientiousness. After three years of unemployment individuals high in conscientiousness experienced a 120 per cent greater decrease in life satisfaction than those at low levels. Individuals who score highly on commitment are more likely to succeed, but are also more likely to suffer if they fail.

Apply yourself. Get all the education you can, but then, by God, do something. Don't just stand there, make it happen. (Lee Iacocca)

Goal setting

A goal is a dream with its feet on the ground. (Frank Vizarre)

Goal setting is a very important psychological technique. Its practical applications will be discussed in some detail in Chapter 26. It was initially developed by Edwin Locke (1968), who conceived it as a cognitive process, with a person's conscious goals and intentions the primary drivers of behaviour.

Goal setting has had a major impact on all walks of life, leading Mento *et al* (1987) to write: 'If there is ever to be a viable candidate from the organizational sciences for elevation to the lofty status of a scientific law of nature, then the relationship between goal difficulty, specificity, commitment and task performance are serious contenders.' However, as is the case with the underlying trait of conscientiousness itself, the story is a little more complex. First, individual differences play a part in the use of goal setting techniques. Individuals low on commitment often find goal setting difficult and attempting to set goals can create very high levels of anxiety. Whilst these problems can be overcome with appropriate and individualized training it is important to recognize that one size does not fit all.

Similarly, whilst the research evidence into the effectiveness of goal setting in the workplace has been impressive, other areas of life do not seem to show this clear pattern. For example, research within the sporting domain has been equivocal at best. As this world is dominated by the ability to measure almost every aspect of performance this, at first sight, seems inexplicable. The problem seems to stem from a whole host of methodological inadequacies of the studies that have been undertaken. Where these have been addressed the findings appear to be more consistent with those emanating from the world of work.

It is clear that goal setting works but:

- some individuals, for example those scoring low on the commitment scales, need more help in using this technique;

- the goal setting process is complicated and the goals set say as much about the individual as they do about the task to be performed; and

- poor goal setting not only does not work, it has a negative impact on performance.

David Beckham is Britain's finest striker of a football not because of God-given talent but because he practises with a relentless application that the vast majority of less gifted players wouldn't contemplate. (Sir Alex Ferguson)

STICKING TO A BORING TASK A case study

A study sought to investigate the relationship between mental toughness (as measured using the MTQ48) and vigilance as a measure of performance under mental stress.

What was done

Twenty-two healthy participants (eight males and 14 females) with a mean age of 21 years took part in this study. Participants were grouped as either high or low mentally tough in relation to their MTQ48 scores.

FIGURE 7.1 Mean number of errors in a vigilance task for low and high mental toughness groups

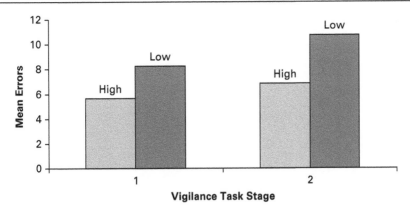

Participants carried out a vigilance task under both normal and stressed conditions. The vigilance task consisted of watching a computer screen on which a circle of 20 points would progressively illuminate one by one, similar to the second hand advancing round a clock face. This is widely known as the Mackworth Clock task.

Participants watched for a 'missed' advancement, where the point supposed to illuminate does not, and the next one does. When this event occurred, participants were to respond as quickly as possible. The task lasted 10 minutes, during which each point was highlighted for 0.7 seconds and 40 'misses' would occur. The number of errors (missed responses and incorrect responses) was calculated for comparison.

Following completion of the first experimental 10-minute stage, participants were asked to place their hand into a cold water bath, keeping it open, for three minutes, but were informed that they were free to withdraw their hand at any time if it became too uncomfortable. The second stage of the Mackworth Clock task was identical to the first stage, and was completed immediately after the end of the cold pressor test.

Results

High mentally tough individuals performed significantly better on the Mackworth Clock task, reporting higher levels of vigilance than lower mentally tough individuals. This was apparent in the significantly lower number of errors for high mental toughness participants for normal stage 1 and stressed stage 2 when compared to low mental toughness participants for stage 1 and stage 2; see Figure 7.1.

And the conclusion...

The MTQ48 successfully predicted performance on a standard test of vigilance. High mentally tough individuals were more vigilant under both normal and stressful conditions. It can be argued that they were more committed to an intrinsically dull task. They were less likely to lose focus and concentration, not allowing themselves to become distracted.

Challenge

08

> *Accept challenges, so that you may feel the exhilaration of victory.* **GEORGE S PATTON**

This component of mental toughness addresses how we, as individuals, respond to challenge. A challenge represents any activity or event we see as out of the ordinary and which involves doing something that is stretching.

For someone in the workplace it might be doing a presentation to senior managers, being put in charge of an important project, representing the organization in a negotiation, or delivering some output in an uncomfortably tight timescale. For students, exams and coursework represent challenges. For athletes, achieving personal best times and performing in competition (especially in front of a crowd) are good examples. For someone who is unemployed getting a job can be a challenge. For others it could be giving up smoking, recovering from illness, etc.

Probably the most important type of challenge everyone faces is the need to deal with change (and in some cases, variety and flexibility). How we perceive challenge is key to how we cope and deal with it. For some a major challenge or a major period of change will be considered exciting, even welcomed. The individual is likely to view the challenge in a positive light. This will be an opportunity to push back the boundaries, to demonstrate to oneself, and perhaps to others, that one can deal with the unknown or the risk entailed in dealing with a significant change. This could be a chance to prove something to yourself.

Others (who might have the same or even higher levels of ability) will see the same situation as threatening and almost certainly not an opportunity for positive self-discovery. Change and facing significant challenge are likely to be considered as negative opportunities – 'this is something that will find me out and will expose me'.

If we look at the example of being asked to do a presentation, the immediate reaction for many will be to be fearful of the experience. They visualize a presentation where things go wrong rather than well. They visualize a situation where notes are lost or dropped; slides are in the wrong sequence; they forget what comes next; they stutter in the wrong places and worst of all, someone asks trick questions that leave them speechless. The biggest fear is that everyone there will know more about the subject than they do.

> To dare is to lose one's footing momentarily. Not to dare is to lose oneself.
> (Soren Kierkegaard)

Small wonder then that the prospect of doing a presentation can terrify some people. And it impacts in a negative way that reinforces the fear. As much as they try to prepare, nothing seems to work and it only serves to convince them that they will do a very poor job and will be humiliated by the experience.

A more positive outlook will create an entirely different picture in the mind of the would-be presenter. This time individuals see it as something that provides an opportunity to impress or to get an important message over to some key people. In their mind's eye they see everything going smoothly. The presentation is well received; they anticipate most questions, acknowledge the questioner and respond firmly and convincingly. Even if asked an unexpected question, they have the confidence to deal with it. They look forward to the presentation and, for them, even preparing for the event is enjoyable and comes easily. The difference between the two is in the mind.

Challenge – defined and applied

Defined: individuals differ in their approach to challenge. Some consider challenges and problems to be opportunities, whereas others may be more likely to consider a challenging situation as a threat.

This subscale measures the extent to which an individual is likely to view a challenge as an opportunity. Those scoring highly on this scale may have a tendency actively to seek out such situations for self-development, whereas low scorers may avoid challenging situations for fear of failure or aversion to effort.

Applied: at one end of the scale we find those who thrive in continually changing environments. At the other end, we find those who prefer to minimize exposure to change and the problems that come with that – and will strongly prefer to work in stable environments.

This concept of challenge emerges as a significant factor in a wide range of applications. Essentially it describes how we approach a variety of different situations. The term 'challenge' doesn't mean that the situation itself has to present a big challenge. It can be something that many people might recognize as comparatively insignificant. However, for the individual, and in his or her mind, it does represent something significant. It can explain why, on occasions, a perfectly competent individual may underperform and why a moderately competent person may perform better than expected. They will 'punch above their weight'.

The situation itself doesn't have to be unduly threatening or stimulating. The individual must see it as such. It is the individual's perception of challenge and change that determines how he or she behaves and how he or she performs.

We often see this clearly in school years. Those whose challenge scores are low will see examinations, tests and coursework as opportunities to expose how little they know about a topic. Just the thought of this will create anxiety. Studies indicate that language plays a part here too. If the prospect of examinations creates anxiety then simply the word 'exam' can create that anxiety. Alternatively, there are those who see the same situation as exciting, as an opportunity to show the examiner what they know and that this provides the opportunity to achieve some recognition for their effort.

In the world of sport we see athletes who are excellent technicians but who fail to succeed on the big day. Others of more modest ability will emerge as champions because they are geared up for the big event. The big game player is not a myth. In recent years, we have seen Tiger Woods dominate the golf world. He is certainly the most successful golfer in recent times but there are few that would say he is the most gifted golfer, although all would agree he is a very good golfer. That difference – the ability to optimize his talent on the big occasion – can partly be explained by his mindset as he approaches major competitions. His approach to challenge is nothing but positive.

In business there are very many applications for the concept. If we look at commonplace business activities such as meetings and negotiations, success is often not down to innate ability nor does it even reflect the quality of work done in leading up to the activity. It will just as often be down to entering those activities with the right frame of mind: 'I am going to do a great job... this is my chance to show what I can do... I know enough to deal with it' as opposed to 'This won't go well, I know my stuff but I can see someone will try to trip me up... I'll get it over with as fast as possible.' An increasing proportion of white-collar work is project based. Entering a project on a 'can do' (not a 'gung ho') basis is likely to produce better results than a sense of intimidation and seeing the challenge as overwhelming.

As with mental toughness generally and with each of the components, we can be forgiven for thinking that being very mentally tough is always good. It is certainly the case that on the whole, the more mentally tough you are the better you will perform and the more likely you are to enjoy better wellbeing. However, being strongly oriented towards challenge (typically achieving sten scores of 8, 9 and 10 in MTQ48) may also have potential downsides.

Someone strongly focused on challenge may like it so much that they will put themselves (and others) forward for challenges that are either extremely difficult to achieve or perhaps, for most people, impossible to achieve. Similarly, if they like change and variety they are unlikely to be happy in a stable and slowly changing environment. They may provoke change for change's sake and may prove disruptive in a well-regulated environment.

They are also likely to be the type of person who comes into work each morning with a new idea. This may be a positive quality in many situations but in some it can be a problem. If these are managers or leaders (and they often are) they may be guilty of creating 'initiative overload'. They may take on too many challenges and too much change on behalf of the team and may take on tasks that others simply find intimidating. If others in their team aren't so oriented then they will find this type of behaviour extremely stressful and may find they cannot deal or cope with it. This can produce the paradox where the most creative person on the team does what is required but finds that his or her own behaviour affects the behaviour of others to the extent that his or her own performance and the performance of others is adversely affected.

So the challenge for people who score high on any of the scales is to capture the essence of this and play to their strengths whilst understanding the potential impact on the behaviour of others on whom they may depend, and learn to develop tools, techniques and behaviours that mitigate the unwanted responses and encourage positive responses. Sample descriptors and behaviours that are often associated with extreme positions on the challenge scale are shown in Table 8.1. This is not an exclusive or comprehensive list.

TABLE 8.1 Sample descriptors, challenge

Lower Scores	Higher Scores
Don't like sudden changes	Like challenge
Don't like shocks	Easily bored – will seek change
Fear of failure	Provoke change
Avoid effort	Like problem solving
Intimidated by challenges	Work hard
Tend to achieve minimum standards	Happy to commit to projects, studies, etc
Respond poorly to competitive people	Volunteer for projects (and tend to commit others?)
Dislike being in new situations – new colleagues, new bosses, new premises, etc	Enjoy competition and show it
Prefer routine	Happy to receive attention
Avoid risk (particularly, of failure)	May not always be content with daily life and routines
Uncomfortable with competitive sports	'Addicted' to adrenalin
Worry about the views of others	Can appear arrogant
May get things out of perspective	May have little regard for the impact of their ideas or activities on others

The psychological context of challenge

Put simply, the challenge component of mental toughness relates to individuals' view about what challenge has to offer them. High scorers see a challenging situation as an opportunity to show off their talents and as a way of developing themselves. A number of psychological models relate to this.

- achievement orientation;
- fear of failure;
- competitiveness; and
- the adrenalin junkie.

Achievement orientation

Murray (1938) defined the need to achieve as the desire to 'overcome obstacles, to exercise power, to strive to do something as well as and as quickly as possible'. This obviously has a major resonance with mental toughness. Murray was in many ways a pioneer in performance psychology, which is reflected in his approach to measuring achievement orientation. He devised the radical Thematic Apperception Test (TAT). This was basically a series of pictures from which respondents had to produce a story. So for example one of the pictures is of an old woman and a much younger one. A very achievement-oriented individual may tell a story about the younger women being held back by having to look after the older one. An individual higher on affiliation may interpret the picture in a different way, for example focusing on a supportive relationship between the two characters.

> Do not give up, and always create your own momentum... Build on every success to get more successes. And never quit. (Mark Victor Hansen)

McClelland's learnt needs theory (1962)

McClelland's theory suggests that individuals learn needs from their culture. Three of the primary needs in this theory are affiliation, power and achievement. The need for affiliation is a desire to establish social relationships with others. The need for power reflects a desire to control one's environment and influence others. The need for achievement is a desire to take responsibility, set challenging goals, and obtain performance feedback.

McClelland's impact has arguably been in the area of achievement motivation. He adopted an experimental approach to his work. The basic paradigm was that during the experiments participants were asked to throw hoops over pegs. No rules or parameters were set by him, but he noted a small number of highly achievement-oriented people had a particular approach to goal setting. They would set their hoop performance goals in a way that was not too easy but also not too hard. He coined the term

'Balanced Challenge', which is an excellent way of understanding the challenge component of our mental toughness model.

Research looking at people with a high need for achievement has shown that they are more persistent, work harder and are medium risk takers. McClelland identified a number of other core characteristics of achievement-oriented individuals. These include the following:

- Achievement is more important than material or financial reward.
- Financial reward is regarded as a measurement of success, not an end in itself.
- Feedback is essential, because it enables measurement of success, not for reasons of praise or recognition (the implication here is that feedback must be reliable, quantifiable and factual).
- Achievement-motivated people constantly seek improvements and ways of doing things better.

McClelland's work has been very influential. It is possible to use the theory to generate an action plan for developing a positive challenge-focused orientation. This includes:

- allowing feedback;
- using achievement heroes – publicize the successes of similar types of people;
- working to improve the self-image of individuals – a confident person is a productive one;
- introducing realism – people should think in realistic terms and think positively.

McClelland's theory has one fundamental difference from the other need theories: it suggests that needs can be acquired or taught, and therefore provides a less deterministic view of motivation. An individual who finds an activity challenging but rewarding will seek out more of this type of action. Individuals with a high need for achievement tend to come from families where achievement was positively rewarded. Often individuals within this environment report that their parents were not particularly warm, emphasizing achievement rather than affiliation.

Another important voice in the area of achievement is that of John Atkinson, a student of McClelland. Atkinson was drawn to an expectancy-value approach. Basically he attempted to understand why people do things on the basis of three components:

1 *Valence* – the attraction of psychological objects.
2 *Instrumentality* – the relationship between outcome and other outcomes.
3 *Expectancy* – probability estimate of the relationship between action and outcome.

He felt that McClelland's achievement theory was not complete. He emphasized the role of the balanced challenge, focusing particularly on the key balance between the need for achievement and the fear of failure. He was aware that linking achievement orientation to performance is not quite as straightforward as it would seem.

People high on achievement orientation are not always drawn to the most difficult tasks. Instead they tend to be drawn to moderately difficult activities, ones in which they have a good chance of succeeding. Motivation to perform an activity is a complex interrelationship between need to achieve and the need to avoid failure.

Fear of failure

The importance of confronting failure was well described by Theodore Roosevelt who stated: 'It is hard to fail, but it is worse never to have tried to succeed.'

It is widely understood that you cannot succeed or win every time. The old adage that 'you learn more by your mistakes' is undoubtedly true, but perhaps not for everyone. The less mentally tough individual may in fact find the experience of failing so traumatic that he or she simply withdraws from the situation.

> Failure is the opportunity to begin again more intelligently. (Henry Ford)

The research evidence suggests that there are significant differences in the levels of fear of failure experienced. It is unclear why this variation occurs, but many authors have relied on a psychoanalytical approach. This tends to suggest that differences in parenting behaviour and other socializations can have a profound effect.

A major force in developing the concept of learnt helplessness was Martin Seligman (1972). His initial work with animals led him to consider the wider implications of this important concept. He wrote:

> I was stunned by the implications. If, dogs could learn something as complex as the futility of their actions, here was an analogy to human helplessness... helplessness was all around us – from the urban poor to the despondent patient with his face to the wall.

Learnt helplessness is obviously highly related to the *control* component of our model as well as challenge. The 4 Cs are distinct in their own right, but there is a degree of overlap.

What of competitiveness?

Competitiveness is certainly an identifiable characteristic. We meet competitive people every day. The challenge component of our model includes an element of competitiveness – the desire, or even need, to win.

This particular aspect of the challenge component can obviously be both a positive force for good and a negative. It can be a driver for success but it can also be a disrupting influence, especially when working with other people.

> If I had to single out one element in my life that has made a difference for me, it would be a passion to compete. (Sam Walton)

In a study carried out with 200 students at the University of Hull, MTQ48 scores were compared to a measure of personality, the ICES scales in the Prevue Assessment. This is a reliable and validated measure of ability, interests and personality. Within its personality scales there is a measure of trait competitiveness. It has been shown that the challenge component of the MTQ48 is significantly correlated with the competitiveness subscale.

> The difference between a successful person and others is not a lack of strength, not a lack of knowledge, but rather a lack of will. (Vince Lombardi)

Research has shown gender differences in competitiveness. It is often assumed that males are more competitive than females. These differences helped prompt the development of a rather interesting model of achievement orientation by Spence and Helmreich (1983). They noted that there were not really gender differences in the desire for achievement or challenge but rather the differences lay in the type of achievement orientation displayed. Their model of achievement had three main strands:

1 Satisfaction with the performance itself: basically getting a buzz from a job well done.
2 Sense of completion: gaining satisfaction from getting something finished.
3 A sense of competitiveness: the enjoyment derived from winning.

Spence and her co-investigators repeatedly identified that males were more competitive, defined by them as 'the enjoyment of interpersonal competition and the desire to win and be better than others', but the two other dimensions did not have any gender variation.

In their research programme it became clear that objective measures of success, for example salaries and academic achievement, were higher for individuals who had higher levels of performance satisfaction and completions, as long as they were lower in competitiveness. Higher levels of competitiveness led to performance decrements, perhaps because these individuals focused more on winning than on doing a good job.

Our challenge component tries to take a broad perspective, ensuring it incorporates all aspects of achievement. Support for this approach is apparent in the fact that no gender differences exist in the component or in mental toughness as a whole.

Mental toughness and risk

The challenge component certainly has a risk flavour about it. It is clear that individuals high on challenge are drawn to controlled risk.

Maddi (2004) examined risk taking from what might be called an existentialist perspective. He argued that life was a series of decisions. In making decisions, individuals face a choice between repeating the past by choosing the familiar path, or striking out in new directions (ie, more risky but also potentially more rewarding).

Nesti (2004) developed a similar theme, but related this to sports. He argued that choosing the past 'tried and tested methods and approaches' can be comforting but it tends to lead to stagnation. Regularly choosing the past can mean missing important opportunities for personal growth, and appears to be linked to individuals who do not learn to operate outside their own comfort zone.

Crust and Keegan (2010) argue that hardy individuals appear to be future-oriented decision makers who seek out challenges, take risks and approach, rather than avoid, potential anxiety-producing situations.

> You'll either step forward into growth or step back into safety. (Abraham Maslow)

Crust and Keegan (2010) carried out a study examining risk-taking attitude and mental toughness (using scores from MTQ48). They concluded that a willingness to take risks was an important attitude that characterizes mentally tough athletes. They also found that overall mental toughness and the subscales of challenge and confidence in abilities were significantly and positively related to attitudes to risk. However, these relations were limited to attitudes towards physical risk taking. Indeed, only the mental toughness subscale of interpersonal confidence was found to be significantly related to attitudes towards psychological risk.

Confidence

09

It's not who we are that holds us back, it's who we think we're not. MICHAEL NOLAN

'Confidence' measures the extent to which we have self-belief to see through to a conclusion a difficult task that can be beset with setbacks. This scale has two component subscales. Overall it describes how we deal with setbacks or with challenges that threaten setbacks. These setbacks can be physical, mental or they can be oral (such as oral challenge or criticism from others).

Those with high levels of overall confidence will accept that setbacks are part and parcel of everyday life. When these occur, confident people will take them in their stride. A setback or a vigorous challenge from others may stop them in their tracks. But the overall response is likely to be that they will pick themselves up, dust themselves off and continue with even greater determination. The setback may spur them on to try harder to ensure success or to recover lost ground – 'this isn't going to beat me!'

Those with low levels of overall confidence will see the same setback or oral challenge in a different way. They are more likely to feel defeated and accept that what has happened is so significant that it will prevent them from achieving the goal or task. They are more likely to give up and feel that they 'have given it their best shot' and will do no more.

Twenty years from now you will be more disappointed by the things that you didn't do than by the ones you did do. (Mark Twain)

Confidence – defined and applied

Defined: individuals high in confidence have the self-belief to complete successfully tasks that may be considered too difficult by individuals with similar abilities but lower confidence.

Applied: for example, individuals at one end of the scale will be able to take setbacks (external or self-generated) in their stride. They keep their heads when things go wrong and it may even strengthen their resolve to do something. At the other end, individuals will be unsettled by setbacks and will feel undermined by these. Their heads are said to 'drop'.

Continuing research has identified two subscales for this component:

1 Confidence (Abilities) – Individuals scoring highly on this scale are more likely to believe that they are a truly worthwhile person. They are less dependent on external validation and tend to be more optimistic about life in general.

2 Confidence (Interpersonal) – Individuals scoring highly on this scale tend to be more assertive. They are less likely to be intimidated in social settings and are more likely to promote themselves in groups. They are also better able to handle difficult or awkward people.

When we first started to examine the confidence scale, our first thoughts were that confidence was largely down to the extent to which someone had confidence in their abilities. This has some kind of simple appeal. However, at the same time we were managing and running a major development centre programme for HM Customs & Excise in the UK. This involved assessing around 700 senior managers through a series of observed exercises that required groups of these managers to work together to solve problems and carry out tasks.

All of the managers were well-educated and well-qualified. Some were exceptionally well-qualified. As time went by, we noticed that the most effective managers weren't always the best qualified. It became apparent that many of these very knowledgeable managers would barely contribute to discussions and take a lead even when they were the acknowledged 'expert' in the matter at hand.

Curiously, at about the same time we were carrying out a similar exercise with several hundred middle and senior managers in a major automotive component manufacturer, AP Lockheed, where we observed exactly the same phenomenon. In both cases we would see individuals playing a major role in a discussion and often being highly influential even though it was apparent that they were not particularly able in the area in question.

In both cases the client organization had agreed that we could use the experimental mental toughness questionnaire to gather data on participants. What emerged was an understanding that interpersonal confidence was a significant component of overall confidence. Confidence therefore had two subscales:

1 *Confidence in abilities* – the confidence that you have the intellectual toolkit – knowledge, skills, education and experience – to attempt and to complete a particular task or action, even if this task was difficult in some way and had the potential for setbacks or failures along the way to completion.

2 *Interpersonal confidence* – the confidence to deal with oral challenges that might interfere with successful completion of the task. These include dealing with criticism and adverse comments when problems arise as well as having the oral confidence to represent your views and your position compellingly, often in the face of alternative views expressed by others. The ability to hold your own when you know you are right to do so.

Again we see the relevance of the confidence scale in all walks of life.

It is commonly said of the most successful sports teams, 'they expect to win and go out there believing that'. There may be a narrow line between arrogance and confidence but it is difficult to be a successful athlete unless you have that confidence.

Any educationalist will give you hundreds of examples of the ordinary students who 'over-achieved' because they believed in themselves and of the impossibly bright students who 'under-achieved' because they didn't have the confidence to express themselves. Under-confident students will look at a question in an exam paper and believe they can't provide an answer even when they know everything they need to know. They may even minimize their response because providing a full answer carries for them a risk that this might not be what the examiner is looking for – and so the examiner never sees what the student does know.

In the workplace, examples are equally common. In one extreme example a few years ago, whilst involved in a selection interview we could hear the applicant mutter, 'This is not going well. I am not going to get this job.' As Henry Ford once suggested, 'if you think you can't, you're probably right'.

Confidence in abilities

Confidence is a measure of self-esteem, identifying the extent to which you feel worthwhile and in need of external validation; see Table 9.1.

Interpersonal confidence

This measures the extent to which we are prepared to assert ourselves and our preparedness to deal with challenge or ridicule; see Table 9.2.

The psychological context for confidence

Self-confidence is a very fuzzy term. A number of constructs have been related to it but it is fair to say that the picture is rather messy. In this section we

TABLE 9.1 Confidence scores

Low Scores	High Scores
Low self-belief	Can believe they are right... even when they are wrong
Not confident that they know your subject matter even when they do	Little or no need for external validation
Produce minimal responses when asked	Happy to ask questions
Will be reluctant to express a view in discussion or debate	Happy to provide full responses to questions and in tests/exams
Will be reluctant to ask questions 'in case it makes me look stupid'	See critical feedback as feedback (no more and no less)
Reluctant to do presentations or oral work	See competence and excellence in others as a motivator 'I can aspire to that'
Inner belief missing – need others to build that	Happy to draw in their experiences into what they do
Unsure whether they have grasped a subject or not – feel you are still missing something	
Will take critical remarks as confirmation of their self-limiting beliefs	
Can be inhibited by competence or excellence in others – feel they don't measure up	
May try to bluster, over-talk	
May be inexperienced and underestimate their own capabilities	

will describe and discuss some of the main constructs that have been related to confidence. Overall mental toughness is clearly related to a number of the constructs that can be, and have been, labelled confidence. For example, in a sample of 200 managers the correlations shown in Table 9.3 were found (all significant at the $p<0.001$ level).

Self-efficacy

Self-efficacy is perhaps the most influential theoretical idea in the area of confidence. According to Albert Bandura, self-efficacy is 'the belief in one's capabilities to organize and execute the courses of action required to manage prospective situations' (1977). In other words, self-efficacy is a person's belief in his or her ability to succeed in a particular situation.

Bandura described these beliefs as determinants of how people think, behave and feel. Many authors use the terms self-confidence and self-efficacy interchangeably and it is not unusual to find the sentence 'for self-efficacy

TABLE 9.2 Interpersonal confidence scores

Low Scores	High Scores
Easily intimidated	Will stand their ground
Won't express themselves in class/ debate even when they know they are right	Will face down criticism, etc
	Will easily engage in class and group activity
Lack the confidence to express that they know in writing – will understate a position	Will use this quality to argue down others more knowledgeable
Won't ask questions – low engagement	Can be aggressive
	Not easily embarrassed
Will accept criticism and ridicule even when not warranted	Comfortable with negative situations – can deal with the fallout
Will back down quickly when challenged	Tend to be more risk-oriented
Will allow others to dominate debates – even when they are more knowledgeable	Comfortable working in a group and making a contribution
Will have difficulty dealing with assertive people	Happy to ask for help and support – won't see this as a shortcoming – it's just something that is needed
Not good with negative situations	More likely to be involved in lots of things
Will minimize communications – 'won't ask for help when needed'	Won't be 'shy coming forward'
May fail to see opportunities as they arise	
Will tend to be less successful	
Can be shy or self-effacing	
Will seek to avoid risk or making mistakes	
Will miss out on opportunities	
A passive team worker – may not contribute as well as they can	

please see self-confidence' in a number of publications. Professor Bandura was very clear about the distinctions between the two:

> It should be noted that the construct of self-efficacy differs from the colloquial term 'confidence'. Confidence is a nondescript term that refers to strength of belief but does not necessarily specify what the certainty is about. I can be supremely confident that I will fail at an endeavour. Perceived self-efficacy refers to belief in one's agentive capabilities that one can produce given levels of attainment.

> A self-efficacy assessment, therefore, includes both an affirmation of a capability level and the strength of that belief. Confidence is a catchword rather than a construct embedded in a theoretical system.

TABLE 9.3 Correlations between mental toughness and confidence

	Pearson's Correlation	Scale
Optimism	0.48	Life orientation test
Life satisfaction	0.56	Satisfaction with life scale
Self-image	0.42	Self-esteem scale
Self-efficacy	0.68	Self-efficacy scale
Trait anxiety	0.57	State-Trait Anxiety Questionnaire

Advances in a field are best achieved by constructs that fully reflect the phenomena of interest and are rooted in a theory that specifies their determinants, mediating processes, and multiple effects. Theory-based constructs pay dividends in understanding and operational guidance. The terms used to characterize personal agency, therefore, represent more than merely lexical preferences.

This clearly reflects a frustration about what can be perceived as the inherent emptiness of the term 'self-confidence'. However, in developing our model of toughness it quickly became apparent that confidence, although poorly operationalized, was a key factor. We conceive it to be a heritable, generic trait. It does share many characteristics of self-efficacy, and Table 9.3 shows they are quite clearly related.

Bandura felt that there could be no such thing as general self-efficacy. People are confident about doing some things but not others. This must be true to some extent, but we would suggest that underpinning these variations is a foundation of confidence that permeates across a broad domain of activities. There is a little evidence that self-efficacy might be more generalizable than it is usually represented. Holloway (1988) found that increased self-efficacy of adolescent girls through strength training generalized to more dispositional attitudes and confidence levels about their bodies and self-esteem.

Bandura was convinced that people learn through observing others' behaviour, attitudes, and outcomes of those behaviours (Social Learning theory). The necessary conditions to learn are:

- *attention* – various factors increase or decrease the amount of attention paid;
- *retention* – remembering what you paid attention to;

- *reproduction* – reproducing the behaviour;
- *motivation* – having the motivation to imitate.

It is argued that levels of self-efficacy within an individual are the product of this social learning process.

People with a strong sense of self-efficacy:

- view challenging problems as tasks to be mastered;
- develop deeper interest in the activities in which they participate;
- form a stronger sense of commitment to their interests and activities;
- recover quickly from setbacks and disappointments.

People with a weak sense of self-efficacy:

- avoid challenging tasks;
- believe that difficult tasks and situations are beyond their capabilities;
- focus on personal failings and negative outcomes;
- quickly lose confidence in personal abilities.

Bandura has suggested that people avoid potentially threatening situations not because they experience anxiety and arousal but, rather, they fear they will be unable to cope. This coping relates to the actual behaviour and the underlying cognitive processes. These latter processes are perhaps the key to the impact of low confidence on performance. Individuals fear they will not be able to control perturbing thoughts.

This type of observation is often criticized as lacking scientific rigor. In the case of negative thinking at least there is a wealth of hard data underpinning the research findings. For example, there is a strong link between adrenalin and noradrenalin levels and doubt. As doubt increases, these two catecholamines increase – both are closely intertwined with the generation of feelings. High self-efficacy is associated with low levels of adrenalin and noradrenalin when someone is put under pressure.

It is clear that higher levels of self-efficacy are an advantage to an individual and the model, based on social learning, clearly identified ways in which learning could take place:

- *Performance accomplishments* – successfully completing a task.
- *Vicarious experiences* – seeing other people succeed. The closer these individuals are to the type of the person the observer is, the more powerful the impact.
- *Verbal persuasion* – this is the basis of many of the cognitive behavioural therapies available and is the bedrock of coaching.
- *Techniques that reduce emotional arousal* – dispersing the emotional fog can allow an individual to more rapidly develop.

These techniques are very valuable and form the core of the mental toughness interventions described later in this book. Bandura also emphasized the reciprocal nature of the mastery–performance link. Feelings of mastery lead to performance improvements which lead to greater feelings of mastery – the virtuous circle.

Confidence and anxiety

These two areas are closely linked. Bandura argued that reducing anxiety increases self-efficacy and this principle has been adopted by many practitioners working in this field. If you are unable to control your anxiety levels you are unable to control yourself.

This linkage has been made even more explicit by Martens *et al* (1990). He and his colleagues developed the Competitive State Anxiety Inventory (CSAI and CSAI-2). The CSAI-2 is the most frequently used measure of state anxiety in sport. State anxiety is simply the term used to reflect how an individual feels at a particular point in time. Marten included a subscale within the CSAI-2 to measure self-confidence. He therefore suggests that anxiety is on a continuum. At one end of the scale he has high anxiety; at the other he has confidence. This topic is very hotly debated – but it is certainly interesting.

Optimism

> A pessimist sees the difficulty in every opportunity; an optimist sees the opportunity in every difficulty. (Winston Churchill)

The trait of optimism has received considerable research effort. Again, it is clear that mental toughness and optimism go hand in hand. Greater levels of optimism have been found to be associated with better mental health, a greater striving for personal growth, better moods, academic and job success, popularity and better all-round coping.

Optimistic individuals tend to adopt a problem-based coping style that is also typical of mentally tough individuals. Optimism and pessimism are not two ends of the same continuum. It is clear that pessimism is associated with neuroticism and negative moods whereas optimism is principally linked to extroversion, positive moods and happiness.

Extroversion

Extroversion, one of the big five personality traits, is clearly linked to mental toughness in general and interpersonal confidence in particular. This is shown in Table 9.4.

Both confidence in abilities and interpersonal confidence relate to extroversion. It can be seen that interpersonal confidence has particularly strong relationships, especially with assertiveness and independence. The core of extroversion is based on how people interact with others.

TABLE 9.4 Correlations between MTQ48 and prevue personality instrument

	Independent	Competitive	Assertive	Conscientious	Conventional	Organized	Extrovert
Overall MT	0.30**	0.11	0.34**	−0.09	−0.16	0.01	0.33**
Challenge	0.38**	0.26**	0.33**	−0.33**	−0.32**	−0.19	0.30**
Commitment	0.20*	0.11	0.22*	0.17	0.04	0.22*	0.22*
Control	0.03	−0.03	0.06	−0.06	−0.15	0.01	0.08
Control: life	0.11	−0.11	0.21*	−0.05	−0.18*	0.06	0.15
Control: emotions	−0.06	−0.08	−0.05	−0.09	−0.07	−0.10	0.15
Confidence	0.39**	0.12	0.51**	−0.06	−0.17	0.03	0.41**
Confidence: in abilities	0.15	0.05	0.19*	−0.03	−0.09	0.03	0.27**
Confidence: interpersonal	0.46**	0.23*	0.50**	−0.16	−0.20*	−0.08	0.28**

*Correlation is significant at the 0.05 level (2-tailed)
**Correlation is significant at the 0.01 level (2-tailed)

Eysenck (1967) suggested that the engine behind extroversion was arousal. He suggested that extroverts have a low arousal level whereas introverts have a much higher one. On average extroverts need more external energy, meaning they are much more likely to seek out social contacts. Social interactions are strongly related to positive moods, but the interactions obviously need to be positive themselves. Confident individuals both seek out opportunities to interact with others and maximize the impact of these contacts.

The success of social interactions is closely linked to assertiveness. It is clear that the 'everyone wins' core of most assertiveness techniques maximizes the effectiveness of social interactions.

THE IMPORTANCE OF INTERPERSONAL CONFIDENCE
A case study in a UK Police Force

The practical implications of interpersonal confidence were demonstrated by Honey Langaster-James in some of her postgraduate studies.

Police performance and behaviour is of continued critical interest. Of particular interest is police officers' willingness to participate in stop and search activities, regardless of the risks involved in such actions. This study assessed police officers' stop and search behaviour whilst on the beat.

Stop and search responsibilities and actions are a key performance criterion for the beat police officer. Such actions are difficult to perform and are often carried out in difficult and dangerous settings. As such, there have been concerns that some officers may be avoiding this activity to reduce their stress levels.

The study gave 110 police officers hypothetical scenarios about stop and search. All completed the MTQ48.

Results

TABLE 9.5 Relationship between the MTQ48 and the desire and usage of stop and search

	Overall Desire	Overall Use	Overall Anxiety
Total mental toughness	0.19*	0.24*	−0.59*
Challenge	0.15	0.21*	−0.53*
Commitment	0.18	0.18	−0.40*
Control	0.15	0.19*	−0.51*

TABLE 9.5 Continued

	Overall Desire	Overall Use	Overall Anxiety
Confidence	0.18	0.26*	−0.60*
Emotional control	0.16	0.14	−0.29*
Life control	0.10	0.19	−0.59*
Confidence (abilities)	0.11	0.15	−0.61*
Confidence (interpersonal)	0.22*	0.33*	−0.42*
Overall desire		0.81*	−0.15
Overall use	0.811*		
Overall anxiety	−0.11	−0.15	

*Significant correlations

What did this tell us?

First, it is important to note that actual use of stop and search activities was associated with an increased desire to carry them out.

In relation to mental toughness: higher levels of overall mental toughness were associated with an increased desire to carry out and actually use the stop and search activities. Additionally, desire to stop and search was associated with high levels of interpersonal confidence. This can be explained as follows. Officers who had high levels of interpersonal personal confidence believed that they could defuse potentially volatile situations. They believed that that could control the social situation.

Self-esteem

A final theoretical construct that can be linked to confidence is self-esteem. This is a little more removed from the concept, but still pertinent. The key to self-esteem is pride.

This pride is related to oneself and is based both on individuals' strengths and on an acceptance of their weaknesses. Pride in young people, like so many things, can be enhanced or destroyed by parents and teachers. If others take credit for individuals' achievements and/or blame them for their shortcomings then the ability to feel pride can be greatly reduced.

Low self-esteem can be easily related to feelings of shame and lack of self-worth. Low self-esteem people believe that they lack skills and have little to offer the world. They will often actively resist attempts to bolster their esteem, for example failing to acknowledge positive feedback. In addition they set low goals, again perpetuating their feelings of inadequacy.

Self-esteem seems to be a critical component of how people deal with the world. Its pervasive effect on people has been linked to terror management theory. This theory attempts to explain human behaviour by placing it within the context of a deeply rooted fear of death. Basically, self-esteem allows us to deal with the inevitable end of life by allowing us to recognize our importance and what we have contributed to the world.

A pursuit of self-esteem is not without its pitfalls. It has been argued that pursuing self-esteem may in fact limit learning. Individuals could avoid challenging situations that threatened their self-image. This sort of self-validation relies on inappropriate behaviours such as making excuses. This type of approach would be clearly linked to low scores on the challenge scale of the MTQ48.

Innovative insights into the education and development of young people

10

In 2007 a lone pilot exercise on Year 10 (aged 15–16) pupils in a secondary school in Knowsley, England, produced some hugely interesting results. There emerged a clear link between the mental toughness of individual students and many aspects of their academic lives. At the same time work in universities and business schools began to provide similar evidence.

In hindsight this should not have surprised anyone. If mental toughness is the quality that determines how we deal with stress, pressure and challenge then this neatly describes central elements of the life of a student at all levels of education. Furthermore if the purpose of education is not only to deliver students with good qualifications but to prepare them for life after education then there is even more relevance to mental toughness.

Within a remarkably short period of time mental toughness has emerged as a significant factor in the development of young people. It is the subject of more research and case studies than any other area of application at the present time and pilots are beginning to show consistently that mental toughness is an important factor in the areas discussed below.

The positive impact of mental toughness

Performance

Studies carried out in schools, colleges and universities in the UK and in Holland show that there is a close link between mental toughness and the performance of young people in exams and tests. These studies consistently show that up to 25 per cent of the variation in a person's performance in exams can be explained by their mental toughness (as assessed by MTQ48).

It therefore seems possible to develop an individual's mental toughness which then translates into better exam and test performance. Early small-scale studies in education are beginning to confirm this.

Again this should not surprise anyone. Studies in the occupational world show exactly the same thing. It is likely that mental toughness is also a factor in teacher/tutor performance and the attention of many in education is turning to this application too.

Wellbeing

The higher the level of mental toughness, the more individuals are able to deal with the pressures, stressors and challenges of everyday life. They are able to deal more easily with even the most difficult days. Pilot work shows that this translates into outcomes such as better attendance, less stress and lower reported bullying.

A 2010 study at the Depression and Sleep Research Unit at the University of Basle in Switzerland (carried out by Serge Brand, Nadeem Kalak, Peter Clough, Markus Gerber, Sakari Lemola and Edith Holsboer-Trachsler) showed that in adolescents, favourable sleep patterns and favourable mental toughness seem to be related. The study also looked at exercise and sleep patterns and found no significant correlation. Whereas the underlying mechanisms remain unclear, the study concluded it seems conceivable that improving both sleep and mental toughness should confer increased wellbeing.

Positive behaviours

The higher the level of mental toughness the more individuals demonstrate positive behaviours. They will adopt a 'can do' attitude and there is clear evidence that the higher the level of mental toughness the more likely the student will engage in the class and the school (asking questions, engaging in discussion, etc). Again, studies in the occupational world show exactly the same thing.

Curiously, studies also indicated that some teachers in secondary education routinely discriminate between male and female students in terms of engaged behaviour. This is often perceived as a 'good' behaviour when demonstrated by males but as 'troublesome', 'difficult' or 'lippy' when demonstrated by females. This appears to be the case whether the teacher/tutor is male or female!

Completion/dropout rates

Several studies show that there is a strong link between mental toughness and the extent to which a student will stick with a programme of study or work and will see it through to a conclusion. This is particularly significant in Further Education (for example the NEETS programmes aimed at those Not in Employment, Education or Training) and Higher Education (where UK undergraduate dropout rates are on average around 16 per cent across the board).

Application of mental toughness assessment and development for this purpose can produce significant economic returns for FE and HE. The second part of this chapter describes a disciplined and highly structured approach being adopted in Scotland that is beginning to produce impressive results.

Aspirations

Studies show that the higher the level of mental toughness the greater the level of aspirations of the individual. This is particularly significant in areas of social and economic deprivation, where feelings of 'helplessness' and patterns of 'worklessness' can develop.

Figure 10.1 shows the pattern of mental toughness scores (MTQ48) for year 10 students at a Merseyside Secondary School and their career aspirations in four broad categories: blue collar, eg manual and craft work; white collar, eg office, administration and retail; professional, eg technical and professional; and performing arts (the school specialized in performing arts). The analysis shows that the more challenging the career area (professional and performing arts) the higher the mental toughness of the young people who aspire to those careers. Interestingly, the more mentally sensitive tended to opt for white collar careers (which include jobs such as shop working, etc).

FIGURE 10.1 Patterns of mental toughness scores for Year 10 students and their career aspirations

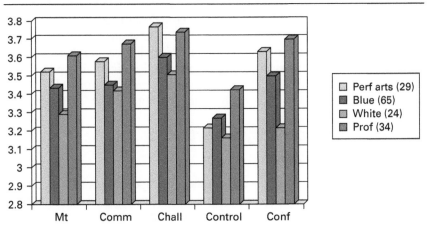

Employability

Pilot studies again show a clear relationship between individuals' mental toughness and their ability to get a job and (often) to get the job they want. Higher mental toughness people are more likely to recognize the recruitment process as a competitive one.

They will approach important elements of the process in a more positive manner. For instance they will enter an interview with the mindset that they will show the interviewer(s) what they are capable of offering. Less mentally tough people will see an interview as a trial. The mentally tough will also recognize they need to compete and outperform others to get their job. They will also be more realistic about the job hunting process. This is very clear in Higher Education.

MTQ48 and mental toughness can therefore be usefully explored in career guidance and career planning. This is discussed elsewhere in this book.

Transition

In a sense this theme runs through much of the above. Studies and research are beginning to provide a consistent picture that the mental toughness of individuals influences how effectively they deal with major transitions in their lives.

Moving from junior to secondary education

A Dutch study showed that more mentally tough students managed this transition more effectively than mentally sensitive students and performed better in examinations after the transition.

In 2009 a study was carried out in Roermond in Holland on students in transition between junior and secondary education. At that point pupils complete a CITO examination which has a significant impact on determining their career in secondary education. The study used MTQ48 to measure the mental toughness of students, accessed their CITO scores and asked pupils to self-assess how they felt they had coped with aspects of life during their transition year.

The study showed a correlation of +0.53 between mental toughness scores and performance on the CITO tests. This indicates that there is a very strong association between mental toughness and individual pupil's CITO scores/results, and mental toughness emerges as a predictor for CITO. Basically the MTQ48 explains 25 per cent of the variation in the CITO score.

Moving from secondary to further and higher education

This is a likely explanation for the significant dropout rates in UK colleges and universities, where in recent years up to 16 per cent of students have dropped out of study within 10 weeks of starting a new course.

In 2010/11 Adam Smith College in Scotland carried out a pilot exercise on 400 students who had enrolled on courses that had a track record of higher than average dropout rates. Using the MTQ48 to assess mental toughness and directing appropriate interventions to whole groups (classes) produced an improvement in retention of 28 pupils compared with the average for the previous three years, an improvement of 7 per cent. The benefits – cost savings, waste reduction and income improvement – massively outweighed the cost of the interventions – test and workshops.

Moving from education into the workplace

More mentally tough people make this transition more effectively.

The link to productivity

A productivity and employability study in Scotland showed a relationship between mental toughness and the productivity of young graduates in a new job. The more mentally tough employees were more likely to tell their employer about their capability, skills and knowledge. The employer was then better placed to harness this, leading to a more productive employee. A mentally sensitive employee is less likely to tell the employer about his or her capability, etc. The employee's potential is then more difficult to harness.

(Anti-)social behaviour

Studies with young offenders show that the lower the level of mental toughness the more likely the individual will adopt anti-social behaviours. A possible explanation is that these individuals are less able to deal with life's stressors, pressures and challenges and either respond poorly to them or are more easily influenced by gang leaders who appear to be more effective at dealing with life pressures, etc.

It is likely that assessing and developing mental toughness in young people can translate into valuable outcomes such as better social behaviours and reduced reoffending.

Other considerations

Developing psychological or emotional resilience and mental toughness is a very important life skill. As Damian Allen, Director of Children's Services put it, 'Not only can we, in many cases, enhance a young person's performance; these particular skills are useful for just about everything else that person is going to have to do in life.'

Returning to the themes of performance, one useful observation from the early research is that the MTQ48 generally emerges as a good predictor of exam success – sometimes a better predictor than the tutors' assessment. In some ways this is not surprising. In the occupational world there is similar overwhelming evidence that judicious use of psychometrics helps managers to make better decisions about people – even when they have worked for some time with those people.

It is important to add the standard cautionary note that tests such as MTQ48 should never be used on their own. They are not designed for that. A psychometric measure is most effective when teachers, tutors and counsellors use it with other sources of information to make the best assessment of the person in front of them.

In summary, the evidence overwhelmingly suggests that examining mental toughness as a factor in the development of young people has the potential to be a valuable and rewarding activity. The development of the measure enables the concept to be better understood and allows the users to make better assessments. Moreover the concept is reasonable accessible to most practitioners in this field and many of the appropriate interventions are known to many. A common observation from many is that this has helped them to better direct their efforts to help the student or young person.

The three chapters that follow each pick up one of many applications with young people and serve to illustrate the value of the concept in that work. The first describes the original pioneering work in the secondary education system at Knowsley Borough Council in the UK, which continues to take a lead in development activity. The second describes the work in the Scottish Further Education Sector. This is led by Adam Smith College which is also proving to be a leading player in looking at applications in the development of young people. Finally we look at career guidance and how mental toughness can prove to be an important concept in this arena.

Mental toughness and its application in secondary education

11

DAMIAN ALLEN AND DAVID AYRE

Introduction and background

Since 2007, Knowsley MBC has been at the cutting edge of a significant initiative to use the concept of mental toughness in the development of young people to explore the barriers to learning. Knowsley became the first local authority in the UK to use Mental Toughness Development in an educational setting. It has proved to be a very useful experience for everyone involved.

Knowsley MBC covers an area of some 76 square kilometres and a population of around 150,000 people. The area has significant areas of economic (and social) deprivation. It has seven secondary schools, which, during the course of this work, have been transformed from traditional secondary schools to Centres for Learning in modern pupil-friendly buildings. Together with other initiatives these make a conscious and determined effort to engage with the community to improve academic performance, a sense of wellbeing and, very important, aspirations. The use of mental toughness, the model, the questionnaire and the interventions is one of the innovative ways in which Knowsley MBC is addressing the issue of embedding ongoing improvements in educational attainment. The latest studies in other areas consistently show that there is a link between mental toughness development activity and improving mental toughness development scores and that this, in turn, is positively linked to improved performance and behaviour.

Mental toughness was first established in Knowsley as part of the then Targeted Youth Support Pathfinder in 2006. This project aimed to test the hypothesis that mental toughness is related to performance, behaviour and wellbeing.

This also embraced considerations of career aspirations and perceived bullying. The whole mental toughness concept was originally used with Year 10 and Year 11 pupils in helping them to achieve maximum attainment and to fulfil their potential. Initial pilots, using selected interventions after assessing a young person's level of mental toughness, allowed us to increase pupils' self-confidence and belief in their abilities, building enthusiasm, drive and passion.

Knowsley MBC next produced a Mental Toughness Strategy in 2009/10 which outlined its commitment to championing the case for greater understanding and development of mental toughness practice in schools. This approach was part of a wider strategic shift during the move from schools to Centres for Learning, which aimed to provide a more holistic support for their students.

Our own research indicated that many factors contribute to one's resilience but studies demonstrate that the primary factor in resilience is having caring and supportive relationships within and outside the family. For young people these relationships are critical in a school setting. Relationships that create trust provide encouragement and reassurance and help bolster a person's resilience.

The approach commenced in 2007 and has involved six Knowsley secondary schools. At the time of writing, the local authority has been negotiating with all secondary schools in the borough the ways in which mental toughness can be further embedded in everyday planning and delivery. The work was conducted with AQR and under the guidance of Dr Peter Clough, Head of Psychology, University of Hull, who is also the developer of the mental toughness concept and measure.

Initial engagement – Targeted Youth Support Pathfinder

The initial engagement of Dr Clough and AQR in Knowsley came about as a result of the borough being identified as a Targeted Youth Support (TYS) Pathfinder in 2006. The Greater Merseyside Connexions Service had previously undertaken similar research with its staff with AQR and Dr Clough and through that had come to understand that it had applications in its work with young people. GMC had advocated its further use as part of the TYS Pathfinder. This was agreed by Knowsley Children's Services and Halewood College (the secondary education provider).

The study was established in the context of a wider 'Risk and Resilience' strand within the overall project. Because the concept of mental toughness is closely associated with resilience, the mental toughness questionnaire, MTQ48, and the mental toughness model were used to test and investigate a number of hypotheses. Resilience can be considered a component of mental toughness.

The study and the hypothesis

The hypothesis to be tested was simply that mental toughness is related to performance, behaviour and wellbeing. This embraced considerations of career aspirations and perceived bullying.

The study covered the entire Year 10 group (age 16 years), some 240 pupils. All pupils participated – no self-selection was permitted. The following data were collected from each pupil:

- mental toughness score – through MTQ48;
- careers aspirations – short structured questionnaire;
- perceptions of bullying – short structured questionnaire.

The following data were provided by the college/year tutors about each pupil:

- year tutors' assessment of students' mental toughness – structured assessment;
- school behaviour records;
- attendance records;
- Cognitive Ability Test measures – CATs for verbal, non-verbal and quantitative abilities.

The data were analysed by researchers at the University of Hull under the guidance of Dr Peter Clough, Head of Psychology.

The results

What emerged was a fascinating set of results. The study showed the following.

The students' assessment (through MTQ48) was broadly in line with the tutors' assessment of their mental toughness – but there were important differences. The differences between teacher and pupil ratings of mental toughness are related to behaviour. The students' assessment (ie MTQ48) was significantly better at predicting negative behaviour than the year tutors' assessment (see Figure 11.1).

MTQ48 was able to explain 13 per cent and 25 per cent of variance in negative behaviour for males and females respectively. Year tutors' assessments were able to explain 12 per cent of the variance in female behaviour and none of the male behaviour. This simply means that the MTQ48 questionnaire emerged as a good predictor of negative behaviour and was better at predicting negative behaviour than the teachers' assessment of the pupils.

This is not a criticism of teachers/tutors. The same type of results are achieved in the workplace, where managers consistently make better selection and development decisions about their staff if they use psychometrics than if they use only their judgement. It does reinforce the value of using

FIGURE 11.1 Mental Toughness Scores (MTQ48) for males and females correlated with negative behaviour scores

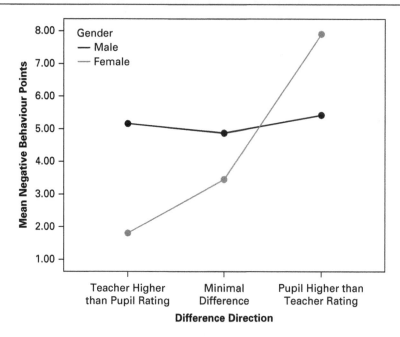

psychometric measures in education provided those measures are reliable and valid (and preferably normative).

There was a significant difference between mental toughness scores for females and for males. Generally female scores were lower. This was particularly interesting since this is the first study on any group that has shown a significant difference between male and female mental toughness. Coincidentally a separate study was being carried out concurrently with a large employer in the same borough on people of working age. This showed the usual pattern – no difference between male and female scores. This is being examined more closely to identify why these results should emerge in a fairly large sample. One hypothesis is that there is a cultural element in the school or in the local area that treated young men and young women differently. This is possibly indicated with the next observation.

Analysis of the MTQ48 results and the tutors' assessments of mental toughness and the behaviour data showed that tutors viewed males and females differently. Where MTQ48 indicated a high level of mental toughness, tutors were significantly more likely to identify negative behaviour amongst females than amongst males. It seems that challenging behaviour (a sign of mental toughness) is more likely to be regarded as negative behaviour in females than in males.

Conversely, where MTQ48 indicated a low level of mental toughness, tutors were significantly more likely to identify negative behaviour amongst

FIGURE 11.2 Mental Toughness Scores (MTQ48) correlated with verbal ability – note that female ability scores are higher than male ability scores

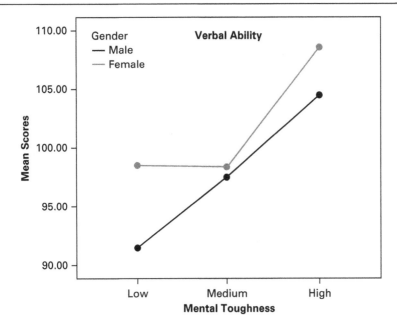

males than amongst females. It seems that quiet, compliant behaviour is more likely to be regarded as negative behaviour in males than in females. These patterns emerged irrespective of whether the tutor was male or female!

Our partners in the project, GMC, arranged for a confirmatory exercise to be carried out in a nearby all-girls secondary school to determine whether the finding in Halewood College reflected that it was a mixed gender school. Exactly the same pattern emerged. Female students who were more mentally tough and who asked more questions in class were more likely to be considered 'difficult' and 'awkward' by tutors and staff.

Analysis of MTQ48 scores showed that in every case – verbal ability, non-verbal ability and quantitative ability – there was a direct, almost straight line correlation between mental toughness and ability. Analysis showed that the patterns were virtually the same for males and females with non-verbal and quantitative abilities. With verbal ability there were two straight lines, almost in parallel, showing that females consistently scored higher at each level of mental toughness; see Figures 11.2 and 11.3.

This confirms results achieved elsewhere. Improving mental toughness can lead to better ability scores. It is thought that the more mentally tough a person is, the more likely they are to do well in a test (because they are more confident) and the more likely they are to absorb learning because they are more confident and feel more in control.

FIGURE 11.3 Mental Toughness Scores (MTQ48) correlated with quantitative ability

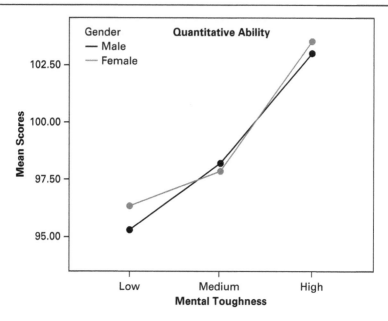

Deep Support programme

The second deployment of mental toughness came in 2007 as part of a wider programme known as 'Deep Support'. On this occasion a different secondary school in the borough, All Saints Catholic High School, was the focus.

The purpose of the Deep Support Pilot Project (DSPP) is to use innovative practice as a means of bringing about further change in learning and teaching to improve the achievements of young people in secondary school. All Saints Catholic High School has already implemented creative practice with regard to the implementation of emotional intelligence for members of staff and students, particularly the use of the Learning Mentor Team to support learning and the sharing of good practice between primary feeder schools and All Saints School.

The programme was set up as a project within the wider 'Change for Children' programme initiated by Knowsley to affect changes in working practices as part of the approach when implementing the then government's 'Every Child Matters' agenda. The wider aims of the Deep Support programme were to:

- increase the students' level of self-worth;
- develop their levels of resilience so that they have greater influence over their futures within a changing world;

- increase their aspirations;
- enable the students to be involved in developing their learning programmes so that learning is relevant, engagement is maintained and potential is realized;
- open doors of opportunity previously not considered.

What we did

The project was targeted at all 181 pupils in Year 7. This was an innovation in another sense. It was the first time that the MTQ48 measure was used with pupils as young as 11 years old. The reading age of the questionnaire is as assessed as 11 years, so most were able to complete it with minimal support. Some needed more support. Each pupil completed a mental toughness questionnaire and, from this larger sample, a smaller cohort of 39 pupils was chosen to take part in further pilot interventions.

Further application of mental toughness assessment and interventions was used as part of the DSPP at All Saints. In 2007 the school was chosen to represent the North West as a hub school and to build on the existing work to take forward the DSPP. The objective of this second phase was to develop innovative methods of integrating the Every Child Matters agenda with the Personalized Learning agenda.

As well as the pupils themselves, the parents, carers and form tutors of this cohort were assessed for resilience (using MTQ48) and emotional sensitivity. The lessons learnt are now being applied to practice in other schools across Knowsley.

Although as yet we do not have evidence to show the impact of the pilot programme on examination results as the learners involved are only in Year 10, we can say that throughout the duration of the programme the behaviour of some of the more challenging learners in the group improved and improvements relating to the students' attitude to learning were noted on their term progress reports.

The group were re-tested at the end of the programme using the MTQ48 (27 out of 29 were present on the day the questionnaire was completed) and in terms of confidence 70.5 per cent of the group had an improved confidence score, 18.5 per cent had stayed the same and 11 per cent had decreased.

Firm Foundations programme

Following on from the two school-specific studies, the local authority advocated successfully with secondary schools to establish a multi-school approach.

Consequently, in 2009 the Firm Foundations programme used the MTQ48 with a large cohort of Key Stage 4 pupils. The Firm Foundations programme is a cross-borough programme across secondary schools focused on Key Stage 4 pupils. Key Stage 4 is the legal term for the two years of school education that incorporate GCSEs and other exams, known as Year 10 and Year 11 in schools in England and Wales, when pupils are aged between 14 and 16. These pupils had been identified by their Centre as potentially at risk of underperforming at GCSE.

Each Centre nominated a lead representative who received a full training session and was then equipped with the tools and techniques to deliver a range of interventions across this group of pupils. Each Centre then had the opportunity to develop its own approach to delivering this programme. This was particularly valuable because it enabled local tutors to bring their own knowledge and experience into play. This in turn reinforced their commitment to the programme.

As part of the 2008/09 Firm Foundations programme over 370 Year 11 pupils completed the MTQ48 assessment between November 2008 and January 2009. In addition to the measure, at least one member of staff from each school attended a training session on providing feedback and delivering interventions. As a follow on from the training, each school received a workbook of interventions (UCanPass) and three Biofeedback Tension takers to be used in school.

During the 2009/10 academic year a significantly larger cohort of KS4 pupils were tested using the MTQ48. Results show that the only area pupils scored above the normal distribution (5.5) was *confidence,* 51.2 per cent of pupils scored 5 or above. Average scores for *challenge* and *life control* were the lowest with 48.7 per cent of pupils scoring below 3 for challenge and 46.8 per cent of pupils scoring below 3 for life control.

In comparison to the previous year's results, *confidence in abilities* and *interpersonal confidence* of this year's cohort were lower. *Challenge* scores are significantly reduced with the majority of pupils' scores falling in sten 2 compared to the majority scoring in sten 5 in the previous academic year.

Nevertheless the results from the application of the Firm Foundations programme and the associated mental toughness interventions have been both effective and impressive. They can be summarized as follows.

1. Academic/exam performance

One of the key goals for the programme was that all schools in Knowsley achieved results above the National Challenge benchmark, which required that at least 30 per cent of pupils achieved five A*–C grade GCSEs including English and Maths.

Knowsley schools moved above the National Challenge benchmark during the period in which mental toughness had been initiated. Improvements of 3.4 and 3.6 per cent were made in the years 2007–09, and this trend continued with another rise in the 2010 results.

A pattern that was observed was that pupils who had higher mental toughness scores tended to achieve better scores than predicted, while those with low mental toughness scores tended to achieve lower grades than predicted.

2. Assessment of mental toughness and its link to ability

Analysis of MTQ48 scores show that in every case – verbal ability, non-verbal ability and quantitative ability – there was a direct, almost straight-line correlation between mental toughness and ability.

3. Wellbeing and aspiration

The link to aspiration was one of the core objectives of the study, to see if there was any explanation why there has statistically been a propensity for students in Knowsley to struggle to address the circumstances that frequently accompany a disadvantaged background. If aspirations are low then achievement is also likely to be low.

The study showed that the more mentally tough the student, the higher the aspirations. The most mentally tough aspired to professional careers, the next most mentally tough aspired to careers in drama and entertainment. Both these sectors are demanding. This shows a clear link between mental toughness and career aspiration. Mental toughness could usefully be incorporated into career guidance activity.

4. The importance of MT for staff and parents

Learning and teaching consultants are able to produce lesson plans to encompass the four areas of control, commitment, challenge and confidence to allow a more practical demonstration of mental toughness application to school staff.

All activities delivered by the Firm Foundations programme will encompass mental toughness as part of their delivery. This also ensures that all practitioners working with Year 10 and Year 11 pupils have access to their MTQ48 results and feel equipped to fully support them in a personalized approach.

The parents, carers and form tutors of this cohort were also assessed for resilience and emotional sensitivity. Work on this project is still continuing and has begun expanding lessons learnt across other schools in Knowsley.

The key finding was that the overall MT score for the Year 7 cohort of pupils in All Saints as part of the Deep Support programme presented a negative result. In evidence which corroborates this information, when their parents were given the test they displayed a similar negative score for their overall MT score. This suggests that there is a strong environmental conditioning effect.

The work links in with wider work Knowsley MBC has done on resilience in the community, including ethnographic work in Stockbridge Village, Huyton and Kirkby, and work with Demos in North Huyton in 2007.

5. Managing change in the world of education

The data from All Saints School and Halewood College reveals that both achieved a great deal through access to mental toughness and the MTQ48, but in different ways.

All Saints adopted an intervention-based approach, using MTQ48 to identify issues and from that diagnose direct interventions. Staff at Halewood College decided that instead of focusing on interventions, they would use MTQ48 as a tool to make the Personal Development Review (PDR) process more effective. This proved to be an impressive tool. Staff found that it is extremely effective in guiding feedback and getting pupils to relate mental toughness to their own behaviour and performance.

They found that with careful feedback, the students would often illustrate with examples of their own behaviour and experience what a particular label of mental toughness might indicate. Specific scores were never released to students – only a general indication of their mental toughness to which they were invited to provide examples of behaviour that either supported or contradicted that assessment. Staff found that students were, on the whole, more willing to participate in the PDR process in this way than in the traditional format where the tutor fed back examples of behaviour and asked students to comment on and to discuss it.

Perhaps the most significant study here, which in hindsight should have surprised no one, was the observation that the MTQ48 feedback or reports could be effective interventions in their own right. Tutors reported that feeding back to students that their mental toughness assessment was above average but that their performance in some way did not reflect that, would often provoke the required improvement in performance or behaviour. It is as if their innate mental toughness 'kicks in' and produces the desired response.

Feedback to those with lower mental toughness scores than the average required careful handling. The converse of the above could emerge, negative feedback confirming to the student that he or she was indeed a poor performer. However, this is a challenge for all forms of feedback and not just MTQ48.

The net effect is that assessment of mental toughness patterns in large groups could be useful in another sense. With often scarce resources for intervention, assessing mental toughness could guide tutors, etc as to where they should direct most of their effort whilst achieving impact across a whole group.

The results show that mental toughness is a valuable concept in understanding how young people perform and how they behave in education. Moreover, we know that we can develop mental toughness with most people. Mental toughness could have a key role to play in developing people at all levels.

From the Firm Foundations work, Knowsley ascertained that in order to implement an authentic needs-driven approach to the Deep Support Pilot

Project for families, provision needed to be flexible, barrier-free and proactive. It was essential to ensure that provision was available on an early intervention basis so that needs didn't escalate, and that it could be consistent and quality assured. To achieve this, service providers on occasion needed to revisit and/or redefine their criteria for intervention so that it was based on the identified needs of the cohort's families. We ensured that signposting of service provision was communicated in a coordinated and easily accessible way, which meant that service information was delivered in a multi-faceted manner, such as via websites, hard copies of a service directory and other signposting mechanisms.

This work can be seen to have links to the wider work that Knowsley is doing on education reform, including 21st Century Skills and the work of the Global Educational Leaders Programme, which seeks to root such issues in the wider global educational economy.

Mental toughness in the complex world of further education colleges

12

CRAIG THOMPSON

In this chapter, mental toughness is considered from the FE college point of view. A pilot project is described, which was designed to improve levels of retention and to achieve a positive impact on student attainment and employability.

An overview is also included of work being carried out to determine how an understanding of mental toughness can improve the contribution of staff in small businesses, including work-based learners. Reference is also made to the use of mental toughness in international leadership work with post-secondary institutions around the world.

The specific context for the work described is the college sector in Scotland. The chapter begins with a description of that sector before moving on to describe and consider the challenge of improving student performance, particularly as reflected by retention and attainment. Furthermore, detailed description of these issues is then covered prior to shifting the focus to look outside the college at the contribution that mental toughness might make to improving productivity in Scotland's workforce.

The college sector in Scotland

Colleges in Scotland play a broad, central role in post-secondary or tertiary education. Spread across the country in a network of 41 autonomous institutions that extends from Dumfries in the south to Shetland in the north, the college sector provides a wide range of further education programmes, supports the vocational education work of schools and occupies a central position in the national higher education system, with over one in five of HE students pursuing their studies in or with a college.

Colleges also act as the main access institutions in tertiary education with a significant proportion of students coming from Scotland's most deprived postcode areas. Part-time students in colleges outnumber full-time by three to one, but in terms of full-time equivalence, over half of the work of the sector is with full-time students. The average age of students in the college sector is around 28.

While the sector shares a broad mission relating to individual development and to economic and social development, the emphasis of the work of individual institutions varies in line with the local and regional economic and social context within which they operate. The curriculum and wider service offer of some is skewed towards community provision, while others have a stronger vocational focus. Thomson (2003: 49) describes the college sector as one that:

> defies simple definition or description. It is here that vocational education meets and integrates with academic and recreational learning; employee training sits alongside personal development; and higher education finds seamless integration with further education. This is also the point in Scotland's lifelong learning infrastructure where many school-based learning experiences are extended and enhanced and where work-based and community-based learning are linked most effectively into the mainstream.

Colleges can be characterized as places where diverse groups of learners of different ages from a range of (often non-traditional) backgrounds come together to pursue a wide variety of programmes of study. Policies aimed at improving student retention and attainment recognize that college programmes have value in their own right and are the key to further study.

The Scottish Funding Council (SFC) emphasizes the importance of supporting initiatives 'aimed at improving the retention of students and their progression to further learning opportunities' (SPICe, 2010). In addition, for many learners the basic link between retention and attainment is, quite simply, the fact is that those who stay on course achieve their qualification outcome.

Understanding and working with this range of different learners and learning objectives is part of the challenge faced by professional staff in colleges as they endeavour to ensure that students stay on programme, succeed and move on to appropriate internal or external destinations. Evaluation of colleges' success in achieving these outcomes is carried out internally and by external agencies using a number of different key performance indicators, in particular covering retention, success and progression.

The main external agency working with colleges in making these judgements in the UK is Her Majesty's Inspectorate of Education (HMIe), which acts as a contractor to the Scottish Funding Council, the main funders of the college sector. Analysis of HMIe reports (HMIe, 2009) on all colleges in Scotland in their most recent four-year cycle of review reveals that: 'Almost all subjects reviewed over the four-year review cycle demonstrated either good or very good learning and teaching processes.'

However, the HMIe work also highlights the importance placed on, and the variable practice evident in, learner retention and attainment. These twin issues also appear prominently in individual college reports[1] with specific comment made on particular subject areas or levels of provision where concern (or praise) is being expressed.

General approaches to improving retention and attainment

The nature of the review carried out by HMIe, a system designed in partnership by HMIe and the college sector, frames the approach to quality assurance that is evident in most, if not all, colleges. A strong emphasis is placed on self-evaluation and ensuring that the focus of teaching and supporting services rests firmly on the learner experience. Retention and attainment are used as central, critical indicators of institutional and course success with retention measured and analysed both in relation to early retention and full course retention. Early retention, measured as retention for the first 25 per cent of the course, also enjoys prominence in college operations as a result of the funding model within which colleges operate. Colleges are not funded for students who fail to cross the 25 per cent threshold.

Interventions by colleges to address retention and to support work that is being carried out to underpin attainment typically encompass support and guidance with a range of generic areas such as financial and personal issues. The interventions also often include timetabled sessions in which designated staff provide guidance as required along with structured support with activities such as personal learning planning. Support is extended further by peer support systems based on mentoring and other similar schemes.

Most colleges have also carried out programmes of curriculum redesign to ensure that students engage with learning in a balanced and appropriate way with, for example, the move from general study to specific or more detailed vocational options timed to take place when the learners understand fully the choices open to them and how these match their own skills, attributes and preferences.

From the general to the specific

Over the past decade, colleges have become more focused on and adept at dealing with issues that might impact negatively on retention and attainment. Despite the fact that performance has improved, a number of factors have added to the importance of making further progress with these issues.

First, the continuing success of colleges in penetrating 'deprived postcode areas' has extended the college student community to a larger number of non-traditional learners who tend to be more transient and less likely to stay the course. Secondly, recession has led to significantly increased levels of demand for full-time college places and losing students early in the academic cycle is particularly problematic when others have failed to gain a place due to the course initially being full. Thirdly, significant reductions in college funding resulting from public spending cuts have focused institutions on the need to avoid the additional costs or loss of revenue associated with losing students prior to the 25 per cent cut-off point.

The focus on improving retention and attainment has therefore heightened and colleges have increasingly introduced specific individual as opposed to general interventions to help them address the challenge. Rather than providing broad guidance and support, staff are seeking ways of identifying and supporting specific learners and working with them on the issues likely to lead to them either dropping out or failing.

In Adam Smith College,[2] this led to a research project being set up with the aim of using the Mental Toughness Questionnaire (MTQ48) to direct a range of interventions with learners. Adam Smith's quality record is excellent. HMIe expressed complete and uncaveated confidence across all areas of the college in its quadrennial review in 2011 (HMIe, 2011). However, retention remains an issue which is recognized by the college as a priority for further development.

The business case for the initiative was a straightforward one. As one of the largest colleges in the country, Adam Smith's exposure to loss or additional expense was assessed. Potential loss of income due to early departure of students was quantified as being in excess of £1 million. While compensating action by the college (in the form of offering additional programmes and recruiting additional students) can be taken to minimize this type of loss, this involves significant additional unplanned spend.

The plan put in place for the 2010/11 academic year involved testing 10 per cent of the college's full-time FE learners (FE provision in the college has tended to show weaker levels of retention than HE, and full-time FE is, in turn, weaker than part-time). The class groups involved in the pilot were selected to reflect a range of different curriculum areas and to cover SCQF levels 4 to 6.[3] The intention was that, once the initial test was administered, post-test interventions would be carried out with all groups.

In focusing on groups, the college departed from the more standard approach adopted in interventions directed by MTQ48, where the focus is solely on the individual. This was done to allow the initial pilot to play a dual role. On the one hand, it was aimed at achieving improvement with the pilot groups; on the other, it provided the opportunity to familiarize staff and students with the approach and to allow open consideration of how the move to an individual focus might be achieved.

Staff were initially concerned that the approach might 'single out' or place an inappropriate focus on vulnerable learners. The research design therefore included a communication and engagement strategy to ensure that discussion and developments were clearly understood. This strategy focused on:

- a clear description of the purpose of the project (what and why);
- the benefits for staff and students;
- details of how learners and staff would be supported;
- Continuous Professional Development (CPD) that would be available prior to the tests and the interventions.

The initiative also grappled with the difficult issue of nomenclature. 'Mental toughness' was considered to be an explicit but stark term and the project was named in line with its core intention, adopting the title 'Stay and succeed'.

As described elsewhere in this book, the instrument used was the MTQ48 product from AQR. This involves those taking part rating each of the 48 test items on a 5-point Likert scale. Test results were analysed and teaching staff were provided with group analysis for each of the classes involved, showing results on a scale of 1 to 10 with 5.5 as the mean. An overall score and a score for each of the components of mental toughness were provided. The interventions employed were at the group level with results for the class discussed with the group as a whole. The next step was to hand out the UCanPass workbooks produced by AQR.

The UCanPass workbook is a learner aid that provides an opportunity for creating self-awareness about one's own mental toughness. It also provides descriptions of very accessible interventions the learner can adopt to develop mental toughness. (All of these are described in the intervention chapters elsewhere in this book.) Staff then determined whether to work through the book as a class, as groups or with individuals.

Learners were helped to think across the 'Stay and succeed' components, ie, control, confidence, challenge and commitment, and to reflect and work on how they could:

- be better prepared for what life 'throws at them';
- cope with difficulties and challenges;
- be more resilient;
- be better organized and able to plan their life;
- adopt positive thinking;
- consider how they perceive things;
- bounce back from setbacks.

Records of subsequent CPD sessions held with staff show that the outcomes of the interventions and student/staff discussions helped to move the debate within the college community on from concern about individual interventions to consideration of how the interventions could be individualized.

While the methodology employed did not focus on individuals, the results in terms of improved early retention in the 2010/11 academic year have been encouraging. The 18 class groups involved in the pilot covered courses in construction, a range of creative subjects, sport, engineering, welding, hospitality, hairdressing and access to nursing studies.

The results were initially analysed in three dimensions, comparing them with figures for the previous year, college averages and sector averages. Eleven of the 18 courses showed improvement with previous years, 11 improved relative to sector averages and 13 showed improvements when compared with college averages. Although these results can be viewed as encouraging, suggesting that the interventions had a positive effect, they cannot yet be presented as conclusive. As with most research and development activity each layer of progress raises another layer of questions that need to be answered.

Further analysis was therefore carried out with retention figures for each course compared to three-year averages for the course. Figures for each of the academic years 07/08, 08/09 and 09/10 were extracted from college records and average retention rates were established. Three-year averages could not be calculated for five of the courses as these had not run over the full period, having been established in their current form relatively recently. For the remaining 13 that had been in place for the full three-year period, 11 showed improvement while two did not. When these results are scrutinized within the context of the performance of other full-time FE courses in the college, they offer further cause for optimism relating to their potential impact.

In 2010–11, early retention rates for those full-time FE student groups not tested for mental toughness fell from 85 per cent to 84 per cent. In contrast, early retention results for the groups tested for mental toughness increased from a pre-intervention average of 81 per cent to a post-intervention average of 88 per cent.

An associated trend can be found from a small sample where there were dual occurrences of the same course. In three cases, courses selected for the project were run in two distinct class groups, one of which was given the mental toughness test while the other was not. The average early retention rate for the three groups not tested for mental toughness was 74 per cent while the average for those who were was 92 per cent

The first phase of the Stay and succeed pilot also offered encouragement on a number of other more general as opposed to statistical fronts. The introduction of the pilot triggered debate in the college professional community about the concepts and techniques involved. Records of CPD events also show debate on how interventions relating to mental toughness could be integrated with a range of other initiatives including the training of groups of staff in 'Critical skills' (Weatherley, 2006) and the college's engagement with the training the trainer element of the Deloitte Employability Initiative (Deloitte Foundation, 2007). It has also helped to validate activities already used by many of the college's more experienced staff as they had designed and implemented their own approaches.

The wider debate and the specific outcomes of the pilot have each contributed to the college's developing approach to dealing with retention and, in parallel, addressing attainment and improving employability. The challenge has been to ensure that the range of initiatives and activities employed by the college fit together in a coherent and effective way that is understood by all staff, is accessible to new recruits to the teaching workforce and can be simply and appropriately described to learners. As this broad approach is planned and developed further, mental toughness will play a central role with interventions increasingly focused on individuals as opposed to groups.

Working on mental toughness with part-time and work-based learners

In addition to work being carried out with college-based learners, Adam Smith has taken forward a research and development project to determine how assessing and addressing mental toughness can contribute to improvements in skills utilization in the workplace. In conjunction with Stevenson College Edinburgh, the Alliance of Sector Skills Councils in Scotland, Skillset and People 1st, work has been carried out to explore how assessing and addressing mental toughness can contribute to performance in the workplace.

This work has been stimulated by broad concerns in Scotland about poor levels of productivity and their impact on economic growth. Scottish productivity, measured as gross value added per hour worked, lags significantly behind OECD and wider UK levels. Figures are almost 5 per cent lower than the UK average and the last decade has seen an ongoing relative decline (UKCES, 2010). These negative movements in productivity have taken place at a time when general skill levels in Scotland have increased.

While the overall shape of the workforce in Scotland (that is, the distribution of skills across lower, intermediate and higher levels) shows significant imbalance (UKCES, 2010) with too few people with intermediate skills and knowledge and too many people with low or no skills, skill levels stand up very well against international comparators. This combination in which rising levels of knowledge and skills sit alongside low and faltering productivity raises questions about the link between these factors. It has prompted deeper consideration of how skills are applied or utilized in the workplace. As part of this, efforts have been made to understand better how levels of skills utilization can be developed and improved. Skills utilization can be viewed as resulting from a complex mix of factors including the technical and physical environment in which work takes place, the managerial and supervisory context, and the contribution of the individual worker.

The initiative in which Adam Smith College has been engaged with its partners has endeavoured to understand (and create a model to represent) complex issues relating to the work contribution of individuals. It is here

FIGURE 12.1 Outline of the Adam Smith Skills Utilization Model

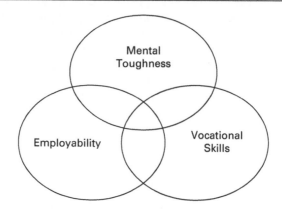

that mental toughness is argued to have a strong contribution to make. Based on workshop activity with staff from Adam Smith and Stevenson colleges, the Alliance of Sector Skills Councils and the Scottish Funding Council, the model developed by staff at Adam Smith brings together three critical factors that are considered to influence the extent to which workers, particularly younger workers and work-based learners, utilize their skills; see Figure 12.1.

The assumptions behind the model are that the propensity of individual workers to apply their skills appropriately and effectively in the workplace will be influenced significantly, on the one hand by their level of employability skills and on the other by their mental toughness, that is, the extent to which they see challenges as opportunities, their levels of personal and vocational confidence, the extent to which they feel in control of their work and the environment in which they work, and their commitment or 'stickability'. The level of mental toughness is also assumed to exert a strong positive influence on employability.

The Working with Attitude project explored aspects of skills utilization that could inform future curriculum and training course development. The project represented a partnership between education and industry aimed at developing a deeper joint understanding of how employees' skills are used in the workplace. It also worked on the premise that a number of elements including mental toughness are contributory factors to an individual's skills utilization.

Working with partners, two occupational groups were selected: 31 company employees and four managers working as Creative Media Editors were selected via Skillset; and 39 Hotel Housekeepers and 32 Hotel Managers were selected by People 1st. Almost 70 per cent of the Creative Media Editors Group fell within the mid-range for overall mental toughness, suggesting they were generally confident, able to cope with challenges, focused on goals and comfortable in most situations. The results did indicate, however, that these qualities may be tested in more difficult situations and in the specific category of interpersonal confidence. A number of low scores suggested that this may be an area for development.

A similar profile emerged for the Hotel Housekeepers with overall mental toughness peaking in the mid range. However, for every category of mental toughness, a significant minority of at least 21 per cent scored in the lower range, suggesting that developing the mental toughness of these housekeeping employees may help them cope with the stresses and challenges of the workplace and improve their performance.

It is hoped that work on the skills utilization initiative will continue into a further stage, providing the opportunity to explore the model and the complex relationships further. The results of the first stage provide an interesting and encouraging basis on which to build.

MENTAL TOUGHNESS AND LEADERSHIP –
an international case study

As the work described above moved forward, opportunities for using MTQ48 as a tool in leadership development were explored. This work was carried out with CEOs/principals/presidents and tier-2 post holders from colleges, community colleges and polytechnics in Canada, the United States, New Zealand and the UK. Those taking part completed two online psychometric instruments: the MTQ48 and one on leadership style.

Individual feedback was provided and the aggregate data set has been used to construct an international post-secondary leader profile that is now being compared with global profiles from leaders in other sectors. The work is ongoing and has two primary objectives. The first is to establish a Mental Toughness Profile and a Leadership Style Profile for leaders in post-secondary education. The second is to determine the potential value of these instruments for recruitment, review and wider benchmarking.

While this remains work in progress, the debate generated among those taking part has been informative, helping to refine and develop plans for international leadership benchmarking further. The work has also shown the potential of this type of instrument in relation to international testing. The use of online instruments is not limited by geography or time zone. Each of those taking part logged on from their own desk, completing MTQ48 and ILM72 (the leadership style instrument). AQR then undertook all administration remotely, sending scores and personal development reports to each individual taking part.

The profile that emerged on the mental toughness measure showed high levels of mental toughness overall but with underlying variables such as confidence and emotional control tending to fall into the high end of 'average or normal' levels. Mental toughness tended to be higher in areas such as control and commitment. These results were consistent with those for populations of other senior managers whose results are reported by AQR.

The inference is that the more senior you are the more challenging the work and therefore you expect the populations to become progressively 'tougher' as you rise though the organization. Work on this aspect of mental toughness in the international college and polytechnic sector is continuing, including plans to compare populations at different management levels.

In conclusion

Work on the skills utilization initiative has proved encouraging and will continue into a further stage. This will provide the opportunity to explore the model further and to gain a better understanding of the relationships between mental toughness, vocational skills and employability skills.

The results of the first stage provide an interesting and encouraging basis on which to build. They point to opportunities for post-school institutions to use mental toughness as part of more broadly based programmes aimed at improving employee performance and retention.

Turning to the use of MTQ48 in college-based programmes of learning, the first phase of the Stay and succeed pilot at Adam Smith College has proved very positive. The work has been and is being formally evaluated by the College Research Unit. Focus group discussions that have already taken place, combined with anecdotal evidence from both staff and students indicate that the project is having a positive impact. In particular, the work suggests improvement in the experience of individual students as reflected by positive changes in retention and prospective attainment. Although the work is at a relatively early stage, qualitative feedback from the focus groups suggests that the work is proving positive and effective.

More research within Adam Smith College and other colleges in the sector can now be carried out. This will aim to determine how the results achieved to date can best be replicated and how mental toughness can develop further as a key to significant and sustainable improvements in retention and attainment.

As indicated above, staff were initially cautious in their view of the MTQ48 instrument and the use of results to guide interventions. Subsequently, the confidence of many staff has increased as they have become more familiar with the approach. Students have reported that the test and interventions have strengthened the framework (personal development plans) against which they can reflect on their abilities and capabilities and understand how they can develop these during their course of study.

Overall, the work on mental toughness at Adam Smith College provides a number of pointers to successful implementation of this type of initiative.

As described above, communication is critical. Experience at the college suggests that a simple strategy for this can focus on clear descriptions of:

- the purpose of the work (the 'what' and the 'why');
- the benefits for staff and students;
- how learners and staff will be supported;
- the CPD available prior to the tests and the interventions.

More generally, the Adam Smith College experience suggests a number of other points that can usefully be taken into account at the preparation and implementation stages. In preparing or establishing an initiative based on MTQ48, it is important that:

- teaching staff are involved from the outset in planning and design;
- a comprehensive set of briefing and familiarization events are held;
- the opportunity is provided for staff to engage in less-formal discussions, helping them to share views and to generate a shared professional view of the objectives and approach to implementation.

During implementation of the initiative, further positive actions include:

- ensuring that students are aware of the aims and gains of the work;
- encouraging a wider debate in the college professional community about the concepts and techniques involved;
- holding staff and student focus groups as part of overall evaluation;
- also using focus groups to provide opportunities for further shared professional development and consideration of the fit of other related work with this specific initiative.

By way of these and other steps, Adam Smith College has established a sound foundation on which the continuing work on mental toughness can now be based.

Notes

1 Individual college reports are available at http://www.hmie.gov.uk/ SelectEstablishment.aspx?typeid=4.
2 Adam Smith College works from campuses in three towns in Central Fife and from a range of community-based locations; see http://www. adamsmith.ac.uk.
3 SCQF is the Scottish Credit and Qualifications Framework. Details are available at http://www.scqf.org.uk/.

Applying mental toughness to career guidance and career planning

13

KIERAN GORDON

The career guidance industry has focused its attention on assisting individuals to make decisions about their preferred job or career based on an assessment of their interests, abilities, aptitudes and needs.

The profession traditionally breaks this down into two distinct but related processes: 1) careers education or career skills development – promoting individual self-development, career exploration and career management; and 2) careers guidance – made up of one-to-one or small group activities (either face-to-face or online) with a skilled and knowledgeable professional to enable individuals to make plans, choices and decisions.

In the 21st century a career is increasingly becoming a journey through a range of opportunities that include education, training, work (paid or unpaid) and career breaks. Individuals may experience some or all of these during their lifetime, including periods of unemployment; indeed most people can expect to have a number of different jobs and even changes in career pathways during their working life. The career professional's role is to help the individual navigate this range of options or eventualities when called upon.

This process can start in school as early as the age of 14 when individuals are faced with choosing their curriculum subjects for national examinations. These may have a bearing on the career direction they take. Career horizons can become limited when essential subjects that are prerequisites for certain careers are dropped, for example, physical or biological sciences in the case of medical studies.

The process of career planning and decision making continues beyond school and will continue throughout life for many people as they adapt to changes in employment brought about by external factors such as variations in the economy or as a consequence of their own career aspirations and ambitions. There are internal (to the individual) factors that will also develop and alter as he or she grows older and takes on additional dependencies. This adds complexity to change – together they represent a considerable challenge. We are now faced with continuous change:

- By 2020 there will be 5 million fewer low-skill jobs in Britain than today.
- Today's learners will have between 10 and 14 jobs on average by the age of 38.
- Many of today's graduate courses did not exist 10 years ago; most of these are in the areas of technology.
- The top 10 jobs in demand in 2010 did not exist in 2004.[1]
- In the United States it is estimated that up to 30 per cent of jobs in the economy did not exist 10 year ago and that process is ongoing.
- In 10 years many jobs that now exist won't. We are now training and developing people for new jobs that don't yet exist.

And competition will increase; China will have a fourfold increase in its postgraduate population by 2020! We are no longer protected in any way from international competition. Most jobs can be carried out effectively from anywhere. As people are presented with career choices at one point in time they may make decisions that are more risky than imagined.

Traditional approaches to careers education, advice and guidance have placed particular value on:

- the skills and abilities of individuals as measured by qualifications and achievements;
- the quality and relevance of careers and labour market information in informing decisions;
- the awareness of the individual in 'matching' their interests and abilities to certain job roles.

As the careers guidance market has developed so too has the range of tools available to assist the individual and the professional careers adviser in the career planning process. These tools include interest inventories through which a person can assess his or her suitability for a certain career or job types based on a range of preferences and dispositions, and psychometric assessment which tests important abilities and aptitudes as well as, in some cases, personality types in suggesting suitable career options. All of this helps to provide a wider base of information on which to make decisions. However, they do not automatically generate ideal or acceptable career suggestions in every case.

The careers advice and guidance process therefore has classically concentrated on the relevant characteristics of the individual and the characteristics of the job or career type under consideration and it has done so with positive effect for many people. Yet, it is the case that individuals, despite this level of support and reflection, can often still make job or career decisions that do not fulfil their interests or their needs, or which are just not suitable for them. There are many reasons as to why this may be the case. The fact is that individuals are exactly that: they are individuals, and what motivates or excites one person can be a complete 'turn off' or struggle for another. We have to look deeper than the typology of the job or career in helping people make choices and make the choices work for them. We also have to look more at the individual's capacity to succeed in given job or career settings.

There are many factors that bring success, from job satisfaction, reward (financial or esteem), to advancement or progression opportunities. Equally there are many factors that limit success: lack of realism, lack of drive, lack of self-confidence, lack of commitment, etc. The careers advice and guidance profession is turning more to examining the personal aspiration and capacity of individuals in assisting their journey and this is important in helping to inform or guide a person's decisions.

On a personal level, after 30 years in the careers profession working with people with a wide range of interests, abilities and personality types, as a careers adviser and latterly as an employer, it is evident to me that just wanting or needing to do a job is not necessarily enough to enable one to succeed. Similarly, having the 'right' qualifications and skills are not the only determinant of whether an individual is suited to or even good at that job of choice.

This is due in part to the fact that the job that people enter is rarely static; it will change as technology, markets, or employer expectations change. We know that this is increasingly the case as all sectors of the employer and employment market strive to keep up with global competition, higher levels of customer demand or expectations and, inevitably, technological changes to processes, systems and products. These can and do create increased stresses for all concerned, not least the individual, whether as employer or employee.

So how do we take account of this ever-changing world of career or job? Well, we need to do more than just equipping people to understand the dynamics of the labour market and where they fit in. The careers professional could and should do more to assist individuals to survive and thrive in it.

To do this we must look beyond the traditional or familiar career planning techniques that are prevalent in most programmes of support. We must look at the way in which we can help individuals cope with changing demands, changing pressures, and the changes even brought about by loss of employment, whether voluntary or forced.

I would like to claim that an analysis of how the careers professional can provide a more rounded and sustainable career strategy for individual customers led me to look at these factors in more detail and discover the application of mental toughness to the careers guidance process. However, it was actually as a result of undertaking a review of the leadership and management capacity of my company's senior team for the challenges that lay ahead that I began to understand more fully some of the critical components of career success and individual wellbeing at work. It was at this point that I was introduced to the concept of mental toughness as a management development tool.

By undertaking a review of the pressures that managers were working under and their individual capacities to deal with them, the company was able to help individuals identify negative stressors and cope with them by building their resilience to them in their everyday lives. The use of the MTQ48 assessment technique provided a unique, reliable and valid tool for giving individual feedback on levels of mental toughness normed against a wider population. It also provided individual insight into how people cope with daily occurrences through an understanding of:

- *Confidence* – how they see themselves as effective managers.
- *Commitment* – how they are able to stick to a task or project and get it done well.
- *Challenge* – how they deal with challenging situations and people.
- *Control* – how they remain in control of situations and their feelings and keep on top of things.

The process proved rewarding for each individual and the feedback was overwhelmingly positive. We benefited from a cohesion and joint determination to succeed by directing people to deliver key goals; by working with people to develop their capability to perform and be productive and by working through people to harness energy and capability to solve problems and make decisions at the right level.

Some time later when looking at the challenges that we faced as a careers advice and guidance company supporting individuals to take a more informed view of opportunities, it was apparent that resilience is an increasingly important factor in how people manage their career. Our aim was to build it into our programmes of support from an early age to develop young people's awareness of the increasing demands of growing up and of working life and to better prepare them for coping with these challenges.

The programme has now been used in secondary schools across a range of ability levels and also with specific programmes targeted at groups of similar ability. Whilst it is in its early stages of use in this context it is already showing its value in helping learners and their tutors in making choices and planning and preparing for transition. By integrating the mental toughness programme into the learning and review cycle of the school, careers advisers have been able to prepare individual learners for the challenges and choices ahead as well as inform their tutor's base of evidence in conducting learner reviews.

Helping learners to look at how being mentally tough can increase their performance in school, their wellbeing and their ability to make successful transitions as measured by achievement and improved employability was at the core of the programme. An example of its use has been with learners who were facing the prospect of going on work experience from school. In this particular instance learners cited motivation and self-belief as two of the biggest challenges facing them, and the programme focused on these areas. The MTQ48 assessment generated individual profiles that were interpreted and fed back in learner review meetings with tutors. The results were used in coaching sessions designed to develop coping skills and positive attitudes as part of their preparation for work experience. School feedback pointed to the learners being more engaged and motivated in this particular aspect of the curriculum.

The strategies developed with the learners looked at the importance of planning: preparing for the big event. It focused on setting realistic goals, taking control and staying positive. It also covered managing stress by identifying and practising relevant tips and techniques such as breathing, planning, positive thinking, prioritizing and laughing. Learners were keen to explore motivation: what inspires and fuels success. Learners identified positive role models and considered what inspired them; they discovered that having a vision and a goal are great motivators. Their conclusion was that by achieving goals individuals gain a great sense of personal achievement and that being successful can increase one's opportunity and choice.

As in all good practice the views of the learners themselves were testimony to the effectiveness of the mental toughness programme:

> The coaching sessions were good. I learnt techniques to help me concentrate and block out distractions. It will help me get on in life. I told my friends about it because I think it would help them too. (Dylan, aged 15)

> The mental toughness programme helped to improve my confidence – it made me feel stronger. I really enjoyed the brain training activities and learnt to do things step by step. My friends should do it too. (Scott, aged 15)

> I thought the mental toughness sessions were very good. It taught me to think about how I organize my time better. I told my friend about it because I think it will help her. (Danielle, aged 15)

From these few examples of the many positive reflections undertaken the striking note is the eagerness to spread the word to friends.

Personal advisers who ran the programme also commented positively:

> The mental toughness programme raises levels of self-awareness and self-understanding – essential skills to help inform the decision-making process.

> The resulting reports of the mental toughness assessments were a real eye-opener to the young people I work with – they loved finding out more about themselves. Motivation levels really improved following their one-to-one feedback sessions.

> The true benefit of mental toughness for me lies in its social mobility factor: helping young people to build their confidence and self-esteem, providing greater career awareness and helping young people stay in learning.

By piloting approaches with young people it was clear that there was identification with the mental toughness paradigm. Those who scored higher on the control scale were more in control of their emotions and their lives; this helped them understand the importance of identifying those factors in their life that enabled control so that behaviours could be modelled to this effect in a programme of self-development.

Some people perceive a challenge as an opportunity, others as a threat. Enabling young people to understand that life will be full of challenges means we are better able to equip them to accept this inevitability and help them to see how challenges can be tackled to positive effect.

Commitment is an area where criticism of young people is most prevalent when it comes to application of self to work or education. How often do you hear that young people are unreliable or not equipped with what it takes to be reliable employees? For the most part this criticism is unwarranted, but we must recognize that there are times when young people, as well as adults, find it difficult to stick at things. This can often result in the primeval response of fight or flight; neither strategy is ideal and often comes at a price for the individual as well as those around them. Finding out why people respond in this way can be an aid to helping them to deal with the eventuality. Often a fear of the different and what is seen to be threatening (not necessarily physically threatening) situations can intimidate people, particularly where they feel they are outside their familiar environment and support structure.

The response has been to build mental toughness programmes into the careers assessment and guidance process, enabling individuals to step outside of a linear job-matching approach to look at the demands of working life and given situations, which looks beyond the job description. The evidence so far is impressive. Research shows that there is a clear link between a young person's mental toughness and his or her education attainment levels. Equally there is a correlation between the realistic and high-aspiring young person and his or her level of mental toughness. Those young people who had clearer career aims and who have based these on a more informed view of their own abilities, interests and resilience have a higher level of mental toughness as indicated in the MTQ48 assessment.

In demonstrating this correlation, we are better able to diagnose some of the components of what makes people more successful in a work situation. By showing that these components or resilience factors can be worked at and strengthened we are able to take proactive steps in addressing how individuals can become more mentally tough and be better able to cope with or maximize the outcomes of challenges that they face. Where this technique may be at its most powerful is when working with people who are able to see the need for help with improving their levels of self-confidence, of taking control of their lives, being able to identify and rise to challenges as new experiences as well as having the staying power to see a challenge through.

Too often the qualities that are under examination are characteristically less evident in young people whose perception of themselves and their situation is borne out of a poor educational experience and where their family or life circumstances lead to a lack of opportunity to excel and progress in educational and employment terms. This is more likely (though not exclusively) the case for young people who grow up in poorer neighbourhoods, where poverty of aspiration as well as economic poverty is most pronounced. For these young people the idea of aspiring to a professional career (other than perhaps a footballer or entertainer) is rarely present. So too is the aspiration to consider a university education, where there is little or no history of family or friends having taken this path in life.

The challenge then, in working with young people from areas of high deprivation or from weaker family/social environs, is to help them to lift their sights and to believe in themselves, creating the necessary self-worth they need to aspire and set goals and set out to achieve them in a positive and constructive manner.

Their conditioning needs to be challenged and a good place to start is with the four building blocks of mental toughness: control; challenge; commitment and confidence. If we can help young people to master or at very least improve their approach to these aspects of life management we are better able to introduce a wider range of career possibilities and opportunities.

Evidence from the use of MTQ48 with different academic ability groups and socio-economic areas does not suggest that there is a pre-conditioned disparity in the levels of mental toughness between the two. The application of MTQ48 within a grammar school setting in a relatively affluent area demonstrated a similar range of mental toughness across the learner body. The range of mental toughness is evident in both settings. A common factor between the two, however, is that the higher the level of mental toughness the higher the realistic aspirations and determination to achieve.

The MTQ48 measure provides a reliable, valid and non-threatening tool for helping young people to identify some of the components of successful living that are applied to the world of work. By providing individual feedback with ratings of where individuals are against the four components of mental toughness it is possible to identify how they can address each of these and apply them to their strategy for planning a career or maximizing a job opportunity.

That it doesn't measure ability or intelligence in a way that formal examinations do and that there is no pass/fail answer to the measure or its outcome helps to provide a non-threatening 'examination' or assessment, which can go a long way to identifying strengths that are not accredited elsewhere as well as inform the steps that can help an individual improve his or her personal effectiveness.

Note

1 *14–19 Briefing – Making Change Happen,* Department of Children, Schools and Families, UK Government.

Mental toughness and the world of work

14

The world of work is a major source of stress, pressure and change for most people. Even if the work itself is not particularly stressful, the environment can often provide the stressors and pressures. People tend to work within organizations, large and small, and there are very few organizations that are so secure that they do not feel the effect of competitive pressures. The Stress Model shown in Chapter 2 illustrates the fact that stressors can arise from almost anywhere and from almost anything we do.

Since its launch in 2003, the MTQ48 has been used in occupational settings more often than any other. This has provided a rich source of case studies and in recent times the beginnings of carefully controlled research. These consistently show that mental toughness has a significant role to play in the performance and wellbeing of individuals, amongst other things. However, equally important has been the observation that assessing the mental toughness of groups has been useful and revealing. The performance and behaviour of groups seems also to be influenced by the prevailing mental toughness of the group.

From the organization's perspective a key requirement is most often to acquire and develop a workforce who perform to the best of their abilities and who develop a positive attitude towards the commercial and operational challenges that need to be dealt with. There is a growing awareness of the importance of culture in determining organizational performance. A consistent component of most organizations' preferred cultural position is to have a 'can do' attitude throughout the organization. Having such a positive attitude is always likely to bring about a better performance than without it.

This is perhaps more important these days given that most individuals and organizations have access to the same plant, equipment and technology. It used to be possible for organizations to achieve competitive advantage through unique access to these factors and in a few cases they may still be important. Similarly, as education, training and development have improved, equal access to skilled and competent employees has produced a more level playing field. But you can still have two sets of employees with equal or equivalent skill, knowledge and experience working with similar equipment in similar environments and yet they will deliver two distinctly different performances. And generally the more motivated the workforce and more positive in outlook, the more likely it will consistently emerge as the higher performing workforce.

We now understand very well that the motivation and mindset of a workforce are crucial ingredients for success. More and more time, money and effort are spent on examining and developing this aspect of the organization. Developing mental toughness is a significant part of the answer to creating a high-performance organization. This appears particularly so when it combines with and supports other solutions. It's not the whole answer to every such question: nothing is. But it does emerge consistently as a core component which few organizations can choose to ignore.

So we now see much more attention given to leadership development. Leadership is a quality that provides motivation to followers to give up their discretionary effort and to do it willingly and enthusiastically. Discretionary effort is that part of what we do which is going beyond what we have agreed to do in, say, a contract of employment – in 'old money' what we used to call 'going the extra mile'.

The more that a leader can do to develop that, the more likely that the leader's highly motivated followers will achieve better performance and provide competitive advantage. The best organizations develop leadership at every level. The ability to deal with challenge, change and pressure is what mental toughness is all about. Mental toughness has a vital role in enabling both the leader and the follower to respond positively to the challenge of leadership.

Probably the fastest growing area in organizational and individual development is coaching. In particular organizations are taking up performance, leadership and executive coaching with an extraordinary zeal. The belief is that coaching is a superior way to develop individuals and an excellent vehicle for engendering employee engagement (a core competency in leadership development). Again, the main goals for most coaching practice are performance, wellbeing, personal development and managing change. Mental toughness is relevant for each of these. We are beginning to be clearer that mental toughness is important for the coachee – and the coach!

The most valuable outcomes for mental toughness activity

Performance

At every level of analysis we see a close relationship between the mental toughness of individuals and performance, however it is measured and assessed. Not surprisingly this reflects the components of the model – the 4 Cs.

Mentally tough people show greater commitment to setting and achieving goals and targets, they respond more positively to challenge, they deal with adversity and setback with greater confidence and have a stronger sense of being able to control their ability to achieve.

Exercises and studies in all sectors of the economy consistently return the same results. Chapter 16 describes a case study in a call centre which shows the link between mental toughness and performance and, most valuably, the link between development activity and improving mental toughness and, through that, performance.

In 2011, a major employability study in Scotland showed that the productivity of graduates in their first employment was closely related to their mental toughness as measured through MTQ48. Quite simply, the study showed that, although the graduates were knowledgeable and skilled, if their interpersonal confidence scores were lower than average, they were more unlikely to tell their employer about their capability, so the employer was unable to access their capability.

An interesting related finding was that the mental toughness of some managers in some of the employers was also a factor in productivity. They, too, appeared to lack the interpersonal confidence to ask new recruits about their capability!

Wellbeing

The more mentally tough the more likely the individual would be able to deal with everyday stressors. They were less likely to report being stressed and were more likely to report being able to complete stressful and challenging days at work and feel satisfied or content.

Perhaps one of the more interesting findings which is the result of formal study is that more mentally tough people emerge as less likely to report bullying behaviour (ie less likely to report being bullied) (Coyne *et al*, 2006). This mirrors a study carried out in Secondary Education, which also showed that the mental toughness of the individual was related to the extent to which he or she reported being subjected to bullying behaviour.

Both cases showed that it was possible to have two groups of people, one mentally tough and another mentally sensitive, who see exactly the same behaviour in two different ways. In being asked to described examples of bullying behaviour both groups would describe a manager, fellow colleague, student or teacher as 'shouty': 'They looked at me when they were making a point', 'They rolled their eyes when speaking to me', 'Addressing me in a loud voice', etc.

The mentally sensitive group would feel that these actions were directly specifically at them. They thought they were being picked on. The mentally tough group, often observing exactly the same behaviour at the same time for the same people, would simply see a shouting manager or teacher, etc who was adopting a behaviour to control a workgroup or a class. They didn't take it personally.

This is not to suggest that deliberate bullying and careless bullying don't exist. Bullying does occur and when it does it has to be dealt with; being subjected to bullying is hugely destructive. But it does raise some interesting questions. Is bullying really as widespread as is sometimes suggested? Almost certainly not. Is the solution always to deal only with the bully? Often it is, but it could often equally be the case that showing the individual how to deal with behaviours and incidents that he or she had found disturbing may be equally or more effective. Curiously, in some instances we find that the bully is also a victim and has in the past been the recipient of bullying behaviour.

What is needed is more careful examination of this area and avoiding emotional content when discussing it. There is a serious issue here that is not well served by treating all bullying incidents as if they were all of the same type.

Positive behaviours

People who were more mentally tough were more likely to be described or describe themselves as having a 'can do' approach. They would tend to assess risk and to accept risk with a more positive mindset. The mentally tough tended to be more aspirational than the mentally sensitive. They appeared to set higher goals and targets and be more confident about achieving them.

The above is very much focused on the individual. Aggregating mental toughness scores to examine patterns of mental toughness in organizations can also be revealing.

GROUP MENTAL TOUGHNESS

In 2008, we worked with a UK local authority based in the North of England, which employed around 7,000 people. The organization had, in the previous three years, made significant progress in transforming itself from an organization that had been assessed as underperforming to one which was now seen as a high-performance operation. This transformation had also stirred an ambition amongst the top tier of the organization to achieve recognition as an excellent organization.

The first part of the journey had been achieved through the vision and commitment of the chief executive and a small group at the top of the organization. The culture had been variously described as 'top down', 'highly centralized' and even 'autocratic'. Senior management had correctly assessed that, although this had been appropriate to move the organization from its poorly performing past, this would not be sufficient to move it to an excellently performing future. A more participative and teamwork-oriented culture was needed to engage everyone in the organization in its success.

A substantial visioning and planning exercise was launched which involved all 97 members of the senior and the senior/middle management structures. The plans, though ambitious, were deemed realistic. However, when implemented, there was a poor response from the employees across the organization. The suspicion was that one element of this was the behaviour of the wider senior management group.

All 97 senior managers completed the MTQ48 measure and the results partially confirmed the original suspicion. Figure 14.1 shows the pattern of overall mental toughness scores.

Studies by Marchant *et al* (2009) amongst others had shown that the more senior the manager the greater the level of mental toughness. We would have predicted that this group should show scores with a mean somewhere in the region of stens 7–8. The actual pattern is skewed to the left. Feedback and discussion with managers in the local authority confirmed that they thought the scores provided a reliable reflection of the situation at the time. One plausible suggestion was that the leadership style hadn't changed. Although all of these managers had participated in the visioning and planning stages of the organization development programme and had therefore been involved in its development, they didn't feel involved.

One interesting observation is that most managers didn't realize it was part of their role to champion and to implement the programme. One director observed, 'These are the results from self-report questionnaires. This is how we see ourselves. It's not going to be a surprise that the staff see us that way too!'

Analysing the scores for the individual scales was equally revealing. Figure 14.2 shows the pattern of scores for the challenge scale. This is, if anything, more skewed to the left than the pattern for overall mental toughness. This indicated that most senior managers (those scoring 7 and below, 72 out of 97), although they had been involved in developing the change programme, did not necessarily see the challenge as an opportunity to show what could be achieved.

The pattern of scores for commitment showed a similar pattern; see Figure 14.3. This was lower than expected.

FIGURE 14.1 Overall mental toughness

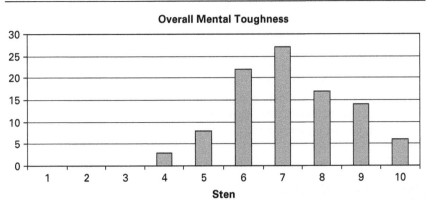

FIGURE 14.2 Mental toughness – challenge scores

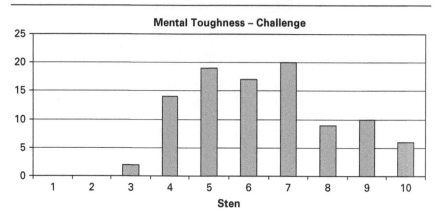

FIGURE 14.3 Mental toughness – commitment scores

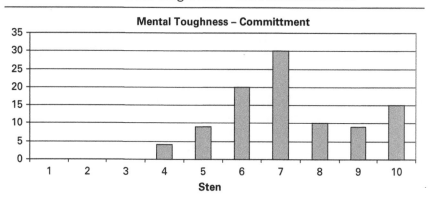

The analysis provoked a review of the organization's development strategy. Amongst actions taken were the provision of coaching opportunities for managers in this group and more attention to ensuring that managers better understood their role as managers and leaders in the organization. To some extent they had not moved their thinking from seeing themselves predominantly as functional managers. Although appreciating the value of developing culture, atmosphere and attitude, this had always been 'handled by the HR department and senior management'.

Other analyses revealed that most managers didn't feel engaged with the organization and with other managers and that there was a poor focus on delivery of key organizational goals. Mental toughness wasn't the only factor in the failure of the programme but it was a significant one. The analysis also indicated strongly what might require attention to make the desired breakthrough.

By 2010 the organization had achieved its desired excellence (4 Star) status.

Applications in the workplace

There are several areas where the model adds considerable value. First, it provides a practical description of core competencies for many jobs. This means that it has value in recruitment, selection and especially in succession planning and promotion. When used in recruitment and selection, it must be used with care. Mental toughness must be shown to be a key requirement for the role.

The MTQ48 measure is a valid and reliable measure and it is a normative one, and therefore has potential to be useful in recruitment and selection. Like any high-quality psychometric instrument it should not be used in conjunction with other sources of information about the individual's mental toughness.

Its greatest value perhaps lies in employee development, in leadership and management development, and in coaching activity to which it is very well suited. This is examined further in Chapter 19.

In training and development generally, work has been carried out that confirms that the effectiveness of much training and development activity is due in some part to the mindset of the individual entering training and development programmes. Unsurprisingly, if individuals enter a training or development programme with trepidation and perhaps even fear, they may not get from the programme what they could. This is particularly true in organizations where staff and managers are 'sent' on training programmes.

Those who adopt a positive attitude will inevitably optimize the learning experience. Their approach is to get the most out of the time they have to spend. These differences in attitude and approach can arise for a variety of reasons. Where there are mergers, acquisitions and managerial changes, staff can often view a good deal of activity with suspicion and concern.

Assessing an individual's mental toughness can also help to assess their readiness for learning. Investing in this assessment and attending to issues emerging can make a significant difference to the effectiveness of training and development activity. This will both minimize waste and improve the chances of running a successful programme.

In some forms of education and training, eg apprenticeship programmes, there is a link between mental toughness and completion rates or, in more common parlance, dropout rates. This is one of the areas of greatest waste in many organizations but it can be reduced through assessing a learner's mental toughness and responding accordingly. In 2011 Adam Smith College carried out a pilot on 400 students and found that it could reduce dropout rates by 28 students (7 per cent overall) compared to the previous three years.

Finally, understanding mental toughness and incorporating relevant material into most soft skills programmes can significantly enhance the content of those programmes. This will include leadership and management programmes (the Institute of Leadership and Management has endorsed the

MTQ48 measure) and interpersonal skills programmes of all types. It is especially valuable in presentation skills and time management programmes. Individual mental toughness is relevant to the way individuals approach both of these activities.

As we have seen in the local authority case study above, there is a significant application in organization development activity. Almost everyone is today engaged in change programmes or in commercially competitive activity or in merger/acquisition/downsizing. These are all activities that provide a source of stressors, pressure and challenge. The mental toughness of the organization as a whole will be as important as individual mental toughness in dealing effectively with those stressors and in bringing about a successful outcome.

Mental toughness as a concept is made for application in the world of work.

Mental toughness and team working

15

We have often found ourselves, when operating as organizational development consultants, engaged in business improvement programmes that have the development of team working as a core component and belief. Curiously, a casual observation in many instances has been that senior management teams, which decide they would like to see a team working culture develop throughout the organization, often provide the least compelling example of team working.

Our work with developing mental toughness within organizations and within teams has led us to some interesting and potentially useful observations. First, we are generally convinced of the benefits of effective high-performance team working. We interact with others all day long. We are important and we influence others. We can be helpful, supportive or destructive. The way we behave sets standards for the rest of the organization – especially when we are in leadership and management positions.

So what do teams do for organizations? They:

- accomplish complex tasks – they tend to achieve high levels of performance;
- enable problems to be solved close to their source – usually more efficiently and more effectively;
- can be very good at coordinating the efforts of diverse but related groups and individuals;
- cover weaknesses by the strengths of others.

Developing team working can be a key component of the business strategy for many organizations. It figures widely in leadership and management theory and practice.

Mental toughness can have a big impact on both the performance of the organization and how team working and team building are developed. Our experience suggests that there are two issues to be considered: organization development and culture, and team working behaviour and individual mental toughness.

Organization development and culture

When organizations are concerned with improving their performance it can be a very effective tactic to set about developing the mental toughness of their people. However, it is possible to develop the mental toughness of an individual or individuals and find that their effectiveness is limited because of the pattern of mental toughness within the organization.

The function of the Organization Development report available with the MTQ48 is to show the pattern of mental toughness within selected groups. This report will often show that a group whose overall mental toughness is comparatively low can, over time, impact on the mental toughness of performers who are higher than the norm and 'wear them out'. Those with exceptionally high levels of mental toughness will not necessarily wilt but they may respond to a mentally sensitive culture with frustration and annoyance.

The challenge here is to support the development of mental toughness across the group or the team. One solution is to consider the use of coaches or mentors who, equipped with a toolkit of suitable interventions such as those described elsewhere in this book, work with members of the team to develop their mental toughness.

Another is to provide learning and development on mental toughness to the whole team and not just selected individuals. In the world of education the Scottish colleges have been experimenting with just these options. Do you provide support only to those whose scores suggest they need it or do you provide a broad range of support to everyone?

Team working behaviour and individual mental toughness

People who rise to the top of an organization are almost inevitably more mentally tough than the average person. However, being mentally tough usually implies a degree of personal achievement and mental insensitivity – a tendency to be 'thick-skinned' and not too sensitive to things that might get in the way of performance. Not, at first sight, the best recipe for team working!

Senior management and board meetings can be interesting affairs. Conversation and exchanges can be very blunt and direct – to the point of appearing rude. Yet the participants will often take it in their stride and think no more of it.

I well remember my first presentation as a junior/middle manager presenting a proposal to develop our operation with my colleagues. We had

FIGURE 15.1 Characteristics of a 'world-class' team

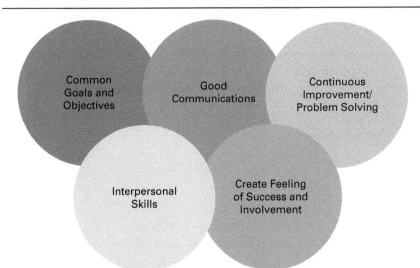

15 minutes to put our case, the questioning was incisive, pressured and bruising. We were down-hearted on leaving the presentation only to learn later that the board had approved our proposal.

Team working is often more effective in the lower reaches of the organization than at the top. Paradoxically it is usually the top team that grasps the importance of developing team working and will make it a key plank of an organizational development programme – and will then provide the worst example of team working in terms of their own behaviour. The challenge is to maintain the mental toughness of these high performers whilst helping them to develop the behaviours that are consistent with effective team working.

Examining the behaviour of high-performing teams – whether they are from the sports, social or the business world – shows that there are certain characteristics that are consistently present if that team is truly 'world class'. These characteristics fall into five broad and interrelated areas, shown in Figure 15.1.

A truly first-class team must perform well in all five areas – anything less is not highly productive, effective and efficient team working. If we examine each area in more detail we can see more clearly why these are critical areas for success.

Developing team toughness

There are a number of actions that a team of mentally tough individuals can adopt that will enhance their team working. It is not necessarily desirable to change the mental toughness of the team members. It is after all one of the qualities that has taken them to the top of the organization and it may be a significant contributor to their individual and their group success.

The key here is to develop self-awareness and to enhance their understanding of their impact on others, and finally to enable them to agree to adopt a common set of behaviours that better represent team working and send a stronger signal to others that they believe in team working and are prepared to adopt at least some recognizable team working behaviours. This can be expressed as a team charter.

Typical activities adopted to enhance team toughness and team working include the following.

Control

- Agree on who is doing what.
- Accept that setbacks are normal occurrences.
- Agree on a plan together and support each other in sticking to it.
- Give each other the space/time/support each needs to recover from setbacks.
- Some things will always be outside your control – work as a team to get round what you can't change.

Challenge

- Review and prioritize work together.
- Communicate with each other.
- Identify each other's strengths and weaknesses – coach and delegate where necessary.
- View challenges and obstacles as opportunities at both team and individual levels.
- Break down assignments into smaller manageable chunks and delegate.
- Recognize when you need to take time out and recharge as a team and as individuals.

Commitment

- Take time to recognize each other's contributions and give praise where due.
- Accept that some tasks can't be completed. Review resources and energy – could they be better directed?
- Identify what motivates you as a team and as individuals and incorporate this into your planning.

- Agree on your goals and deadlines. They should be specific, measurable, achievable, relevant and time bound (SMART).
- Don't be afraid to ask each other for help when you need it and encourage each other to suggest ideas.
- Have regular meetings/contact to monitor progress. Things change and so might your goals.
- Listen to each other and ask each other questions. Communicate.

Confidence

- Recognize each other's strengths, acknowledge them and use them.
- Don't dwell on mistakes and over-generalize them. Not everything is black and white – mistakes can be learnt from.
- Beware of over-confidence.
- If confidence is knocked, recognize the need for time off to recover. Give each other the additional support you need.
- Give constructive criticism, corrections and encouragement instead of verbally beating someone down.
- Give teammates the support they need to improve their skills and increase their confidence.
- If a teammate or colleague needs chastising do it in private and provide him or her with the opportunity to remedy the error.

A team must have a shared sense of purpose, aspiration, effective ways of working with each other, a willingness to work together, personal independence, and a collective identity.

If a team behaves carefully it can improve things for its colleagues and show others, by example, how to be more effective. There are two steps to be taken; first to reflect on and discuss with colleagues key issues. Once done, this should lead to the completion of a team charter. Typical issues for reflection include:

- What can we do as a team to increase team toughness for others and ourselves?
- What can we do as a team to reduce stress for others and ourselves?
- What can we do as a team to achieve peak performance?
- How can we work more effectively with each other?
- How can we work more effectively with others outside the team?
- Can we genuinely commit to doing something about it?
- How will we implement and publish it?
- Which actions are absolutely key?

A typical team charter might look like the following.

Team Charter

Set out here are the key behaviours everyone in the team will adopt to improve the way the team performs:

1   We will avoid the use of strong language at all times.

2   We will publicly support all group decisions.

3   We will respond to all questions and queries.

4   We will not apportion blame to any person or group when something goes wrong.

5   We will keep all appointments – and be on time every time.

6   We will visit a department of the business at least once a week for at least one hour.

The world of work – a case study from a major call centre

16

ADRIAN EAGLESON AND JOHNNY PARKS

Introduction

The (2009) investigation shows the impact of a three-month mental tough-ness training programme directed at 28 managers within a large call centre company in the UK. The object was to establish to what extent structured mental toughness development activity was able to change the mental toughness of a group of managers.

Data about individual mental toughness was collected via the Mental Toughness Questionnaire (MTQ48) before and after the programme to assess the measure of difference from the training. A control group of 23 managers was also established. They were tested at the same times as the experimental group but were not offered any mental toughness interventions.

The results show that mental toughness can be developed over time (p = .016) and that there was a main effect for those who undertook the training in comparison with those who did not (p = .045). The study high-lights the importance of such structured programmes and the use of applied psychological skills training.

Participants

All participants were managers in a large contact centre in the UK. The company in question was gem, which is one of Europe's largest independ-ent providers of outsourced multilingual, multi-channel customer contact solutions. The organization had approximately 900 staff deployed over a number of sites. The study took place in its central location with the main business support teams and key operations managers.

Gem had an excellent track record in designing and delivering training and was known for its approaches to coaching and mentoring with staff teams. As an organization it was interested in developing the mental toughness of the management team and had secured the services of a consulting company to deliver an agreed programme over a three-month period.

Training sessions – the core interventions

The mental toughness development programme involved three parts. In the first part (covering two sessions), participants described current stressors, challenges and pressures that they found based on four criteria of individual, team, organizational and extra-organizational. A model of mental toughness (Clough *et al*, 2002) was presented and feedback given based on the results of the MTQ48 scores and development of the key concepts around the 4 Cs model.

For the second part of the programme (covering three sessions) participants practised a range of psychological skills techniques for developing mental toughness. These included attentional control (Maddi, 1987), REBT (Ellis, 1980), visualization and relaxation techniques and the development of psychological capital (Luthans *et al*, 2008). Most of the tools and techniques are described elsewhere in this book.

The final part of the programme consisted of one session where a number of case studies were used to highlight the 4 Cs model and embed learning, and concluded with a series of action-planning activities so that participants had a clear personal development path to engage in after training.

The results

Analysis of the data gathered during the project was carried out at several levels: looking at overall mental toughness, and looking at scores for each of the 4 Cs – challenge, control, commitment and confidence. The results can be summarized as follows.

Overall mental toughness scores

A mixed measures factorial ANOVA was carried out. Means and standard deviations are shown in Table 16.1, and a line graph of the results is shown in Figure 16.1.

There was a main effect for time of measurement $F(1,49) = 6.20$, $p = .016$, a main effect for whether the employees were trained or not $F(1,49) = 4.24$, $p = .045$. There was not a significant interaction effect

TABLE 16.1 Means and standard deviations of mental toughness scores by whether or not employees attended a mental toughness development programme

	Group	Mean	Std Deviation	N
Time 1	Experiment	5.6071	1.70705	28
	Control	5.4348	1.75360	23
	Total	5.5294	1.71293	51
Time 2	Experiment	7.0357	1.89506	28
	Control	5.6087	1.80250	23
	Total	6.3922	1.97057	51

FIGURE 16.1 Line graph of overall mental toughness scores by time of measurement and whether employees undertook mental toughness development training

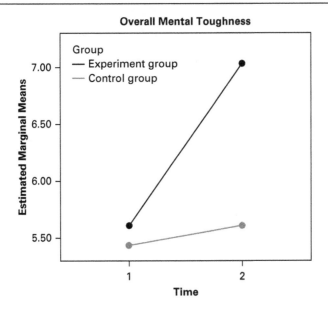

between time of measurement and whether employees were trained or not F (1,49) = 3.80, p = .057. There was a medium to large effect size (d = 0.78).

Examination of the mental toughness scores of both the experiment group and the control group before the training took place shows that the scores were very similar. However, after the training programme the mental toughness scores for those who had participated in the training were considerably higher. This suggests that the training programme had a marked positive effect on developing mental toughness.

Challenge

A mixed measures factorial ANOVA was carried out. Means and standard deviations are shown in Table 16.2, and a line graph of the results is shown in Figure 16.2.

TABLE 16.2 Means and standard deviations of challenge scores by whether or not employees attended a mental toughness development programme

	Group	Mean	Std Deviation	N
Time 1	Experiment	5.2143	1.75028	28
	Control	4.4783	1.67521	23
	Total	4.8824	1.73951	51
Time 2	Experiment	6.8214	1.94467	28
	Control	5.2174	1.80798	23
	Total	6.0980	2.03229	51

FIGURE 16.2 Line graph of challenge scores by time of measurement and whether employees undertook mental toughness development training

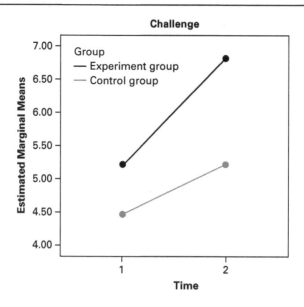

Similar to the findings for the overall mental toughness scores there was a main effect for time of measurement F (1,49) = 16.45, p = <.001, a main effect for whether the employees were trained or not F (1,49) = 7.88, p = .001 and no statistical significance between time of measurement and whether employees were trained or not F (1,49) = 2.25, p = .140.

Control

A mixed measures factorial ANOVA was carried out. Means and standard deviations are shown in Table 16.3, and a line graph of the results is shown in Figure 16.3.

There was no main effect for time of measurement F (1,49) = 2.43, p = .126, a main effect for whether the employees were trained or not F (1,49) = 5.71, p = .021 and for between time of measurement and whether employees were trained or not F (1,49) = 1.487, p = .229 and no major interaction effect.

Commitment

A mixed measures factorial ANOVA was carried out. Means and standard deviations are shown in Table 16.4, and a line graph of the results is shown in Figure 16.4.

There was a main effect for time of measurement F (1,49) = 5.21, p = .027, no statistical effect for whether the employees were trained or not F (1,49) = 1.182, p = .282 and no significant interaction effect between time of measurement and whether employees were trained or not F (1,49) = .820, p = .370.

TABLE 16.3 Means and standard deviations of control scores by whether or not employees attended a mental toughness development programme

	Group	Mean	Std Deviation	N
Time 1	Experiment	5.3929	2.07880	28
	Control	4.8696	2.11712	23
	Total	5.1569	2.09163	51
Time 2	Experiment	6.4643	2.16850	28
	Control	5.0000	1.59545	23
	Total	5.8039	2.04958	51

FIGURE 16.3 Line graph of control scores by time of measurement and whether employees undertook mental toughness development training

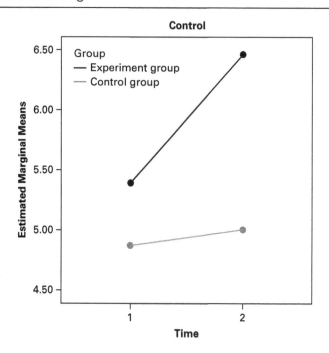

TABLE 16.4 Means and standard deviations of commitment scores by whether or not employees attended a mental toughness development programme

	Group	Mean	Std Deviation	N
Time 1	Experiment	5.7143	1.58365	28
	Control	5.6522	1.55530	23
	Total	5.6863	1.55551	51
Time 2	Experiment	6.8214	1.84699	28
	Control	6.1304	1.96108	23
	Total	6.5098	1.91178	51

Confidence

A mixed measures factorial ANOVA was carried out. Means and standard deviations are shown in Table 16.5, and a line graph of the results is shown in Figure 16.5.

FIGURE 16.4 Line graph of commitment scores by time of measurement and whether employees undertook mental toughness development training

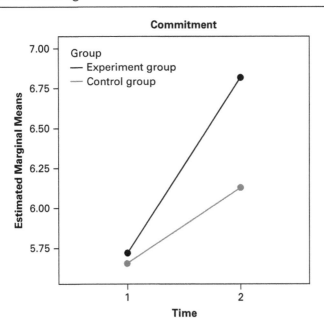

TABLE 16.5 Means and standard deviations of confidence scores by whether or not employees attended a mental toughness development programme

	Group	Mean	Std Deviation	N
Time 1	Experiment	5.4643	1.55116	28
	Control	5.7391	1.48377	23
	Total	5.5882	1.51230	51
Time 2	Experiment	6.7500	1.93649	28
	Control	5.7826	1.80798	23
	Total	6.3137	1.92344	51

There was a main effect for time of measurement $F_{(1,49)} = 3.980$, $p = .05$, but none on whether the employees were trained or not $F_{(1,49)} = .994$, $p = .324$ and between time of measurement and whether employees were trained or not $F_{(1,49)} = 3.476$, $p = .068$.

FIGURE 16.5 Line graph of confidence scores by time of measurement and whether employees undertook mental toughness development training

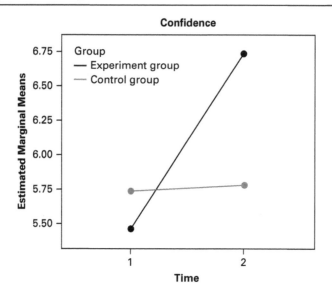

Summary of results

The results from the study show favourable effects of the mental toughness programme for the development of overall mental toughness. At the conclusion of the programme (three months) the total experiment group had significantly improved their overall mental toughness scores and in particular challenge, confidence and control. These results are in line with the conclusions drawn by Clough *et al* (2005), Bull *et al* (2005) and Maddi *et al* (1998) that mental toughness can be developed through the use of applied psychological skills training and that it is best delivered over an extended period of time.

The effect of time showed significance in the areas of challenge (p = <.01), commitment (p = .027) and less significantly with confidence (p = .05). Mental toughness is regarded as being a long-term process that develops in different stages (Gould *et al*, 2002) and in relation to managerial position (Marchant *et al*, 2009).

The population sample that was used during the study consisted mainly of young managers in their first or second management position (mean age 34). This could account for the relatively low scores at the beginning of the study that were below what would be expected for a normative population sample of managers (AQR, 2005).

Research has shown that, following Bloom's (1985) three career phases (early, middle and later years), mental toughness is developed in the early stages of a managerial career by several critical incidents and coaching

(Connaughton *et al*, 2008). The results show the importance of interventions such as the mental toughness development programme being introduced at an early stage in a manager's career to help develop the skills and mindset necessary to deal with pressure, stressors and challenge.

The results also demonstrate that training has a positive effect with a significance being reported of p = .045 between those who had been trained and those who had not. Therefore although mental toughness can be seen as an attribute that can develop over time, the findings show how this can be affected through training and the positive impact of tailored interventions. The study gives considerable weight to the view that mental toughness training programmes are useful in an applied setting (Sheard *et al*, 2009). The results in this study showed that the mental toughness development training had an impact on participants' control scores, p = .021.

Employees' experiences of working in call centres is known to affect wellbeing (Holman, 2005), satisfaction (Houlihan, 2004) and anxiety (HSE, 2003). The techniques used in the training programme drew upon a number of applied psychological skills for developing emotional and attentional control (Maddi, 1987). The study provides further evidence for the inclusion of such psychological skills training in an attempt to improve the psychological capital of individuals (Luthans *et al*, 2008). In an industry that is known for its surveillance and sacrificial HR policies of high staff turnover and burn-out (Wallace, 2000), the implementation of similar programmes could be significantly beneficial in improving employee experiences within a call centre environment.

One key question is, 'Does this translate into improved performance — for the organization and the individual?' Whilst objective and comparatively clean performance data is difficult to obtain, data obtained from gem's employee feedback survey also showed that those who had attended the training programme had a higher belief in their ability to carry out their work effectively (which would support the evidence on the control scores). They also rated themselves higher in regard to job satisfaction. Absenteeism was also shown to have reduced.

Moreover, the study showed that there remained more to be done to improve the performance of managers. The results can also be used to show the importance of senior manager buy-in regarding training programmes and the role of timely feedback from course evaluations to key decision makers. The challenge and commitment scores for both the experiment and control group show an increase at time 2. Whilst it was hypothesized that the experiment group would show an increase, the control group score raises an interesting issue.

A possible explanation can be drawn from factors that occurred during the course of the programme. Once the initial scores were collected for both groups (time 1), the results were fed back to the board of the organization. It transpired that the company was in the middle of some restructuring and there was a certain amount of frustration from the top regarding the attitude of the managers to the change and their commitment to the organization.

The results from the MTQ48 showed that there was a reasonable level of commitment to organizational goals (n = 51, commitment 5.69) but managers in both groups were feeling overwhelmed with their capacity to cope with the challenge of the change (n = 51, challenge 4.88). As a result of this the board undertook a series of engagement meetings with all managers who were taking part in the study to fully explain the change, highlight areas of concern and allow for a fuller exchange of information. At the end of the three-month period (time 2), the challenge scores has moved upward (n = 51, challenge 6.10), which can be explained in part by the board intervention.

Whilst not a primary focus of the study, the findings show the importance of stakeholder management and management buy-in (CIPD, 2007; Sloman, 2007) for organizational training programmes. The results also show the effect that the training programme had between the two groups (p = .001) in relation to developing the aspect of being able to deal with challenge. The study offers some insight for how organizations can navigate change effectively using the three processes that were present during the course of the experiment.

First, a baseline assessment should be taken of key staff's abilities to deal with the change (in this study the MTQ48). Secondly, the information generated should be used by senior management to inform and shape their decisions and communications. Thirdly, the psychological capital of staff should be developed through the provision of structured interventions to enable them to deal more effectively with the change (Luthans, 2008). In this case this was achieved through the implementation of the mental toughness development programme.

Mental toughness in sport

17

DR KEITH EARLE

The term 'mental toughness' has become synonymous with sporting success, from the sinking of a putt to win the Ryder Cup, to victory on the most treacherous mountain stage in the Tour de France.

In the sporting arena the phrase was first coined by James Loehr in his seminal work, *Achieving Athletic Excellence: Mental toughness training for sport* (1982). Loehr's approach highlights the important nature of the psychological aspects of sports performance. He outlines the link between mental toughness and what he calls 'a very specific constellation of feelings referred to as the Ideal Performance State'. These feelings/emotions and the control of them are linked inextricably to the concept of mental toughness (MT) and in turn to sporting excellence.

Since Loehr's work, the concept of MT has become a frequently used term throughout the sporting world (coaches, players, pundits and academics) and the generation and enhancement of MT has seemingly been the elixir of peak performance. Barely a day passes without some reference to mental toughness or mental strength in the sports pages of most newspapers around the world.

However, for MT to become a useful concept that can be utilized by both academics and professional sports it has to be clearly defined and operationalized. Without this, any attempts to enhance MT would lack scientific rigour and possibly lead to inefficient use of the psychologist–client consultation time. The development of a model of MT, and the MTQ, has produced a framework to guide sports psychologists through the sometimes choppy waters of applied sports psychology work.

Entering any professional sporting organization irrespective of the sport can be extremely difficult and surrounded with problems throughout all levels. In his book, *Psychology in Football,* Mark Nesti (2010) proposed that the 'sport psychologist must get ready to be insulted, misunderstood, ignored, denigrated, seen as a mole, a threat, as unreal, not sufficiently performance focused, and peripheral and lightweight'. This rather negative perception of sports psychology needs to be addressed from the outset of any encounter with an interested organization. Having a strong theoretically based concept with a clearly defined relevance to performance outcomes is a good starting point. Certainly the use of MT as a conceptual framework and the use of the MTQ48 as an informational base can be seen to be both theoretically and practically valid and valuable.

I work as part of a team of sports psychologists based at the University of Hull. We have a varied client base, working with athletes from a wide range of individual and team sports. We use the mental toughness structure and assessment in most of our applied sports psychology work. It allows us to quickly identify the issues and provides us with a vocabulary that we, and the athlete, can share. This common ground allows us to move the process forward quickly. This is vital when dealing with elite athletes as often they are faced with imminent key events. Recently we have introduced toughness assessments and development to the following athlete groups: rowers, figure skaters, rugby league and rugby union players, soccer players, elite swimmers, speedway riders, dressage riders, gymnasts, track athletes, field athletes and golfers.

We are often asked how the use of the mental toughness approach differs between team sports and individual sports, or between contact and non-contact sports. The simply answer is that it doesn't in its fundamentals, which can be summarized as:

- *Diagnostics* – what are the issues? These can encompass individual, team, club and organizational factors.
- *Discussion* – confirming and extending the diagnostic stage. Even when the athlete disagrees about the assessment, the act of disagreement facilitates useful dialogue.
- *Tailored interventions* – targeting the resource to meet individual needs.
- *Reviewing and reassessing* – the measure and related interventional techniques provide an excellent framework with which to evaluate success.

All stages are critical, but it is clear that the latter two can sometimes be underplayed. Interventions must be provided on the basis of need and not on what tools and techniques are available. The MT audit is a vital cog, but there are many other aspects of the sports psychology machine. It is wise to bear in mind the old adage, 'If it ain't broke don't fix it.' It is also important that evaluation is carried out. This should never be simply based on sporting results, but should include such things as skills audits, perceptions and wellbeing.

In our work we have not identified a pattern where the MT profiles differ between sports. Elite athletes of all varieties need the 4 Cs, from dressage to rugby league. However, it is clear that different need profiles can exist within a sport. For example, one poorly performing skater could have issues with confidence, whereas another, showing similar performance decrements, could be struggling with commitment.

The MTQ48 produces a number of reports, ranging from an overview through to development suggestions. For example, the new sport-specific reports will, amongst other outputs, produce a list of questions for the sports mentor to probe a problem area. So if a shot putter reported low challenge scores, possible questions would include:

- What is your ideal training environment?
- Describe your last two competitive performances.
- Describe an aspect of your training that you find particularly stretching. What was so challenging about it?

AN APPLIED CASE STUDY A season with Hull Kingston Rovers

A recent example of where the mental toughness framework was used is work with Hull Kingston Rovers. Hull Kingston Rovers (Hull KR) play in the top tier of professional rugby league in the UK (Super League). The following account describes the process of embedding a mental toughness training programme into Hull KR and details some of the applied consultancy work that was undertaken at the club.

In November 2009 a meeting was held that included the HKR chairman Neil Hudgell, coach Justin Morgan, psychologist Dr Peter Clough and Dr Keith Earle. The meeting discussed various items relating to both organizational and player issues within the club. A brief overview of what psychology could offer to the club was undertaken. It was ultimately agreed that Hull KR could benefit from some psychological support.

Of greatest interest to the coach was the concept of mental toughness and how this could be integrated into the training regime. As a former Australian rugby league player, Justin had previously experienced the use of psychologists within the game and was well aware of the potential benefits of incorporating a more psychological approach to the team/individual development. Therefore it was agreed that a multifaceted approach would be undertaken at the club that would incorporate assessment of the players and team development and, where appropriate, would use individual player sessions.

In December 2009 (at the start of pre-season), the players were given a brief overview of sports psychology and the way it was going to be introduced into the club. There was an opportunity at this point for the players to ask questions and make their views known about the introduction of psychologists into the club environment.

Before the MT framework was introduced it was decided that the players should express their views on the concept and what they think MT is and the importance of the concept in terms of its relationship to both team and individual performance.

Players' definitions of mental toughness

'Person's ability to counter any negativity in the mind and keep focused, positive and persist with the activity.'

'Is the ability to perform at the highest level, pushing yourself past its regular threshold despite the internal demons and exterior factors.'

'Pushing your body through the pain barrier. Your mind will tell you to stop; if you are mentally tough you will ignore it and push yourself to levels not yet achieved personally.'

'Perform under adversity and effort under fatigue.'

'How much until you mentally break.'

'Putting your mind to things and getting through the harder things by thinking about it.'

'Blocking things out and playing through the pain barrier. Mental toughness is being able to play through the pain barrier and still perform to your best and overcoming things.'

'The ability to push your body through pain or fatigue. To be resilient to negative people and things that happen around you.'

'Keeping your focus in a difficult situation.'

'Pushing yourself beyond the pain barrier. Not giving up when it gets tough.'

'Overcoming obstacles that are not in your usual routine.'

'Not moaning about things all the time.'

'Maintaining a good attitude, not cracking under pressure.'

'Testing the mind and body and being strong in showing your strength not weakness.'

'Being able to deal with ups and downs in your career and at the same time maintain a high performance every training session in the week to head into a game at the weekend, and then starting to go again Monday morning.'

'Not giving up when times get tough, eg tired, things not going well, mistakes.'

'Pushing through the barrier.'

'Is being able to work mind over body. So whatever challenge faces you, you never give up.'

'No matter what obstacles are put in front of you they won't have an effect on the outcome.'

'The ability to remain relaxed and focused under pressure.'

'Is not giving up when things get difficult and the easy option is to quit.'

'Being able to overcome hard times during training, playing and in your everyday lifestyle.'

'Is like a shield around my mind – in a rugby match people are constantly trying to break the shield, getting me to quit. The thicker the shield the tougher I am.'

'Finding the reason and will to do something your mind and body tell you not to, all for a greater cause.'

'When things get tough, eg fatigue, soreness etc, you block it out and carry on.'

'The ability to continue to carry out the task in the face of adversity and under physical and mental strain.'

'Being able to make hard decisions with no fuss.'

'Mental toughness is being able to contribute significantly to the team when under fatigue.'

'Not giving up when things get hard, never giving up on the task.'

'Is the ability to keep on fighting and keep trying in the worst possible conditions to yourself.'

'Being able to turn on absolute focus when under pressure.'

Irrespective of the actual definitions, they do highlight that the concept of mental toughness is an extremely ingrained psychological construct for the players and that it relates positively to enhanced performance when under extreme physical and/or psychological pressure. Discussions with the players further cemented the notion that mental toughness was an intuitively comfortable model that they would be happy to explore through various assessment and intervention techniques.

Shortly following this initial meeting all first-team squad players completed the MTQ48. From the resultant analysis it was found that nine players scored high (sten 8–10) in mental toughness, 17 players scored in the medium range (sten 4–7), and one player scored in the low range (sten 1–3). This spread of scores is typical of professional sports, as you would expect the enduring process of rising through the senior ranks is usually only successfully completed by athletes who were already mental tough or by athletes who have quickly adapted themselves to the professional environment and performed sufficiently well to pursue a professional career in their chosen sport.

A group session was held with the players to discuss the results and explain exactly what the scores mean (both total MT score and the four subscale scores were detailed to the players). This process included defining MT and its components and describing in detail the key aspects of each of these areas (examples of which are given below):

- *Challenge* – seeing challenges as opportunities rather than threats.

- *Control* – recognizing that setbacks are normal occurrences in a sporting environment.

- *Commitment* – developing a clear goal setting strategy.

- *Confidence* – consciously seeking to build up your feelings of self-worth.

Each player was given their own personalized profile with suggested recommendations for the enhancement of each of the core elements of mental toughness. These profile reports would be used as the framework for the individualized sessions for the players. These individualized sessions were not compulsory and were, in all cases, initiated by the players.

Although the information from the MTQ48 reports was used as a starting point during the individualized sessions, the sessions were not merely restricted to the development of MT. Everyone was encouraged to hold these sessions in an environment where all issues impacting on performance could be freely discussed in an open and confidential manner (strictly adhering to BPS code of conduct guidelines). Although individual sessions cannot be reported in this chapter, it was generally thought (by the players and coaching staff) that they were useful in formulating future action planning in areas such as goal setting and anxiety control.

To further illustrate the importance of mental toughness the players undertook a unique biofeedback challenge that incorporated using the 'Mindball Trainer'. This piece of kit measures, via detecting alpha and beta brainwaves, the ability of individuals to both concentrate and remain relaxed – key features in sport at whatever ability and level. Each player completed the task, which involved wearing a headband with electrodes attached. The electrodes are connected to a biosensor system that measures the electrical activity in the brain (EEG). This was converted into a signal that enabled a small ball to move on a magnetic table. The movement was a function of the extent to which the individual concentrated and remained relaxed.

The goal of the task is to be as relaxed and focused as possible to enable the ball to be moved away from the player to the intended target in the shortest time possible. Players can monitor their levels of relaxation and focus by a connected screen (detailing levels of both relaxation and focus) or by viewing the movement of the ball itself.

Preliminary analysis of the data showed a positive relationship between overall MTQ48 scores and 'Mindball Trainer' times. This relationship was in fact even more strongly shown in the subscale control (incorporating emotional control), which showed a strong statistically significant relationship between the variables of MTQ48 and time.

As well as providing interesting results, this practical demonstration also provided an exciting and interesting method of introducing sports psychology into a team environment. Breaking down the barriers between psychologist and athlete (specifically in male-dominated team environments) is a key factor in the successful implementation of any sports psychology intervention programme.

This initial practical session laid the foundations for the MT training programme. This took place over the whole of the season. The following describes in detail three team activities designed to enhance and increase the awareness of the various components of MT.

1. The Line of Positivity – confidence building

The aim of this exercise is twofold: first, to create an awareness of differing levels of confidence in the squad, and secondly, to provide a sound basis for developing a confidence enhancement strategy.

This exercise involved the team members forming a line, in order of their perception of their own positivity/confidence – this process was most enlightening as debate reached fairly heated levels as a number of scores were considered to be over-inflated. After much discussion consensus was achieved over final positioning for all participants in the exercise.

At this point the players were asked to write down three positive self-affirmation (PSA) statements designed to enhance differing elements of their psychological make-up. These statements were then used as self-affirmation reminders throughout the year. The players were then asked to create self-affirmation statements for any members of the squad that they chose. These statements were collated by the psychologists and then individually delivered to each player where appropriate. This process uses the well-researched sources of confidence building ie, social support and positive self-talk.

2. Performance Profiling – commitment enhancement

This is a technique that uses a structured goal-setting approach to identify important training needs and maximize the motivation levels of the athletes to adhere to the resultant training programmes. The process starts with the squad members dividing themselves into small groups (ideally with a mixture of youth and experience) of similar positional players (eg forwards, backs). Each player independently produces a list of the qualities (both technical and psychological) that typifies a player in his particular position.

The list for a scrum half may include such attributes as speed, good decision making, communication, passing technique, determination and confidence, amongst others. Once this is completed the list of attributes is discussed with the other members of the group to ensure that all the key qualities for that specific position are covered appropriately.

As soon as this is done for the whole group, each player independently rates on a scale of 1 to 10 (1 being not important, 10 being vitally important) each of these attributes in order to create the 'perfect player'. For example, a scrum half may feel that communication is the most important facet of his play and would therefore rate this as a 10. However, he may feel that confidence is not so important and only rate this as an 8. Once all the attributes had been given a rating based on their importance, the player then rates himself in relation to the list of attributes. This self-rating is discussed within the original small groups and a final self-rating is then decided.

As with all good goal-setting techniques the importance of agreed targets cannot be over-emphasized – the ownership of these goals is key to the effectiveness of the future training programme. The final performance profile clearly provides a representation of the player's strengths and potential areas of improvement. This can be discussed with the coach/trainer and integrated into the overall training programme.

3. The Egg-Drop – challenge and confidence

This is an exercise designed to highlight a number of facets within team working. The task itself involves designing a method that would enable a raw egg in its shell to be dropped from a height of 10 metres without breaking.

The squad was split into teams of around six players, and each team given a number of articles that could be used in their design. The materials included 10 sheets of newspaper, a strip of sticky tape, four short/two long pieces of string, an A4 leaflet, a parcel tag, a bulldog clip, two paperclips and a rubber band. The teams were given 30 minutes to build their design and then the eggs would be dropped, in this case from the upper tier of the Roger Millward Stand. Throughout the exercise the teams would be closely monitored to enable a discussion of learning points from the task, although at the time the teams' only task was to protect their egg from gravity and concrete!

Once the 30-minute design phase was completed and the various attempts at dropping the eggs were undertaken (some more successful than others) the whole squad returned to discuss the process. In this instance, the following learning outcomes emerged:

- Generally insufficient planning was devoted to the exercise – some teams had finalized their design within 10 minutes. The whole 30 minutes could have been broken up in to sections to ensure the best use of time (5 minutes individual thinking time, 5 minute group discussion, 15 minutes build time, 5 minutes review).

- The importance of including everyone in the decision-making process. It was noted that in some groups certain individuals looked uninterested and did not become engaged with the task. There were various reasons for this including inappropriate seating arrangements that hindered good working relationships, and lack of leadership that resulted in only limited ideas and views being expressed (quiet thoughtful people also generate ideas – and often the best ideas!).

- Focus on the task in hand. There were numerous occasions where players were spending a great amount of time on irrelevant issues and materials (eg how to use paperclips and what to write on the parcel tag!). These issues further highlight the importance of good leadership and having appropriate interpersonal confidence to be able to direct efforts in a more efficient and productive manner.

- Finally, the design of an 'egg safety device' is all but irrelevant (however, encasing the egg in a cone-shaped crumple zone with a parachute attached seemed to be the most effective design) – it is all about the process: good leadership incorporating ideas gathering and a review process are key in this particular task.

The season-long MT training programme delivered a comprehensive package of psychological skills to the players that could be targeted to enhance any aspect of their overall mental toughness. The toolkit essentially consisted of those tools and techniques described elsewhere in this book. This toolkit for sporting performance created an awareness for the players of how, when faced with difficult circumstances (eg lack of confidence, pre-game anxiety), they can effectively deal with them.

The head coach of Hull Kingston Rovers, Justin Morgan, commented:

> I believe we are the first rugby league club in the UK to benefit from such a comprehensive package of psychological support. The concept of mental toughness and its relevance to our game cannot be underestimated – any attempt to enhance this aspect of our game can only be advantageous to the club.

The 2010 season initially saw mixed results with Morgan's team sitting outside the top eight and out of the playoffs half way through the season. In the second part of the season, the ship at Hull Kingston Rovers was steadied somewhat and it achieved a second consecutive playoff place, ending the regular rounds in seventh place.

This led to a playoff game away at the KC Stadium to deadly rivals Hull FC, which Rovers won comfortably 21–4 to record their first ever Super League playoff win. The 2010 season ended at Wigan Warriors a week later when Hull KR where defeated 42–18 by the eventual winners of the Super League Grand Final.

Health and social factors relating to mental toughness

18

Perhaps one of the most satisfactory achievements in our work with mental toughness has been to broaden its applications from a narrow focus on sports to an understanding that it is a fundamental aspect of human personality and that it has application everywhere.

After all, stress, pressure, challenge and targets are not unique to the world of sport. They impact on all of us at some time. Towards the end of the first decade of the 21st century everyone saw a major global upheaval as the social and economic certainties of the past 15 years of so-called stability suddenly became very uncertain. Whether you were working, studying, at play, dealing with a personal or social issue, the ground rules changed and life became more challenging for everyone.

In the two years running up to the publication of this book we have witnessed an exponential interest in mental toughness as a concept that has a role to play in the health and wellbeing of individuals and society. This has spawned a huge number of research projects and of pilot applications in these areas. It is too early to report outcomes and conclusions from most of these but it is possible to offer a chapter that describes where we are in applying mental toughness in these areas. We are confident, on the basis of the work done in other sectors and the emerging evidence from work in these sectors, that mental toughness is a significant and valuable concept in most if not all of those applications too.

The kinds of issues being examined in terms of a link with mental toughness include, in health:

- recovery rates from trauma and operations;
- general health and fitness;
- treatment of conditions such as eating disorders and ADHD;
- the incidence of mental health problems;

- supporting people recovering from certain forms of mental illness;
- stop-smoking activity;

and in society:

- examining worklessness – where significant work has already been carried out with encouraging results;
- building aspirations in areas of socio-economic deprivation;
- examining anti-social behaviour including offending patterns;
- minimizing reoffending rates for young offenders and adults in custodial sentences;
- developing programmes for carers, etc.

The work is truly global too. For instance, in the UAE we are examining what is locally called the 'Arabization' agenda, which is to do with reducing reliance on ex-pat resources and supporting the development of the local population in the uptake of work and occupations that aren't traditionally in their province.

So what forms the basis of our confidence in these areas?

Mental toughness and health

There has been extensive work on mental toughness and health. Health can be broken down into physical and mental health.

Mental toughness and physical health

It is clear that from our studies that mental toughness and physical fitness positively co-vary. Mentally tough people tend to do more exercise. As Dienstbier showed us, we already know that physiological toughening can lead to psychological toughening. The causal link is unclear at the moment. Mental toughness may drive the exercise or the exercise may drive the mental toughness.

Exercise is for many people physically uncomfortable. In fact this discomfort is the second most cited reason why people don't exercise – the first reason is the fairly empty statement of 'not having the time'. Surely this is a phrase that an individual with a high level of commitment would not use?

Early in the development of the MTQ48 we carried out a study that aimed to assess the influence that mental toughness has on an individual's ability to tolerate physical discomfort. The MTQ48 model predicts that an individual's ability to endure physical discomfort will significantly and positively correlate with mental toughness and its subcomponents.

Forty-one males with a mean age of 21 years took part in this study. All were assessed for their suitability for undertaking the physical endurance task. The task constituted a standardized method of assessing physical endurance.

Participants were instructed to lift a dumb-bell using their dominant arm in an over-hand grip from its resting position on a desk to a holding position, and maintain this position for as long as possible. The dumb-bell was standardized to weigh approximately 1.5 per cent of the participant's own body weight. This low resistance was chosen to produce a gradual increase in physical sensations during the task. The holding position required participants to hold the weight suspended with a straight arm directly in front of their body and over a desk, with a 90° angle between arm and torso. Performance was timed until participants were unable to maintain the holding position.

The findings showed that there was a significant correlation between total mental toughness and duration (r = 0.34). Individuals who scored higher on total mental toughness, control and confidence were significantly more likely to tolerate the physical endurance task for longer than those individuals who scored lower on these factors.

Perceptions of discomfort

Antarctica and the Arctic are some of the most demanding environments within which humans perform. An individual's ability to cope with these demanding environments is of significant importance as not only is performance affected, but both an individual's and team members' lives will be at risk. One study we carried out followed a team of 12 scientists training for a long-haul expedition within the Arctic Circle to collect environmental and medical data. This training took place within the Arctic Circle over 10 days, and consisted of long-distance trekking, hauling equipment and camping. Team members also ran through scientific protocols and procedures.

As part of the study team members completed the MTQ48 prior to starting this training programme. At the end of each day, participants rated their perceptions of the emotional, mental and physical demands during that day. This was achieved through a simple rating 7-point scale; see Table 18.1.

TABLE 18.1 Correlations between mental toughness demands

	Demands		
	Emotional	Mental	Physical
Mental toughness	.008	−.059	−.391*
Emotional demands		.772*	.383*
Mental demands			326*

*Significant correlations.

Total mental toughness was significantly correlated with ratings of physical, but not emotional or mental demands experienced during that day. Specifically, individuals with high levels of mental toughness rated the physical demands they experienced during the day as significantly less than those individuals lower in mental toughness.

Recovery from injury

An athlete's ability to cope with physical injuries and successfully adhere to rehabilitative regimes is of great interest to those looking to improve rehabilitation success and ensure continued participation. The present study followed 70 athletes throughout a 10-week rehabilitative regime for sports injuries (Levy *et al*, 2006).

In the initial stages of rehabilitation, participants completed the Sport Injury Rehabilitation Belief Survey (SIRBS), the MTQ48 and the Sport Inventory for Pain 15 item (SIP-15). Physiotherapists measured adherence via attendance and completion of clinic rehabilitation activity using the Sport Injury Rehabilitation Adherence Survey (SIRAS). Participants were instructed to record their adherence to home-based rehabilitation activities.

A number of external measures were used:

- Adherence. Attendance to scheduled rehabilitation appointments was calculated by dividing the number of rehabilitation sessions attended by the number of rehabilitation sessions scheduled.
- Sport Injury Rehabilitation Beliefs. The SIRBS is a 19-item questionnaire assessing severity, susceptibility (threat appraisals), treatment efficacy and self-efficacy (coping appraisals).
- Pain. To assess pain the SIP-15 was used. This measures three factors concerning how athletes respond psychologically when in pain.

The results are shown in Table 18.2.

In summary, these findings suggest that the more mentally tough an individual is, the less susceptible he or she believes he or she will be to further injury. This finding was replicated with regard to pain in that more mentally tough individuals were better able to cope with pain during rehabilitation by using more direct coping methods.

In contrast, low mental toughness individuals were found to be more likely to dwell upon the pain during rehabilitation and potentially despair when the pain is unbearable. In respect of rehabilitation adherence, greater attendance at rehabilitation sessions was displayed by those who had higher levels of mental toughness and individuals higher in mental toughness also demonstrated higher levels of adherence to procedures whilst within the clinical environment. Importantly, mental toughness was associated with greater adherence to home-based exercises and procedures as well.

The finding that individuals who are low in mental toughness were less able to cope with their injuries and were also less likely to participate in

TABLE 18.2 Correlations table for MTQ48 and rehabilitation measures

Measure	Mental Toughness	M	SD
Susceptibility	−0.31*	23.01	3.83
Treatment efficacy	0.20	71.21	2.46
Rehabilitation value	0.22	5.10	1.10
Severity	−0.30	20.10	2.62
Pain – direct coping	0.43**	17.53	3.55
Pain – catastrophizing	−0.32**	15.46	1.79
Pain – somatic awareness	0.07	10.30	2.16
Clinic adherence	−0.30*	273.10	74.96
Home adherence	−0.28*	89.46	33.95
Attendance	0.25*	91.77	9.04

*$p < 0.05$
**$p < 0.01$

rehabilitation has important implications for both sporting and occupational settings. Of particular importance are the lower perceptions of future injury risks.

For athletes and sports rehabilitators, the knowledge that high levels of mental toughness are associated with successful participation in rehabilitation regimes is important for promoting future programme success. By identifying low mental toughness individuals, appropriate efforts can be made to support them to ensure successful rehabilitation outcomes. This finding also adds weight to the proposition that highly mentally tough individuals are better able to deal with stresses and setbacks. This is clearly a central issue for the mental toughness construct.

In occupational settings, it would be important to note that low mental toughness individuals could potentially be vulnerable to poor health outcomes following illnesses, which represents a double detriment for such individuals: low mental toughness individuals are more likely to report worse health outcomes; these individuals seem less likely to be able to deal with illnesses and successfully adhere to advice.

A summary of the mental toughness and exercise findings

It is clear from the findings reported here, and many others carried out by ourselves and others, that mentally tough individuals are more likely to exercise. They are better equipped to deal with the physical demands.

The study relating to injuries is potentially very important. Although it used a sample of elite exercisers there is little reason to suppose that its findings are not applicable to non-elite athletes and health issues in general. Current research using the MTQ48 is attempting to move the health agenda forward. Dr Lee Crust at the University of Lincoln has preliminary data relating mental toughness with the flow experience. 'Flow', a term developed by Csikszentmihalyi, is the feeling of getting lost in an event. Everything goes right and time just flies by. You lose yourself in the moment. This type of experience is very pleasurable and motivating. Dr Crust's preliminary work shows that tougher individuals are more able to experience flow, offering another explanation as to the draw of exercise for them.

A recurring theme in this book is the need to treat individuals as individuals. Attempts to get the population to exercise or be healthier or to give up smoking have tended to fail or at best produce disappointing results. It is estimated that around 14 per cent of the population exercise on a regular basis. It is reasonably clear that the exercise experience is different for sensitive and tough participants. If we wish to attract more people into a healthier lifestyle we have to tailor the incentives to their experience of the activity.

Mental health

Mental health problems are widespread. Around 1 in 10 individuals will suffer from a significant mental health issue in their lifetime. It is important to be clear here. The MTQ48 is designed to be used in a normal population: it cannot be used with people with severe clinical problems. Similarly, the interventions outlined later in the book are designed for the 'average Joe or Josephine'.

It would be patronizing to suggest that the techniques could be effective with someone who has clinical issues. It is important that if you have significant and recurring depressions or anxiety you seek out the appropriate medical help. This book, the model and the measure may help you identify that you have a problem – but that is as far as we can take it.

In Chapter 4, we discussed the original construct validation work of the MTQ48. Part of this work showed that the measure was positively related to self-esteem, optimism, self-efficacy and life satisfaction, and negatively related to trait anxiety. Each of these variables has been consistently related to mental wellbeing. It is perhaps therefore not surprising that mental toughness scores also link directly to mental health.

Many of the studies we have carried out over the last 10 years have used the General Health Questionnaire (GHQ) as a measure of mental health.

TABLE 18.3 Correlations between the MTQ48 and the GHQ

	GHQ
Overall MT	−0.70
Commitment	−0.52
Control	−0.54
Challenge	−0.71
Confidence	−0.57

The GHQ is a standardized screening instrument to assess the probability of minor psychiatric disorders, and is a common measure used to give insight into an individual's present state of mind. For example, we carried out a small-scale study looking at mental health issues within the prison service (prison officers) and HE institutions (lecturers). A summary of the results is shown in Table 18.3. Correlations indicate that higher levels of mental toughness as measured using the MTQ48 were associated with better mental health.

Similarly, in a sample of 83 teachers there was a clear and consistent pattern relating to the beneficial effects of mental toughness. Tougher teachers were less likely to report being anxious (state anxiety). The high-toughness teachers utilized different coping strategies. They were more likely to use active coping techniques, planning and restraint.

Teaching is widely acknowledged as a stressful occupation. Clark (1980) tried to identify why this is the case, identifying pupil behaviour, time demands, work conditions and staff relationships as key stressors. Borg and Riding (1993) suggested that certain types of teachers were particularly vulnerable. They reported cognitive style and experience as important factors. An opportunity arose to compare teachers in a school specializing in children with emotional and behavioural difficulties and a mainstream school. The results showed that the special school teachers were significantly tougher, as we had hypothesized.

When considering mental health issues in the workplace it is important to recognize the matching of people with the job. Ideally, the job should be fitted to the person. In reality this is not always achievable and rarely happens – it becomes a matter of fitting the person to the job. Some people are better suited to working in stressful environments. It should be noted here that a stressful environment is a subjective term. What you find stressful I might not, and vice versa.

Mental toughness and sleep

There are clear links between mental toughness and physical and mental health. An interesting study from colleagues in Switzerland (Serge Brand, Nadeem Kalak, Markus Gerber, Sakari Lemola and Edith Holsboer-Trachsler) examined the sleep patterns of adolescents. There is clear evidence to show that favourable sleep patterns are related to favourable psychological functioning such as curiosity, lack of depressive symptoms, and to increased physical activity. Ninety-eight adolescents (mean age 18.36 years; 66 females) took part in the study. They completed a series of questionnaires related to mental toughness, optimism, depressive symptoms, perception of pain, physical activity and sleep. Increased sleep complaints were related to low control, low confidence in one's abilities and low challenge, amongst other things.

In adolescents, favourable sleep and favourable mental toughness seem to be related. The authors concluded: 'Whereas the underlying mechanisms remain unclear, it seems conceivable that improving both sleep and mental toughness should confer to increased wellbeing.'

Social responsibility and mental toughness

At first glance the concepts of social responsibility and mental toughness do not seem to go hand in hand. In the opening chapter, the caring side of mental toughness was touched upon. It is true that mentally tough individuals are often driven and dynamic, and the mental toughness stereotype is often seen as akin to the lead character in 'Wall Street'. There is also clear evidence that they are by nature active copers. They are less likely to express, or perhaps even feel, emotion, preferring doing something concrete to sharing their emotions. Neither approach is wrong or right. It's just different. However, sometimes the mentally tough are seen as disinterested onlookers. This is not an accurate stereotype and misrepresents what mental toughness is. You can be a caring mentally tough person, or an uncaring mentally sensitive one. It's not a black or white, all or nothing phenomena.

We are building up our research in this area and the work is at a relatively early stage, compared to other aspects reported in this book. In the remaining part of this chapter we would like to introduce a small number of studies and also briefly describe where this type of work is leading. It covers a wide array of areas including voluntary work, Alzheimer's carers, bullying and anti-social behaviour.

Voluntary work

A study carried out by Kate Halstead and Peter Clough investigated the motivation of student volunteers. It is obvious that people have greatly differing reasons for giving up their time to help others. In this study 71 volunteers completed two questionnaires: the MTQ48 and the Volunteers Functions Inventory. The latter questionnaire looks at six main functions of volunteering: values, understanding, social, career, enhancement and protective functions.

The findings were fascinating. It was the case that most of the students who volunteered to give up their free time to help others were more mentally sensitive. Twenty-five of the sample had low mental toughness scores, 39 had average scores and seven achieved high mental toughness scores. It was also clear that there were differences in why they volunteered. The more sensitive individuals were more likely to do so for social reasons and also to protect their ego. This latter motivational category is all about feelings of guilt and self-worth. At this point it appears that the more mentally tough are unlikely to give up their time to help others. However, the ones who did volunteer were more likely to work longer hours, suggesting that when they do something, 'they really do something'.

Where does this leave us? It is clear that more sensitive individuals are more likely to help out others in society. It is interesting to speculate why this is the case. It's unlikely that the mentally tougher are simply bad people or less caring about others. The data from this study perhaps give a clue towards a better understanding of what is happening here. The tougher individuals are less likely to feel guilty and feel bad about themselves. Much of the promotional and advertising activity used by charities and trusts plays the 'guilt card' fairly robustly. This may be leaving a large percentage of the target audience unmoved.

The second interesting suggestion to come out of this research is that the tougher individuals, when they do volunteer, do and achieve more. It might be argued that the goal of the charitable work is to aid the person who is in need of support, not to make volunteers feel good about themselves. These conclusions have to remain speculative, but they do raise interesting questions. It is the intention to carry out more research into this complex area.

What of the carers?

We are living in a time when our population is ageing rapidly. This has seen a rise in many health conditions, especially dementia. Currently one in six people over 80 and one in 14 people over 65 have some form of dementia. With the growth of this terrible disease comes the growth in the need for carers.

Many carers are not volunteers. They are simply people who find themselves in this dreadful situation. The mental toughness concept was designed to understand performance in high-pressure environments. There can be few higher-pressure environments than trying to help people in the later stages of dementia. The pressure is unrelenting and there is no foreseeable 'good' end point.

Sarah Sykes carried out an investigation into the impact of mental toughness on the wellbeing of carers. Twenty-two carers were asked to complete four questionnaires: The General Health Questionnaire, Carer Strain Index, the MTQ48 and the Ways of Coping questionnaire. The results were illuminating. The carer's scores indicated that they were experiencing high levels of stress, anxiety and depression. There was a clear negative correlation between the mental results and the MTQ48. It appears that mental toughness gives some levels of protection to the mentally tough individual.

Again there were differences in the coping mechanisms involved. Mentally tough individuals were less likely to adopt avoidance strategies. They faced their problems head-on. This clearly links with the findings of Lee Crust and Adam Nicholls, and also to the cutting-edge brain structure approach that identifies the reality testing centres of the brain as being more active in the mentally tough.

In the introductory chapter we were at great pains to point out that mental toughness is not simply about winning at all costs – winning games or making money. It is more fundamental than that. The findings relating to dementia carers raise the possibility that mental toughness training may help them cope better. Both the authors of this book are reasonably mentally tough. We are drawn to the active coping paradigm and have both experienced first-hand the impact of dementia in people close to us. We would like offer a practical way forward: not just sympathy but practical solutions!

Bullying

The subject of bullying has received an increasing level of attention in recent years, particularly in terms of workplace bullying and in school-based bullying. A number of studies have now used the mental toughness model and the mental toughness questionnaire MTQ48 to examine bullying in the workplace and in secondary education. The results have been consistent and provide a valuable perspective on this complex and troubled issue.

The most important result is that there is a strong correlation between mental toughness and the extent to which an individual perceives he or she is being bullied. It is important to understand that this does not necessarily mean that the individual is being bullied. Some involved with dealing with bullying may argue that this is an irrelevant distinction. It isn't. It helps us to understand how bullying arises for many and how it might be handled.

It must be stressed that this does not mean that bullying doesn't exist. It clearly does. In some (perhaps many) instances the act of bullying is a deliberate attempt by one individual to undermine or demean another for some unjustifiable advantage. However, the results show that for many, the perception of bullying may be just that – it's a perception that they are being bullied. In many cases it is entirely possible that the individual is sensitive to the words or actions of another and may attach a meaning to them which may not be there.

The people we meet in our life, our work and our play will adopt a wide range of behaviours. Some people will respond to some of these behaviours by feeling they are being bullied. Others will accept them as normal part of life. Some will argue, with some validity, that simply because some aren't offended by another's behaviours it means it isn't bullying behaviour. Again we are saying not saying it isn't.

The suggestion here is that a bullying situation should be examined carefully from the perspective of the alleged bully's behaviour and the response of the apparent victim to that behaviour to come to a more measured view about what is going on and, importantly, what can reasonably be done about it.

The standard solution to dealing with bullying is usually to find the bully and deal with that person or persons. To take a more complete and more balanced view, we need to consider how the individual is responding to apparent bullying behaviour. It's this internal state that has often been underplayed – it often does not seem to be considered with enough weight when examining a bullying scenario. This is complicated further by an awareness that the same behaviour in one situation may be seen as potentially bullying where in another situation it is seen as normal and acceptable. We are not attempting to blame the victim. We are just trying to better understand the interaction and suggest that, on some occasions, no 'crime' has been committed. In the sports arena a coach or manager will often shout at a person to stimulate a better performance. Back in the workplace, the same behaviour between the same people may be deemed unacceptable.

There is a hypothesis, which has increasing support, that many bullies are in fact themselves the past recipient of bullying behaviour and may also possess a higher degree of mental sensitivity. The bully may be just as much a victim as the bullied.

One important implication is that mental toughness development activity does appear to help individuals deal more effectively with situations where they perceive themselves as being bullied. This helps to provide a more holistic solution to a difficult and complex issue.

Workplace bullying

A study was carried out by Dr Iain Coyne looking at workplace bullying and the role of mental toughness. This was presented at the British Psychological Society's Annual Conference in 2006. It assessed 93 individuals in the workplace using MTQ48 and the NAQ (Negative Acts Questionnaire). The NAQ is a questionnaire relating to the experience of 22 bullying behaviours.

The study showed that mental toughness has a role to play in bullying and in particular a mediating effect on the relationship and physiological distress. Individuals low in mental toughness reported more incidence of bullying-type behaviours, showed more evidence of psychological distress and tended to use less-effective coping strategies. Mental toughness training seems to improve an individual's ability to cope with a stressor.

Perceptions of bullying in a secondary school

The study covered the entire Year 10 group (age 16 years), some 240 pupils, from a secondary college based in an area of north-west England that experiences a degree of social deprivation. All pupils participated – no self-selection was permitted. Pupils were asked to self-assess in terms of being bullied. Tutors were also asked to rate which students appeared to be bullied and to what extent.

Analysis of mental toughness scores and the tutor's assessment showed that there was a clear and strong relationship between the students' belief they were being bullied in some way and their level of mental toughness. Focus groups showed that the same incident would be viewed differently by pupils depending on their level of mental toughness. A tutor who may shout in class to get attention would be seen as a 'shouty' teacher by the more mentally tough who would see it as an aspect of the teacher's behaviours with no specific implication for themselves. The more mentally sensitive would often see the shouting as directed personally to them even where they acknowledged the teacher shouted at everyone.

The likely explanation is that mentally tough people shrug off other people's behaviour or actions and don't feel bullied or threatened by it. Mentally sensitive people on the other hand appear to respond negatively to any level of provocative or challenging behaviour from other people and will feel intimidated by it.

Anti-social behaviour

A final area we wish to explore is mental toughness and difficult behaviour. This work is still in its infancy but it raises exciting possibilities. We have carried out one small study. Twenty-two participants made up the control group, with a mean age of 29.91. The 'troubled' group consisted of 19 participants with a mean age of 30.42 (range = 15–57, SD = 9.32). The delinquency sample was recruited from a Drug Intervention Programme (DIP) and Youth Offending Team (YOT).

A significant difference was observed between the total mental toughness scores of the troubled and the control group; see Table 18.4. The troubled group had significantly lower mental toughness scores, and significant differences were also observed between the two groups on the mental toughness subscales of challenge, commitment and control (life).

Summary

The application of our model and the measure in the wider realms of society and in public and personal health in general is potentially the most exciting area of application.

For many, carving out a living and making a success out of life for themselves and for their families represent a major challenge and opportunity.

TABLE 18.4 Mental toughness and difficult behaviour – group scores

	Troubled		Control	
	Mean	**SD**	**Mean**	**SD**
Challenge	3.5	0.47	3.9	0.31
Commitment	3.4	0.56	3.8	0.28
Control (emotion)	3.2	0.37	3.3	0.54
Control (life)	3.3	0.49	3.7	0.48
Confidence (abilities)	3.3	0.55	3.5	0.57
Confidence (interpersonal)	3.7	0.47	3.8	0.5

It's patently a source of stress for many. In some parts of the world the challenge dwarfs the challenges faced in the UK. Raising a family in central Africa is a vastly different proposition to raising a family in the Western world. But for both it still remains a challenge. The changing role of society and not being able to look to the government to provide us with services will mean that many will have to fend for themselves in a manner not experienced since World War II.

It is interesting that one area where we have seen a rapid growth of interest is in parenting. As we introduce mental toughness assessment and development into schools and colleges, we are increasingly being asked by parents to explain, first, what we are doing and then to help them to apply this to their offspring. There is a realization that this is a vital life skill that all young people should develop and it's not reasonable to expect that they will develop this solely from the input they receive during the comparatively short time they spend at school.

In health, the state of the economy and the way that working life will shape up will ensure that stress management will remain a major issue in health management. Mental toughness already has a major role to play here. The interest in examining recovery rates from operations and trauma also provides opportunity. It is not too difficult to understand that the more mentally tough you are the more quickly you are up on your feet (provided that in doing so you don't undo what has been done). More likely, those who dwell on their circumstances may be supported back to full health more quickly through application of mental toughness. Health services represent scarce and valuable resources in any society. Anything that optimizes their use and delivers great performance has to be welcomed.

Coaching for mental toughness

19

CHRISTIAN VAN NIEUWERBURGH

This chapter considers the role of coaching to enhance the self-reflection, learning and development arising from the MTQ48. More broadly, it proposes an integrated, person-centred coaching approach that is particularly appropriate for working on the development of mental toughness.

Mental toughness

One of the originators of the term 'mental toughness', Jim Loehr, defines it as 'the ability to consistently perform toward the upper range of your talent and skill regardless of competitive circumstances' (1986). To take this sports-related term into a wider arena, it can be understood as the ability to manage our thinking so that we can continue to perform at optimum levels despite challenging circumstances.

Resilience, hardiness and mental toughness are concepts that continue to attract attention and interest, particularly as many of the world's nations face a period of financial and socio-economic challenge. It has been proposed that mental toughness can 'have a buffering effect between stressful life events and illness' (Clough *et al*, 2008: 209). It is in this context that MTQ48 provides a useful, research-based psychometric tool to measure personal resilience.

Coaching for professional development

Coaching is now widely accessed in a broad range of organizations as an important tool for professional development and career progression (Palmer and Whybrow, 2007; Bresser and Wilson, 2010; Cox *et al*, 2010).

It is already used to support clients on a broad range of topics and issues including, notably:

- feeling 'in control', professionally and personally;
- managing emotional responses to challenging situations;
- coping with significant organizational or personal change;
- finding ways of maintaining commitment to processes or change programmes;
- enhancing self-confidence at work and in social settings.

These areas align well with the four key scales of the MTQ48 discussed in more detail elsewhere in this book: control, challenge, commitment and confidence.

Evidence-based research

Initial research into the relationship between coaching and mental toughness is encouraging. A growing body of evidence-based research is showing a correlation between coaching and the elements that constitute mental toughness: self-efficacy, cognitive hardiness, enhanced goal-striving, higher expectations about outcomes and environmental mastery (Grant, 2009).

Most notably a recent study found that coaching can increase cognitive hardiness (mental toughness) and hopefulness in high school students (Green *et al*, 2007). Coaching has also been shown to enhance goal striving (Spence and Grant, 2007), increase self-efficacy and heighten expectations about outcomes (Evers *et al*, 2006). Evidently coaching has an important role to play in supporting people to develop appropriate levels of mental toughness.

Coaching for mental toughness

If we acknowledge that coaching is primarily about increasing awareness and a sense of personal responsibility (Whitmore, 2002), then the potential role of psychometric measures becomes evident.

Reports generated by questionnaires such at MTQ48 are an ideal basis for coaching conversations. Both the process of completing the questionnaire and considering the ensuing client report will focus attention on levels of mental toughness. By providing an opportunity for careful self-reflection and exploration, coaching can support coachees to increase their own self-awareness.

FIGURE 19.1 Three components of coaching

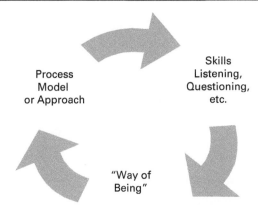

At the same time, the integrated coaching approach and process suggested in this chapter will encourage coachees to thoughtfully consider potential areas for development and take personal responsibility for pursuing these. Before we proceed any further, it may be helpful to outline our definition of coaching.

Three components of coaching

It is helpful to think of coaching as having three distinct but connected components: the skills of coaching, a process or model, and a 'way of being' (see Figure 19.1). Two of the elements can be taught, while the third can only be learnt.

Process: model or approach

At the present moment, there is no convincing evidence to suggest that any one model or coaching approach is more effective than another. It is my view that coaches should instead apply one of a range of approaches or models that best meet the needs of the situation or the client. The integrated model suggested in this chapter is based on the widely used and well-respected GROW model; see Figure 19.2.

Skills of coaching

There is broad agreement about the skills necessary for coaching (Whitmore, 2002; Dembkowski *et al*, 2006; Hawkins and Smith, 2006; Cox *et al*, 2010; Passmore, 2010). The coach needs to demonstrate the following skills:

- listening actively;
- asking good questions;

FIGURE 19.2 The GROW model

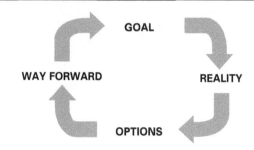

- summarizing accurately;
- giving helpful feedback;
- providing appropriate challenge.

As professionals, many of us already have these skills and it is simply a case of honing them for use in coaching conversations. The market is inundated with publications, online guidance and professional development opportunities for 'active listening', 'giving feedback' and 'managing challenging conversations' amongst others.

'Way of being'

Perhaps the least explicit is the notion of a particular 'way of being' that is helpful for effective coaching relationships. This is the one that might be difficult to 'teach' in the traditional sense. Hopefully this 'way of being' develops with practice.

Using as a starting point the 'necessary and sufficient conditions' for effective one-to-one relationships proposed by Carl Rogers (1957), coaches need to focus on three elements: congruence, unconditional positive regard for the coachee, and empathy:

- Congruence requires coaches to be genuine in their interactions, building the coachee's trust by being open and honest about their feelings and thoughts.

- Unconditional positive regard, perhaps one of the most challenging concepts for many coaches, is the need to be non-judgemental about anything that is raised during the discussion and to remain positive about the coachee as a person throughout.

- Finally, coaches must work hard to maintain appropriate empathy, trying to understand the situation from the coachee's perspective. Obviously, coaching is not therapy, but these conditions form the basis of mutually respectful, trusting and powerful relationships.

If you would find it helpful, take a few moments of self-reflection
to consider how you would rate yourself in these skills.

How would you rate your coaching-related skills? Rate yourself on
a scale of 0–10:

0: No skill at all in this area.
10: Expert at this skill.

Looking down the list, are there any that you would like to develop?
Would others who know you mark you in the same way? Why not ask?

TABLE 19.a

Listening actively
Asking good questions
Holding silences
Summarizing accurately
Giving feedback effectively
Providing appropriate challenge

In practice, this means that coaches must prepare themselves to get into an
appropriate frame of mind before coaching takes place, ensuring that it will
be possible to remain:

- non-judgemental;
- empathetic;
- supportive;
- positive;
- future-focused; and
- respectful.

The directive to non-directive spectrum

There is a broad range of coaching approaches and many writers have found
it helpful to place the various conversational interventions along a 'directive

If you would find it helpful, take a few moments of self-reflection to consider how you would rate yourself with regard to this 'way of being'.

How good are you at demonstrating these attitudes during coaching? Rate yourself on a scale of 0–10:

0: Unable to demonstrate the attitude.
10: Very comfortable demonstrating the attitude.

Looking down the list, are there any that you would like to develop? What would be a good way of practising the attitude?

TABLE 19.b

Being non-judgemental
Showing appropriate empathy
Being generally supportive
Maintaining a positive attitude
Maintaining a focus on the future
Showing respect

to non-directive' spectrum (see, for example, Downey, 2003; Thomson, 2009). Figure 19.3 is one view of where coaching interventions might be arranged along the spectrum, accepting that this is open to further discussion and interpretation. Such a representation can help coaches make conscious decisions about the type of intervention needed for specific situations and with particular coachees.

With a topic such as mental toughness, where there is a clear focus on improving performance and wellbeing through willing participation, it is important to operate in a way that builds motivation, self-esteem and self-confidence. Ultimately, mental toughness is about feeling in control, having a positive outlook, seeing things through and being confident in one's own abilities.

Whilst there are many times when a directive approach (such as mentoring) may be most appropriate, 'instructing' or 'telling' will do little to support the coachee's sense of being in control of the situation. Equally, the provision of advice, suggestions and guidance is more likely to diminish the coachee's confidence in his or her own abilities.

FIGURE 19.3 The directive to non-directive spectrum

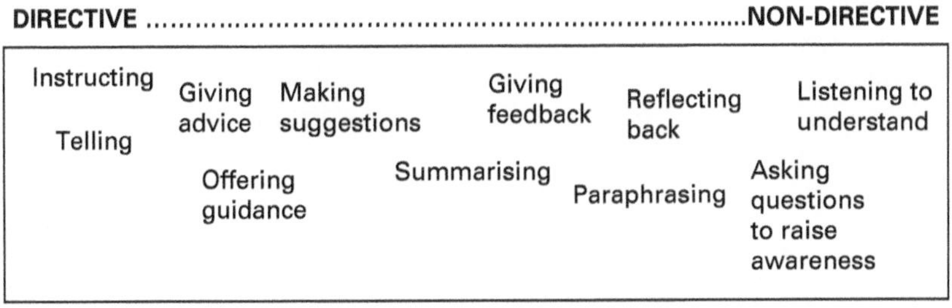

| DIRECTIVE ....NON-DIRECTIVE |

Instructing			Giving		Listening to
	Giving	Making	feedback	Reflecting	understand
Telling	advice	suggestions		back	
	Offering		Summarising		Asking
	guidance			Paraphrasing	questions
					to raise
					awareness

A positive outlook is important for mental toughness and necessary for the coaching process, as any change requires motivation and enthusiasm. With a non-directive coaching approach, the responsibility rests entirely with the coachees, who will find their own answers. They are the expert of their own situation, not the coach. Allowing coachees to discover their own way forward and realize that they have the resources necessary to bring about significant change is therefore an important part of the process. In this context, the type of coaching required is 'the very opposite of telling someone what to do' (Strycharczyk and Brause, 2010: 3).

Coaching for mental toughness: an integrated approach

This section presents a process for supporting the development of mental toughness through coaching. Based on the GROW model (Whitmore, 2002), it contains elements of cognitive-behavioural, solution-focused, person-centred and positive psychology approaches. The process can be used explicitly with the coachee or as a virtual road map for the coach.

Pre-session planning and preparation

It may be helpful for the coach to quickly read through the coachee's MTQ48 report if this is available. However, it is counterproductive to plan the session before meeting with the coachee. Asking coachees to read the report and think about what they would like to bring to the coaching interaction is usually sufficient. As with all coaching, it is important to ensure that the coachee decides the topic of conversation and identifies goals and targets. The coach's responsibility is to manage the process (deciding how much time to spend on the various stages and supporting the coachee to focus on the agreed goal for the session) and create the safe, confidential and supportive environment in which the coachee can explore the topic fully.

TABLE 19.1 Coaching for mental toughness: an integrated approach

Relationship	1	Getting to know one another
	2	Contracting and maintaining the relationship
Goal-setting	3	Agreeing the topic
	4	Agreeing the overall goal
	5	Agree a goal for the session
Awareness	6	Raising awareness of current reality
	7	Explore options
Responsibility	8	Evaluate options
	9	Next steps
Evaluation	10	Review

As discussed above, it is important for coaches to take a few moments before coaching sessions to think about the 'way of being', reminding themselves of the need to be non-directive when coaching for mental toughness.

1. Getting to know one another

The significance of the relationship between the coach and the coachee cannot be underestimated. For this reason, building rapport quickly is essential. Rather than going straight into the session, it is helpful to make the coachee feel at ease by spending a few minutes talking about anything other than mental toughness.

To check before proceeding

> Have I made a 'connection' with this person?
>
> Are we both more comfortable than when we first met?

2. Contracting and maintaining the relationship

This stage builds on the connection made above by talking specifically about the nature of the coaching relationship. Often the 'contract' between the coach and coachee includes the following:

- discussion of confidentiality and its limits;
- confirmation of the length and frequency of sessions;
- permission to take notes.

Once this has been agreed, the coach might outline the non-directive approach, explaining that coaching is one-to-one support for self-directed development. The role of the coach is to ask questions and create the space for coachees to explore their thoughts and feelings. Coachees need to be clear that they are entirely in control of the topic and the goals, while it is the coach's responsibility to manage time effectively and encourage the coachee to leave the session with a clear plan of how to move forward.

At this stage and throughout, coaches should maintain the relationship by being aware of their body language, listening actively (nodding, maintaining eye contact), showing genuine interest in the coachee's topic, focusing on positives and being non-judgemental.

To check before proceeding

> Do we have a shared understanding of the term 'coaching'?
>
> Are we both clear about the boundaries of confidentiality?
>
> Does the coachee appreciate that this is a conversation to support self-directed development regarding his or her MTQ48 results?

3. Agreeing the topic

With agreement about the contract and a shared understanding of the non-directive approach, attention turns to the topic for discussion. This must come from the coachee and will become the focus of the coaching conversation. Some sample questions for this stage:

- What would you like to discuss today?
- What surprised you about the report?
- Which of the 4 Cs would you like to focus on?
- What would be the most helpful area to discuss?

To check before proceeding

> Am I clear about the coachee's topic for this conversation?
>
> Is it possible to articulate the topic in one sentence?

4. Agreeing the overall goal

Once the topic has been selected, the coach can broaden the discussion to include the coachee's overall or long-term goal. In other words, what is the reason that the coachee wants to focus on the topic that has been selected? Once again, the goal is entirely the coachee's responsibility and the coach should accept it without judgement. Remember that ambitious goals and targets can motivate the coachee to make the necessary changes in his or her behaviour or thinking. It is worth exploring the goal further if it does not seem to excite or motivate the coachee.

Thinking point: If it seems to the coach that the overall goal is unrealistic or unachievable, it is worth remembering that, as a coach, our main concern is for the goal to be motivational, not whether we think it is achievable.

Some sample questions for this stage:

- In relation to (the agreed topic), what is your overall goal or ambition?
- In an ideal world, how would you be in relation to (the agreed topic)?
- When will you know that you have achieved what you want in relation to (the agreed topic)?

To check before proceeding

Does the coachee seem to be motivated by this overall goal or ambition?

Have we spent enough time talking about what achieving that goal or ambition would mean for the coachee?

5. Agreeing a goal for the session

While the overall goal, ambition or dream of the coachee should be celebrated and left untouched by the appropriately non-judgemental coach, the goal for the session is a shared responsibility. Both coachee and coach will benefit from agreeing a clearly definable and achievable goal for the session that they both feel comfortable working towards. The coach plays a leading role in this stage, ensuring that the goal for the session is achievable in the time available.

Thinking point: Both the coach and coachee have a shared interest in the success of the coaching session itself. If either party feels that the goal for the session is unachievable, it is important that they share this openly at the beginning of the conversation and set a new goal for the session.

Some sample questions for this stage:

- What would be a good outcome of this session?
- What would make you think this session had been a success?
- When you leave here at the end of this coaching session, what do you want to take away with you?
- If we could achieve one thing during this coaching conversation, what would you like it to be?

To check before proceeding

Have I made a note of the agreed goal for the session?

Are we both convinced that this is something that we can achieve in the time that we have together?

6. Raising awareness of current reality

The first five stages have focused on building a relationship with the coachee, talking about his or her goals and setting a clear target for the session. Stage six focuses on 'current reality' or the situation as seen from the point of view of the coachee. The primary function of this stage is to enhance the coachee's understanding of the situation. This is because we believe that coaching is about raising awareness and a sense of responsibility (Whitmore, 2002). By exploring current reality through discussion, the coachee may discover something new about the situation or be able to see it from a different perspective.

Thinking point: Remember, from a non-directive standpoint, we believe that the coachee is the expert on his or her situation. This means that the coach does not need to know the intricate detail of the 'current reality'. It is more important that the coachee explores the situation to get new insights.

Thinking point: The coachee will be talking about his or her 'current reality' in relation to the MTQ48 report. It may be beneficial to point out to the coachee that the questionnaire is a helpful tool for increasing self-awareness but is not 100 per cent 'accurate'. This may allow the coachee to challenge or question some of the conclusions of the report.

Some sample questions for this stage:

- What is going on at the moment?
- How is your perception of (the agreed topic) impacting on your ability to function at your best?
- What do others (colleagues, family members) think about this?
- What evidence do you have?
- How is your perception of (the agreed topic) helping or hindering you to achieve your goals?
- How is this impacting on our conversation (if at all)?
- What is positive about the current situation?

To check before proceeding

> Do I have enough information to be able to understand the relationship between the chosen topic and the current situation of the coachee?
>
> Has the coachee achieved any new insights into his or her current reality?
>
> Has the coachee had an opportunity to see things from other people's perspectives?

7. Explore options

The purpose of this phase is to allow the coachee to consider as many options as possible. From the coach's point of view, it is important to persevere in this phase, accepting awkward silences as evidence of new thinking. It is sometimes helpful to introduce a drawing, movement or a creative task at this point to unlock new ideas and options. This stage has two purposes. One is to generate a number of options for the coachee to consider. The other, more important purpose is to show the coachee that he or she has a range of options available and that he or she is in a position to make choices and move forward.

Thinking point: Remember, the coachee will have thought about this before, so many of the initial suggestions from the coachee may be ones that he or she has already tried. This is why it is important to keep encouraging the coachee to develop as many options as possible.

Some sample questions for this stage:

- What are your options?
- If you could do anything what would it be?
- What is your heart telling you to do?
- What is your head telling you to do?
- When you look back at this point of your life in, say, five years' time, what option will you be proud that you took?
- What else could you do?
- If you think of someone that you admire, what sort of things would they consider doing in this situation?
- If you had to write down five options, what would you put on paper?

To check before proceeding

Does the coachee have at least three options?
Have I helped the coachee to generate new options?

8. Evaluate options

The point of the previous phase is to generate as many options as possible. In this part of the coaching conversation, the coach should encourage the coachee to narrow down the broad range of options to one or two which, in the coachee's view, are most likely to lead to a better outcome.

Thinking point: The coachee needs to evaluate the various options now available so it is useful to ask him or her to consider what criteria he or she would like to use for the purposes of evaluation.

Some sample questions for this stage:

- Of the options you have identified, which ones would you like to pursue?
- Which option is most likely to be successful?
- If you were to rank the options you have, which would be the top three?

To check before proceeding

> Has the coachee voiced a clear preference for one or more options?
>
> Have I helped the coachee to spend time evaluating the options carefully?

9. Next steps

In this critical stage, the coach encourages the coachee to commit to one or more actions, based on the option or options selected in the evaluation stage. The coach must pay close attention to the coachee's 'intention to act'. This is the extent to which there is commitment to carry out the proposed actions. The ideal outcome is that the coachee has self-selected a course of action based on the options he or she self-generated and that he or she seems motivated and committed.

Thinking point: Whilst the coach should accept, without judgement, the overall goal or ambition of the coachee, it is important that the agreed tasks are realistic and achievable. This is especially the case when coaching for mental toughness as the purpose is to support the coachee to experience success in achieving self-selected tasks and goals.

Some sample questions for this stage:

- So what is going to happen next?
- Having chosen a course of action, what specific actions will you take between now and the next time we meet?
- How likely are you to do what you have just committed to doing?
- What is going to change as a result of this conversation?
- What will be different the next time we meet?

To check before proceeding

> Has the coachee made a note of what he or she has committed to doing?
>
> Have I evaluated the coachee's intention to act?
>
> If the intention to act seems low, have I challenged this appropriately?

10. Review

This final stage provides an ideal opportunity for evaluation and feedback for the coach. Questions can focus on the effectiveness of the coach's interventions and the process itself.

Some sample questions for this stage:

- Have we done what we set out to achieve at the outset?
- How did you feel this coaching session went?
- What would you have liked me to do differently?
- How helpful was this session for you?

The what-ifs: some tips

The self-confidence and mental toughness of the coach are important factors in the coaching relationship. The coach's confidence in his or her ability to support another person can be sensed by coachees and can influence how they perceive the likelihood of success. From this point of view, it is helpful if coaches enter these conversations optimistic about the interaction and free of self-doubt or concern. In reality, that is probably close to impossible for any coach, and especially for coaches who are relatively inexperienced.

The good news is that the more one coaches, the more belief one seems to have in the process and in one's own abilities as a coach. First, it is helpful to remember that most people feel valued when they are listened to in a genuine and authentic way (Kline, 1999). Secondly, the non-directive approach that underpins coaching for mental toughness means that you, as a coach, do not need to 'have the answers' or 'own the problem', leaving you free to be present and support the coachees as they come to their own solutions. Thirdly, the model above can be shared with coachees so that they are aware of the way the conversation might develop with the support of an attentive coach.

Finally, a number of 'what if' situations are listed below with some possible responses that a coach might want to employ.

What if the coachees do not seem to want to engage with the process?

- Take this as data. Their resistance to the process may be a defence mechanism or they may not want to find out for certain something that they have been suspecting.
- Spend more time focusing on the relationship, finding out about the coachees.
- Be explicit about the lack of engagement and discuss the reasons for this in a caring and non-judgemental way.

What if the coachees are not able to articulate a clear goal?

- Again, this is data. Could their lack of ability to articulate a clear goal in the coaching session reflect a similar difficulty in the workplace?
- Spend time finding out what motivates them.
- Find out what they enjoy doing and then return to goal setting. Often, coachees realize that they would like to be doing more of what they enjoy, and this can be a goal.

What if the coachees constantly focuses on all the reasons that they are unable to progress?

- Listen empathetically to the reasons that they are unable to progress. Point out that much of the discussion has been on what is stopping them. Ask what they can do in this situation.
- Taking a solution-focused approach, ask the coachees to imagine what the future would be like if they were able to overcome all the barriers they are facing.
- Highlight any positives that emerge in the conversation. The very fact that the coachees are persevering in the face of so many obstacles is positive. Once they feel a bit more positive about the situation, they may be encouraged to think about taking steps towards a solution.

What if the coachees cannot generate any options at all?

- Use tools to encourage creative thinking. For example, ask the coachees to draw themselves in their situation. The act of drawing it may generate some thoughts. Talking about the finished drawing may also allow for new thinking.
- Ask the coachees what advice they would give to a friend or colleague who was facing the same challenges. Then ask how that advice might apply to them.
- Ask the coachees how someone they admire would deal with the situation.

What if coachees comes to a session without having read their report?

- This is data. What has stopped the coachees from reading the report? This is worth exploring.
- Ask the coachees what they think the report would have highlighted. Use the responses as the basis for the coaching conversation.

What if I do not believe that the coachees can achieve more than they are currently?

- What can you, as the coach, do to change this belief?
- If you believe that another intervention is required (eg counselling), discuss this with a coaching supervisor. It may be that the coachee should be referred to a counsellor.

What if I feel that it would be helpful if I provide a suggestion?

- From the respectful stance of non-directive coaching, it is better to believe that the coachees are resourceful, intelligent and able to come up with their own solutions. Try to withhold advice or suggestions.
- If it seems to you that the coachees would benefit greatly from some information that you have, offer it tentatively after seeking permission. When doing so, present the coachees with a number of options for consideration so that there is still an element of choice.

What if the coachees commit to an action but seem unlikely to actually carry it out?

- If, as a coach, you are unconvinced that the coachees will undertake an action that they have committed to, first check your evidence. What gives you this impression?
- If there is evidence to support this impression (eg the coachees' tone of voice or body language), challenge them by sharing your perception. See if you can agree another action.
- Ask the coachees to rate the likelihood of taking the action just discussed, on a scale on of 0 to 10. If it is relatively low, ask the coachees what they could do to increase their rating by a point or two. If there is anything that can be done in the coaching session, take a few minutes to do this. If not, choose another action.

Conclusion

Using the process described in this chapter, coaching for mental toughness can be a productive and rewarding activity. With the overriding purpose of building resilience to support clients to achieve more of their goals and aspirations, coaching for mental toughness leans towards the non-directive end of the coaching spectrum.

This chapter has highlighted the importance of a 'way of being' as part of the coach's approach when supporting clients who have completed the MTQ48. By combining the integrated approach to coaching for mental toughness with a respectful belief in the coachees' ability to discover their own way forward, there is an increased likelihood of coachees taking ownership of the situation, feeling empowered and making the changes necessary for success.

Whilst the integrated approach recommended in this chapter is designed specifically for use with mental toughness, it is important to bear in mind that it is only one model. De Haan reminds us that 'theoretical orientation evidently makes little difference, while conviction or commitment to the orientation makes a lot of difference' (2008: 43). In other words, the coach's belief in the model he or she is using is more important than the model itself. This is a clear indication that coaches should feel free to adapt and develop the model to suit their preferred way of working.

Mental toughness and resilience emerge from the experience of successfully facing and overcoming varying levels of personal and professional challenge through one's own resourcefulness. This experience obviously comes at the price of hardship, difficulty or discomfort. When considering the question of how best to develop mental toughness in others, it seems perverse to think about creating such difficult circumstances in order to support a person's professional development. Fortunately, coaching creates opportunities to discuss challenges that have already been overcome and to highlight positive examples of mental toughness from one's past. It is also worth pointing out that coaching for mental toughness does not focus solely on discussions about increasing mental toughness. Coaching can be more nuanced, recognizing that there are optimum levels of mental toughness for particular work situations and within different social contexts.

For both of these reasons, coaching provides the ideal supportive intervention. It is a form of personalized professional development that allows for an exploration of the appropriate level of mental toughness for the situation that the coachee has brought for discussion. Even more important, this intervention does not require putting the coachee through difficult or particularly unpleasant situations as a way of building resilience. Through carefully managed conversation within a safe and confidential environment, the coach can support the coachee to selectively remember challenging situations that he or she has overcome in the past to start the process of recognizing and building on existing or forgotten personal strengths and attributes.

The coaching process also allows the coachee to take small steps to build his or her personal resilience in a managed way, with opportunities to reflect and learn at each step. For example, if a coachee finds it difficult to present to large groups of people, he or she may consider finding opportunities to take small steps out of his or her comfort zone by presenting at a non-work related event or to a smaller number of colleagues. This would be stretching and would also build the person's resilience through the experience of having successfully faced and overcome a hurdle. In this way, the level of challenge can be gradually increased to enhance the likelihood of success.

Coaching for mental toughness can unlock the potential of others by developing their resilience and self-confidence. We are all in control of our dreams and ambitions. We are also masters of our own attitudes. Setting ambitious goals for ourselves and adopting a positive attitude about our ability to achieve them can be a large part of our success. Another necessary component is the mental toughness to continue performing at our best in the face of challenges and difficulties. With all three elements in place, each of us can flourish and achieve more of our seemingly unlimited potential.

Fatigue and mental toughness

20

DR FIONA EARLE

Mental toughness and fatigue are closely related concepts. As described at length in the earlier chapters of this book, mental toughness is a multidimensional concept incorporating components of challenge, commitment, control and confidence.

Mental toughness is now a widely accepted 'personality trait', which explains individual differences in the ability to deal with stressful circumstances and the tendency to maintain performance in challenging conditions. There is now a growing body of research (presented throughout this book) that reliably demonstrates the moderating role of mental toughness in the stressor–strain relationship: that is, when people are exposed to challenging circumstances, performance levels are less likely to be maintained by those with low levels of mental toughness.

Fatigue, on the other hand, is intuitively opposed to mental toughness. Like mental toughness, fatigue is also an important part of the stress process. Where mental toughness is known to moderate (and interfere with) the stressor–strain relationship, fatigue is a significant part of the resulting strain itself. In short, fatigue is the subjective state of tiredness that follows a period of dealing with a stressor, eg heavy mental workload or physical demands. So, along with anxiety, fatigue is a core 'product' of the human stress response.

With regard to mental toughness and fatigue, people who are mentally tough may be less likely to suffer the consequences of fatigue or even to experience fatigue. These two propositions have important implications in the worlds of business, sport, education and occupational health.

This chapter will initially present an overview of fatigue, explaining what fatigue actually is and what happens to us when we are fatigued.

Appreciating these issues is essential for developing our understanding of the moderating role mental toughness may have in the stress process. Following this, the relationship between mental toughness and fatigue will be considered, including the presentation of an experimental case study that illustrates the development of the state of fatigue and how the process differs for people with varying levels of mental toughness. The conclusion offers some practical considerations for readers to better understand their own stress response and minimize the impact of their personal stressors.

What is fatigue and why is it important?

Fatigue is clearly an extremely familiar and commonplace occurrence. Most people regularly experience some degree of tiredness following a difficult day at work, a particularly challenging workout, a bad night's sleep, illness, or as a consequence of dealing with a difficult emotional problem. The list of circumstances that can potentially generate feelings of fatigue is almost endless! But, despite the familiarity of the fatigue experience, psychologists working in this field are still debating many of the issues surrounding the concept, even the most basic issue of 'what fatigue actually is'. Also, there is still lively debate as to whether the 'fatigue' that develops after exercise is the same as the 'fatigue' that develops after a difficult work day or emotional challenge.

These intriguing and seemingly simple questions have challenged and infuriated psychologists for over 100 years. As long ago as 1921, Muscio comprehensively outlined the fundamental problems associated with studying fatigue in his presentation to the Industrial Fatigue Research Board (later to be renamed the Medical Research Council). In essence, the problems have always centred on the difficulties associated with measuring fatigue, which have in turn limited the ability of psychologists to study it.

To explain the impact of the measurement issues, consider a hypothetical example. Imagine that scientists could not measure temperature. Without a reliable measure of temperature, it would be very difficult to understand the weather, understand how the weather changes over time and predict changes in the weather. The problem is the same with fatigue. Psychologists have struggled to find an accurate measure of fatigue and without this it has been extremely difficult to understand changes in fatigue and what factors influence these changes.

In the 1920s, Muscio was so very pessimistic about psychologists ever being able to measure and understand fatigue that he recommended that 'the term fatigue be absolutely banished from precise scientific discussion, and consequently attempts to obtain a fatigue test abandoned' (Muscio, 1921: 45). Stark advice indeed! Despite this pessimism, the study of fatigue has persisted. This is not at all surprising as people still experience fatigue and it continues to be associated with poor performance, accidents and ill-health. In response to this enduring and real-world problem, there is a global academic interest in all aspects of fatigue, which can be categorized into the following areas of research:[1]

- Understanding the development of the fatigue state and what makes people tired. What are the conditions in the workplace, for example, that make people tired? How are people affected by factors such as workload, exercise, autonomy, social support, noise and lighting?
- Exploring the personality factors that can moderate the state. Is the development of fatigue different in people who are high in traits such as mental toughness, trait anxiety, or conscientiousness?
- The development of tools and techniques for measuring changes in fatigue. Can questionnaires adequately measure levels of fatigue? Are there any reliable physiological changes that can be used to estimate or even explain fatigue? Can we measure differences in distinct types of fatigue, such as mental, emotional and physical fatigue?
- Understanding and minimizing the consequences of fatigue for performance (in the short term) and for health and wellbeing (in the longer term). What can organizations do to maintain high levels of performance in safety-critical jobs such as those in frontline medical professions, or those in important monitoring roles such as air-traffic controllers? What factors lead to significant health issues, such as burnout?

Each of these areas of fatigue has huge relevance in the modern world, where heavy work demands are ubiquitous and standards for performance are frequently very high.

But what is fatigue? Well, although there is no universally accepted definition of what fatigue actually is, it is now generally accepted that fatigue is a state generated by engaging in some form of heavy or prolonged demands/work. It is characterized by feelings of tiredness and, interestingly, also by a strong desire to stop. Whether or not we listen to these impulses may be influenced by many factors, including mental toughness. The following section will explain the implications of fatigue, before going on to consider the role that mental toughness plays in the process.

What happens to us when we are fatigued?

The process of fatigue should really be considered at two levels or stages: the short-term and the longer-term effects.

Short-term fatigue effects

To understand the effects of fatigue in the short term, it helps to consider the two options that are generally available to individuals who are facing ongoing demands and feeling fatigued; they can choose to 'listen' to their body, submit to the feelings of tiredness and take a break, or they can choose to ignore the feelings of fatigue and continue with the task in hand.

The reasons for choosing to submit to the fatigue or to override these feelings and continue are relatively simple. Consider the conditions that would result in your choosing to stop working on a task when you feel tired, or keep going in spite of these feelings. In essence, the key is motivation – how much do you want (or need) to keep on going? What will be the cost of not continuing with your task? These are the sorts of questions we explicitly and implicitly ask ourselves continuously.

If the answer we provide ourselves is that 'it can wait' and circumstances allow us to take a break and rest, the feelings of fatigue are likely to dissipate. However, we can (and frequently do) choose to override these feelings and continue. Under these circumstances, we are likely to face a number of consequences (for a full description of this process see Hockey, 1993, 1997).

In the first place, the feelings of tiredness are likely to continue and build, and the desire to stop may become increasingly persistent and uncomfortable. In addition to these feelings are the subtle and less well-known changes in the way we think: in essence, being in a state of fatigue typically leads us to increasingly adopt low-effort strategies and ways of working that rely less on higher-level thinking (particularly working memory).

The consequences of this shift are often a tendency to make quicker and less well thought-out decisions and an increase in risky behaviour. Rather than carefully thinking through a series of options, a fatigued person would be more likely to just guess, or make a decision quickly, without fully considering all of the consequences. Furthermore, if the decision requires action, fatigued people are likely to be heavily weighted towards a decision that requires a reduced effort on their part. Therefore, fatigue can influence the actual process of decision making as well as the weighting of the resulting decision.

In general terms, it is this shift towards low-effort strategies of thinking and behaviour that characterizes the fatigued individual. Therefore, it is not difficult to imagine the consequences of fatigue in all working environments, particularly those with implications for health and safety, such as medical or military settings. However, while the impact of fatigue in safety-critical settings is most worrying, this 'low-effort' approach has implications for any environment where performance is an issue. As described above, these changes are more likely to lead to risky behaviours, poor decision making and increased risk of accidents.

Thus, fatigue has clear relevance in all occupational settings, sporting environments and within the educational sector. It also has relevance within the realm of normal life, with driving safety and performance being an area of considerable interest.

Longer-term fatigue effects

While the fatigue state may be uncomfortable, inconvenient and occasionally dangerous, it does have an adaptive value. That is, it can serve to protect us from the development of longer-term health problems.

Although psychologists do not currently fully understand the link between dealing with prolonged strain and the development of longer-term health problems, there is sufficient research and anecdotal evidence to strongly suggest that if we consistently override the feelings of fatigue there will undoubtedly be health consequences. The most commonly reported consequence is that of burnout (Maslach, 1976), which constitutes a significant and enduring health problem associated with emotional exhaustion, depersonalization and a reduced sense of personal accomplishment. Further conditions that have been associated with longer-term stress and fatigue are high blood pressure, heart attacks, stroke, gastrointestinal problems and even cancer.

In summary, fatigue may be a commonplace and familiar phenomenon, but in the short term the state of fatigue can subtly and subconsciously influence the way that you work (sometimes with significant consequences) and in the longer term the decision to consistently override the desire to stop can have catastrophic health consequences.

The chapter will now consider how mental toughness interacts with fatigue, and what you can do to minimize the negative consequences of fatigue.

How does mental toughness impact on the development of fatigue?

As stated earlier, mental toughness comprises a combination of components that have been found to moderate the stressor–stress relationship. However, the relationship between these two familiar concepts of mental toughness and fatigue may be surprisingly complicated.

On first consideration, it seems plausible (although counterintuitive) that mentally tough people are in fact more likely to suffer the consequences of fatigue, as they may be more inclined to override the desire to stop. However, this idea would clearly be contrary to the literature on mental toughness and against the broad underpinnings of the concept – it is a central assumption in the mental toughness literature that mental toughness somehow 'offsets' or reduces the impact of stressors on the individual (Jones et al, 2002). Nonetheless, there is little direct research evidence that explains how these concepts are interrelated. In consideration of this, an experimental study was undertaken to directly investigate the moderating effects of mental toughness on the responses to physical work and the development of fatigue.

EXPERIMENTAL CASE STUDY on mental toughness, workload and fatigue

The study aimed to find out how individuals would respond to physical work and whether this process was different for people who were high or low in mental toughness. How would the demands of the work affect them physiologically? How would they evaluate the demands of the work? How would the individuals differ in their ability to maintain focus on an additional mental task? And what level of fatigue would they experience?

The study – what did we do?

Physical work was simulated by using stationary cycling activity that we could manipulate to represent different levels of activity. This was varied at three levels of intensity or weight resistance, representing low, medium and high levels of workload. This three-level workload approach was used so that we could see how people responded at different levels of demand, as it has been suggested that the advantages of mental toughness may be most relevant under stressful conditions, ie when the 'going gets tough the tough get going'. So, it was considered important to look at the effects of mental toughness across varying levels of stressor.

Furthermore, it was very important to ensure that the physical workloads were equivalent for everyone, ie that one person cycling at the low level would be experiencing the same level of physiological demand as all the other participants cycling at the low level. To set the levels of workload for all, the fitness of each person was tested prior to the experiment. This was done using a fitness test known as VO2 max testing, which essentially measures maximum oxygen uptake as an indicator of cardio-respiratory fitness (Astrand and Rodahl, 1986). The levels of workload were then set for each individual based on their level of fitness – low workload was calculated as 30 per cent of their maximum, moderate workload was calculated as 50 per cent of their maximum, and high workload was calculated as 70 per cent of their maximum.

Each participant experienced three experimental sessions, each representing one of the three levels of workload. Each session included 30 minutes of stationary cycling at one of the three levels, assessment of heart rate throughout the cycling and the additional mental task of an auditory reaction time task. This task required the participants to pinch together their finger and thumb when they heard a high pitched alarm. (The fingers were fitted with electrodes to measure their response times and this measure was taken to represent the impact of the cycling task.) Finally, the participants completed two types of questionnaires. The first of these was the Borg measure of subjective workload (Borg, 1978), which required participants to rate demands on a 20-point scale at three intervals during the cycling. The second questionnaire was the state fatigue scale (Earle, 2004), which uses 15 items to assess changes in state fatigue.

The participants in the study were 24 students (15 males and nine females) with an average age of 24.3 years. Of these, 12 were categorized as being high in mental toughness and 12 were categorized as low in mental toughness. This categorization was based on their responses to the MTQ48.

FIGURE 20.1 Mean heart rate as a function of workload and mental toughness

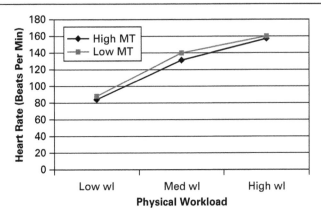

The main findings – what did we discover?

1. With regard to the physiological impact of the cycling, heart rate increased with workload, showing that there was a clear and significant difference in the impact of the different levels of the cycling on heart rate (see Figure 20.1). However, as illustrated in the graph, the average impact of the cycling was not different for those who were high and low in mental toughness. There was almost no difference in the average heart rate for the two mental toughness groups.

The relevance of this finding is that we can deduce that any subsequent differences in either the performance or fatigue may be explained by psychological variables. Interestingly, this is demonstrated, to some degree, in the data for the auditory response time task.

2. The data illustrated in Figure 20.2 highlights a trend that as physical workload increased, the response time (to the auditory alarm) increased steadily for the low mental toughness group, whereas the response times in the high mental toughness group are less affected by workload, and do not increase linearly with the demands of the task. This suggests that the physical task had less impact on the more mentally tough participants, who had greater concurrent mental resources to respond to the auditory alarm.

Furthermore, the largest difference in reaction times between the two groups occurred in the high physical workload period, supporting the argument that mental toughness is particularly important when facing high levels of a stressor. Although these differences were not found to be statistically significant, the data does provide the first layer of evidence that individuals with increased mental toughness can perform more effectively in adverse conditions.

So, while the participants experienced the same level of objective demand of the cycling, with no differences in heart rate, the impact of this cycling was greater for those who were less mentally tough and was found to impact negatively on performance on a simple current task. This objective performance data is further supported by the subjective data of post-task overall workload assessment.

FIGURE 20.2 Mean alarm response times in milliseconds for the two time periods as a function of low/medium/high physical workload and mental toughness

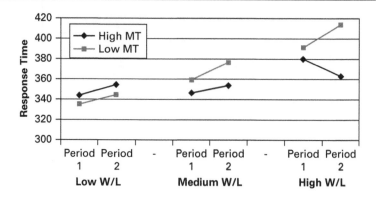

FIGURE 20.3 Mean physical demand ratings as a function of physical workload, period (10 minute intervals) and mental toughness

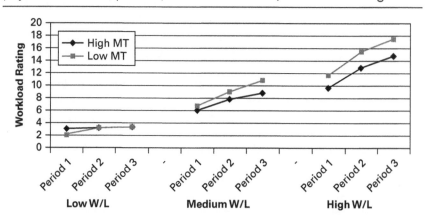

3. As one would expect, there was a significant impact of physical workload on ratings of workload, ie the higher the level of cycling, the more demanding the participants rated this task and both groups reported increased physical demands as the workload increased. However, the positive impact of mental toughness was again highlighted when the individuals were working at the highest physical workload. As illustrated in Figure 20.3, there were no differences between the ratings of workload at low levels of demand for the two mental toughness groups. So when the task was relatively easy, being mental tough did not provide an obvious advantage.

However, there was an increasing divergence in workload ratings, with workload ratings being slightly higher for the low mental toughness group at medium load and the

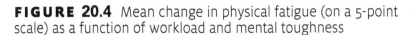

FIGURE 20.4 Mean change in physical fatigue (on a 5-point scale) as a function of workload and mental toughness

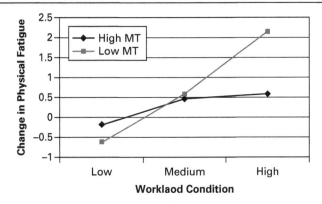

gap between the two groups increased under high load. Although this finding was again not found to be statistically significant, this is a thought-provoking trend.

4. Of particular relevance to this chapter is the reported change in state fatigue. That is the extent to which feelings of tiredness increased as a consequence of dealing with the physical stressor of cycling. The findings shown in Figure 20.4 illustrate that for those who were low in mental toughness, subjective physical fatigue increased as workload increased. However, while physical fatigue in the high mental toughness group did increase from low to medium workload conditions, it did not increase from medium to high workload conditions. (NB: a negative fatigue score indicates a reduction in reported fatigue from the start of the cycling to the end.)

The analysis of these data revealed a significant interaction between mental toughness and workload, with workload having a different effect on those who are high and low in mental toughness (significant at the 5 per cent level). That is, the demands of 'heavy' cycling (at 70 per cent of maximum) only resulted in substantially increased fatigue in the low mental toughness group. This is a very important finding, as this is direct evidence to support the proposition that stressors have less of an impact on those who are mental tough.

In summary, the experimental case study presented here gives us a direct comparison of the stress process in people who are high and low in mental toughness. Following on from the results presented above, the impact of the cycling on the two groups was measurably different. Although the physiological impact was the same (in terms of heart rate), the faster response times of the mentally tough group (under high levels of load) suggest that this stressor resulted in a greater drain on the cognitive resources of the less mentally tough.

This was also consistent with a higher evaluation of workload in the low MT group and a greater increase in the level of resulting fatigue. Therefore, people who are high in mental toughness are less affected by stressors and are, consequently, less vulnerable to the development of fatigue.

Understanding your own process of fatigue: three recommendations for action

We now consider how we can use the 100 years of research on fatigue to understand our own fatigue processes. In a general sense, it is important to understand the changes that you are likely to undergo when fatigued.

1. Monitoring your fatigue

As reported earlier in the chapter, the feelings of tiredness and irritability are often the first indicators of fatigue. They are our warning sign that a rest should be considered. In themselves, they are not particularly worrying, but these feelings are typically associated with changes in the way we think. Although the pattern of these changes may be slightly different for everybody, we are all likely to experience a subtle shift towards low-effort thinking.

An understanding of this is extremely important, as it is often a subconscious process with potentially catastrophic consequences. This shift can lead to reduced attention to detail, risky behaviour and faulty and biased decision making. In a work context, this can result in poor work performance and an increased likelihood of accidents. In education this might mean a reduced capacity to revise and produce good coursework and so on.

An awareness of this process may be sufficient to minimize the impact that fatigue has on our attitudes and behaviours. An explicit knowledge of this process during a fatigued state could offset these changes, at least for a short period of time.

Consider the impact this fatigue state could have at work or at home. If you are aware that fatigue is likely to make you take 'short cuts', this information could be important in deciding whether to take a break or alternatively, consciously increase the care you take over tasks that are important to get right.

2. Identifying its causes

The second consideration worthy of mention is to evaluate what it is that makes us tired. Again, this may be slightly different for everyone. Some people are more prone to physical fatigue, some emotional fatigue and some people are particularly affected by heavy or prolonged mental demands.

It may be a worthwhile exercise to consider what it is that makes you tired, ie, is it certain tasks, particular working conditions or specific times of day? If you can reorganize your work or life demands to minimize fatigue, this may be the best way to stop fatigue developing.

A fatigue awareness exercise:
Understanding your own fatigue patterns

The demands of the modern working world mean that is isn't always possible to take a break when we are tired, so it is important to recognize what makes us tired and how we respond to being fatigued. Consequently, it is important to develop effective coping strategies to minimize the negative effects of feeling tired and/or worn-out:

- Be aware of what makes you tired, ie certain tasks, time of day, etc.
- Be aware of the short-term psychological consequences.
- If you can reorganize your work, do so. If not, be aware that your judgement may be affected and that you may be more inclined to take risks and jump to conclusions.

Use the boxes to identify what makes you tired, how you normally react and what coping strategies you could develop to deal with them better. Remember there are different types of fatigue: mental, emotional and physical fatigue, morning and evening tiredness. You may want to discuss your coping strategies further with your manager/coach/mentor or a colleague, friend or family member.

3. Understanding yourself: are you particularly susceptible?

Finally, in the context of the current chapter, it may be interesting to consider how the process of fatigue may be different for people at the two extremes of the mental toughness spectrum.

First, the people who are low in mental toughness are arguably more sensitive to life's demands. Stressful circumstances and events are likely to lead to a greater stress response in people who are low in mental toughness. Therefore, this group may be more prone to the negative consequences of fatigue and it may be particularly important for them to consider changing the circumstances that lead to fatigue or, better still, to consider ways in which they could improve their level of mental toughness, leaving them less vulnerable to the effects of life's stressors.

Conversely, the people who are high in mental toughness are less likely to experience stress when facing difficult circumstances and are hence less likely to develop fatigue. However, these people may be less likely to listen to the warnings signs that the fatigue state provides. While this may offer regular short-term gains in terms of task completion, there may eventually be a performance cost in the medium term and even a health cost in the longer term. This is particularly true for the people who are high in the 'commitment' component of mental toughness. This group of individuals may persist with their chosen goals in spite of considerable adversity and beyond that which may be reasonable. While this is obviously an extreme picture, it is worth considering the value of the fatigue warning for protecting us in the longer-term.

Note

1 For a comprehensive and lively discussion of current research in these areas see Ackerman (2011).

Can mental toughness be developed? Psychologist/practitioner perspective

21

Introduction

Having defined what mental toughness is and how valuable the concept is in determining individual and group performance, wellbeing and behaviour and understanding better how to measure mental toughness, the million dollar question is, 'Can we do anything about it?'

Instinctively the answer is, 'We can.' Sports psychologists and sports coaches would argue that they have been doing this for many years with significant evidence of success. Coaches, trainers and mentors in other fields might argue likewise. However, a fuller answer is a little bit more complex than this. We need to consider questions like:

- Which are the tools, techniques and interventions that appear to assist in the development of mental toughness?
- Do some work better than others? We know that they all work but they don't all work for everyone.
- Is the person delivering the intervention a factor? Do some people get better results than others?
- Is the recipient a factor? Do some techniques work better with certain types of people?
- What are the conditions needed to make them work?
- Can we explain why these work?

- Quite crucially, in doing this are we changing someone's mental toughness or are we simply equipping someone with tools and techniques that enable them to behave as a mentally tough person might behave?

From a practitioner's perspective many of these questions may matter less than they would to a psychologist or academic researcher. The practitioner may be more concerned that what they do works. The psychologist may be more interested to know why they work. In this chapter we look at mental toughness development from both perspectives.

The psychologist's perspective

There is some evidence that mental toughness has a significant mental component. For example Horsburgh *et al* (2009), using a sample of twins, showed that mental toughness not only has a strong genetic component, but is also influenced by environmental factors. Clough *et al* (2010) reported a positive correlation between higher mental toughness scores (measured by a questionnaire) and more grey matter tissue volume in the right frontal lobe, suggesting a genetic link, but certainly not precluding the influence of environmental factors.

In general, psychology has moved beyond the age old question: are we a product of nature or nurture? The fact is that clearly both have an influence, so some people are born tough, and others may develop toughness. This raises the very interesting question of how mental toughness is developed.

Various researchers have identified that critical life incidents can facilitate mental toughness (Coulter *et al*, 2010). Parental behaviour is clearly a key component in the deliberate or accidental toughening of children. The centrality of the role of the parent is highlighted by Thelwell *et al* (2010) who advocate educational programmes aimed at parents to help cultivate the most appropriate environment to support psychological development.

A truly fascinating study was carried out by Nico Van Yperen (2009) in the Netherlands. His prospective study was designed to identify psychological factors that predict career success in professional adult soccer. Two groups were distinguished: male soccer players who successfully progressed into professional adult soccer, and male soccer players who did not reach this level. Differences between the two groups were examined on the basis of data gathered in the initial phase of their careers, 15 years earlier.

In his discussion Van Yperen writes:

> More remarkable is the finding that, relative to the unsuccessful group, successful participants had more siblings, were more often of non-White (or non-Dutch) ethnic origin, and more often had divorced parents. In speculating about these remarkable results, siblings may form a kin group bound by strong ties of trust and support, and may increase social skills which may be helpful to

progress in team sports in particular. And being a member of an ethnic minority and having divorced parents may help to develop coping skills and attitudes that are helpful in dealing with all kind of problems or drawbacks. (p 326)

This fascinating insight into how people develop clearly shows that the hard knocks of life can bring forward toughness. However, caution must be used. The individuals who experienced difficulties and used this energy to thrust themselves forward may have started with higher levels of toughness. It may be the case that sensitive individuals are more likely to be swallowed whole by traumatic events.

In a recent paper by Crust and Clough (2011) three further factors that might help enhance mental toughness were discussed:

1 Providing a challenging yet supportive environment.
2 Having an effective social support mechanism.
3 Encouraging reflection; emphasizing the importance of experiential learning.

It is clear that genetics and environment both play a role in the development of mental toughness. This leaves many questions unanswered, but the research base is moving forward rapidly and insights are occurring on a regular basis.

One question that we can begin to address is can formal training actually increase mental toughness? There is certainly some evidence that mental skills training programmes can lead to increases in self-reported mental toughness (eg, Sheard and Golby, 2006; Gucciardi et al, 2009a). The mechanism by which these interventions work can be explained as follows. Often mental toughness is described as a mindset. Whilst we feel this does not do justice to a far more complex picture, it does suggest the possibility that cognitive interventions (eg imagery, positive thinking) may be able to influence it. Crust and Azadi (2010) reported that mentally tough individuals use more psychological techniques and skills.

Similarly, Nicholls et al (2008) found mental toughness was significantly and positively correlated with problem or approach coping strategies (ie, mental imagery, effort expenditure, thought control, logical analysis) and significantly and negatively correlated with avoidance coping (distancing, mental distraction, and resignation). This led to the AQR team developing a mental toughness training package. The approach is based on Psychological Skills Training (PST) and Cognitive Behavioural Interventions (CBI). The programme has proved both popular and effective.

A practitioner's perspective

We now know we can understand better what mental toughness is and how important it is in determining our capability to perform to the peak of our abilities, our wellbeing and the extent to which we adopt positive behaviours and a positive mindset. We also know that we are able, through the model and the measure MTQ48, to assess an individual's mental toughness in some useful detail.

The most important question for the practitioner is, 'Can I do something that helps my client develop mental toughness?' We know the short answer is, 'We can!' Other important questions for the practitioner include:

- If I do help someone to develop his or her mental toughness, how sustainable is this?
- In working with people am I actually changing their mental toughness or showing them how to behave in a more (or less) mentally tough way?
- Are some techniques and approaches more effective than others? And is this down to the technique or down to the way it is delivered?

We will address these questions below.

Turning back to examine how we can work with people to develop mental toughness, we find that there are very many tools, techniques and approaches that seem to make a difference to a greater or lesser extent. Most of these appear in other areas of people and HR development; many are to be found under labels such as psychology, sports coaching, Cognitive Behavioural Therapy (CBT), Neurolinguistic Programming (NLP), positive psychology, etc. Some techniques and approaches appear in all of these places. Interestingly, many techniques also appear within and are practised by some of the major religions, most notably Hinduism and Buddhism. In a recent visit to India one response from a student to a description of a visualization technique was to say, 'We do that... we call it prayer!'

We have found that virtually all the tools and techniques can be grouped under five major headings. These are:

1 positive thinking;
2 visualization;
3 anxiety control;
4 goal setting; and
5 attentional control.

The first four are generally well known to most trainers, tutors, coaches, etc and to many competent managers. The fifth, attentional control, is less well understood and less well known. Developing better attentional control can produce some of the most significant benefits for those to whom it is introduced.

One thing that we also know about most of these techniques and approaches is that they all seem to work to a varying degree but they don't always work for everyone and they don't work all the time. So there is a clear need for effective practitioners to be aware of this and to monitor and assess the effectiveness of what they do. Very few do so! Many adopt a 'toolbox' of tools and techniques and use them relentlessly on a 'faith-based' approach often relying on casual anecdotal evidence as the primary source of support for the technique (eg, 'Mary showed Mike how to... and he tried it for a week and it changed his life in these ways...). This isn't good enough. It may seem to have worked for Mike but the change in Mike might also have little to do with what Mary did unless you can show a direct link.

Fortunately it is possible to do something more effective in terms of assessment and research. All of the psychological changes implied in mental toughness and developing mental toughness have a physiological counterpart. So we are able to (easily) measure changes in the body that reflect changes in mental toughness. This is called 'biofeedback'.

Finally, perhaps unsurprisingly, the MTQ48 and good feedback have also emerged as effective interventions in their own right. As in other areas of people development, self-awareness gives individuals better information with which to reflect on their position, which can either help them to do something about it or understand better why something works and other things might not.

Positive thinking 22

Henry Ford is claimed to have said, 'Whether you think you can do a thing or think you can't do a thing, you're probably right.' Essentially he was describing the nature of positive thinking and its importance for our effectiveness. We are what we think. Positive thinking describes an approach that encourages ideas, words and images into the mind that are conducive to performance, wellbeing, growth and success.

We have an extraordinary power over ourselves as everything we know, feel and believe is based on our internal thoughts. We are often more aware of this in a negative sense than in the positive sense. Ask a group of people to list five things they have done well today and five things they have got wrong, and most people will complete the latter fairly quickly but will struggle to complete the first part of the exercise. This occurs despite the fact that most of us get most things right most of the time. That is why any negative or demeaning statements you make about yourself, either to others or yourself, should be avoided. These self-limiting beliefs are reinforced every time they slip into your conversation or mind.

There are now hundreds of tools and techniques that support the development of positive thinking; see the list in Table 22.1. They appear within CBT, NLP, sports coaching and positive psychology. This chapter describes some of those that are consistently found to be effective.

Making affirmations

These are short statements or phrases that mean something to you. When subjected to stress pressure or challenge their use can enable you to adopt a more positive approach. Affirmations are essentially a way of saying to yourself, 'I can do it!' Examples of affirmations include:

- I am a calm, methodical and efficient worker.
- I can make a difference.

TABLE 22.1 Tools and techniques that support positive thinking

Intervention	Description/Comment
Positive Thinking	
Affirmations	Positive statements about oneself that are important to you.
Mental thought stopping	How to say 'No!'
Physical thought stopping – elastic band	Short but painful reminder to stop thinking negatively. Thwack yourself with an elastic band if something negative has happened.
Think three positives	At end of each day, record three good things which have happened. At end of week or month, summarize this to get a sense of all the good that is there.
Turning negatives into positives	Reframe negative thoughts or comments into positive ones (or those which have a positive component)
What will I do tomorrow?	At end of each day, identify one, two or three things that you will accomplish the next day. Must be achievable. Pick up in the morning.
Looking at heroes/heroines	Identify people you admire and their key behaviours. Seek to emulate some of those.
Self-talk	In your head use positive language when setting out to do difficult or challenging things.
Self-hypnosis	

- I can achieve difficult tasks.
- I work well under pressure.
- I enjoy solving problems.
- I love that feeling of having achieved so much in a day.
- I enjoy being calm when others around me are not.

To make affirmations effective they should:

1 Be made in the present tense. Affirmations need to be stated in the 'Now'. There is a temptation to make affirmations in the future sense – describing what you will do. 'I am…' works much better than 'I will…' because the subconscious recognizes 'I am' as something being done now, not in the future.

2 Have an emotional reward. Affirmations that are not personal to you won't work very well for you, so they should be expressed in the first person. Again this helps the subconscious mind recognize that this is something it is supposed to go to work on. Affirmations should begin with 'I' or 'my', not 'you' or 'your'.

3 Be positively phrased. Affirmations rarely work when expressed as a negative. The mind isn't good at recognizing the concept of 'not'. Its use can inadvertently reinforce the behaviour you are seeking to change.

Affirmations work because they are broadly equivalent to someone else telling you that 'you can do it'. If you work with a coach or mentor who consistently reinforces your ability to do something, you will probably come to believe that it is so. You are creating a person 'in your head' who is doing exactly the same thing.

Self-talk

Widely used in sports coaching with considerable success, there is growing evidence that language and the way we process language can have a significant effect on how we approach tasks, work, challenges, etc.

Words often conjure up images and meaning beyond the simple dictionary definition. It is this 'additional' meaning that can influence us. A good example is the word 'exam'. The dictionary meaning might describe it simply as a test of ability. However, use the word 'exam' in conversation with students and you will get a range of responses. These will determine performance, wellbeing and success. Some students will hear the word 'exam' and associate it with an eagerly anticipated opportunity to show the examiner what they can do. They associate the word with opportunity. The link provides a positive experience. Others will hear the word 'exam' and respond quite differently. They will associate it with something to be avoided. In their mind the exam is more than a test: it is a situation that will reveal how little they know about the topic being assessed. The two groups of students may have equal abilities and they may have attended exactly the same classes and programmes but their resultant performance will be quite different.

Where that association has come from is interesting and useful. It is possible that at a young age one group had been told to look forward to exams and to expect that they would do well. The others may have been told not to

TABLE 22.a

Exercise: Self-talk. Think of three positive statements that would work for you.
1.
2.
3.

expect too much and maybe even expect to do badly. We see this behaviour replicated in every walk of life. Whether it is an employee making a presentation, an athlete reaching his or her first championship final, someone being told he or she needs an operation, etc. The way the person approaches the 'presentation', the 'final' or the 'operation' may affect significantly how the event is handled.

Whatever the source of anxiety or pressure, try talking yourself through it. Examples include:

> 'These feelings will fade away – they won't last forever.'
>
> 'I know how to control these feelings. I must concentrate on relaxing myself.'
>
> 'I will begin to feel better soon.'
>
> 'No one is looking at me. I am not going to make a fool of myself.'
>
> 'This is perfectly natural and normal. I know what is happening to me.'

An MRI brain scan study confirmed that the challenge scale in the mental toughness model is closely associated with the fusiform gyrus. This is the part of the brain that is responsible for the visual word form (written not spoken) and semantic processing and language comprehension. These are all likely to play a part in 'self-talk'.

The Positive Thinking (Attitude) Ladder

Fiona Mackay Young has developed an interesting scale which she calls the attitude ladder; see Figure 22.1. It represents 10 points on a positive thinking scale from low to high. It is a useful device for self-reflection and for use by coaches, mentors, managers, etc who want their clients to understand realistically where they are in terms of thinking positively.

This kind of diagnosis provides perspective for the individual as well as indicating what might be useful 'next steps' to be considered. It combines

FIGURE 22.1 The attitude ladder

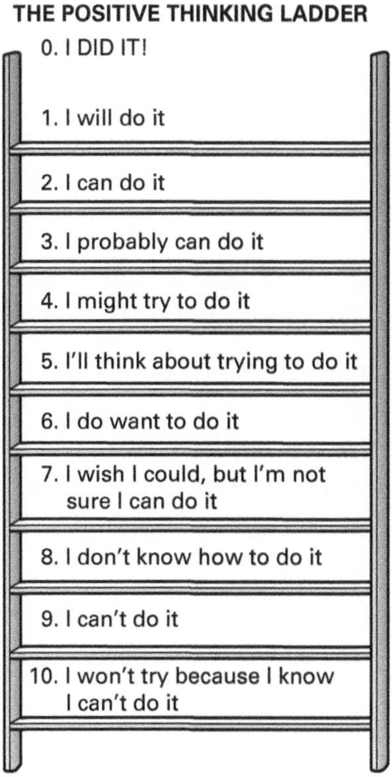

THE POSITIVE THINKING LADDER

0. I DID IT!

1. I will do it

2. I can do it

3. I probably can do it

4. I might try to do it

5. I'll think about trying to do it

6. I do want to do it

7. I wish I could, but I'm not sure I can do it

8. I don't know how to do it

9. I can't do it

10. I won't try because I know I can't do it

self-awareness with goal setting. The ladder breaks a 'big goal' – attainment of a truly positive attitude – into smaller more achievable milestones.

The first question is – Where do you fit right now? Think about the language that you or the individual is most likely to use in most circumstances. Does that affect performance, wellbeing and behaviour? It almost certainly will. When people say to themselves 'I can't', in any form, they are programming themselves for failure. The more often they think or say it, the more they believe it.

Using the mental toughness development tools and techniques described elsewhere in this book and in this chapter and, with the support of others, it is possible to make progress in developing a more positive mindset – and to monitor that using the ladder.

Thought stopping – physical and mental cues

Again widely used in sports coaching, this is a powerful and often quick to apply technique that is closely related to affirmations and self-talk. A cue is a device that you activate when experiencing negative thoughts. It is useful in dealing with worry, panic and anxiety.

The essence of thought stopping is that you consciously issue a 'Stop!' command when you experience negative thoughts. The negative thought is then replaced with something more positive and realistic. The way it works is straightforward. Essentially, it is a form of controlled distraction that abruptly and firmly turns one's thoughts from the negative to something that is more controllable. Without some form of positive intervention, negative thoughts can 'accumulate' and become the normal response. This will influence the way you behave and feel. If coupled with positive and reassuring statements, it is possible to break the pattern of negative thought.

Thought stopping can arise through the use of mental or physical cues or a combination of both. The process is typically as follows:

1 Identify a situation where you frequently find yourself thinking negatively.
2 Identify the negative statement you make when in this situation.
3 Prepare yourself with some form of relaxation.
4 Find a phrase or cue you can use to stop your negative thoughts.

A physical cue can be as simple as pinching yourself. Sports people will use elastic bands on the wrist and 'thwack' themselves when a negative thought arises. Mental cues will include:

- positive statements that are activated when the negative thought arises;
- mentally or even orally shouting 'Stop!';
- replacing a poor image with a positive one;
- associating the negative image with its consequence.

Controlled distraction

By concentrating on something else, this technique allows the individual to be distracted from a negative situation. It is useful because it can be a quick intervention in many circumstances.

It can sometimes be easier to concentrate on something else to take your mind off your anxiety rather than seeking to talk yourself out of it. Essentially this is controlled distraction. By attending to something that doesn't cause anxiety, you can regain control and refocus. Examples include:

- Mental tasks: doing a puzzle in your head, a sudoku, thinking of a poem or the lyrics to a song; imagining a relaxing scene – a beach, looking at pictures, listening to music you really like, etc.
- Concentrating on your immediate surroundings: counting lamp posts, adding up the items in your shopping basket, etc.

- Bringing a pet to work: enabling you to focus on something that is not creating anxiety but demands enough attention for you to be distracted, even for a short while, from the source of the anxiety.
- Breaking routines: doing something differently so that you focus on maintaining the new routine.

Think three positives

Most of us get through most days getting most things right. We can easily, if we reflected diligently, see that we have completed perhaps a hundred tasks perfectly well. Mostly, however, when we get to the end of the day and ask ourselves, 'How did things go?' we will default to thinking about what went wrong. It's probably right to do that but if we repeatedly spend each day dwelling on what went wrong we can easily develop the sense that there is not a lot going right in our lives.

Consequently, a useful and highly effective activity is to write down at the end of each day (or some suitable time) a reminder of, say, three things that you have done well. This tells you that you do get some things right and doing this repeatedly restores a sense of balance – 'I make mistakes but I mostly get it right.' This is especially effective with young people. They are adept at seeing what went wrong before they see what went right. It is a useful parenting activity which, in a structured and systematic way, enables parents to provide positive feedback to their charges. The propensity for negative thought can often be attributed to lack of, or critically negative, comment from parents when their children are in their formative years.

Turning negatives into positives

Inevitably there are times when we do get it wrong. If you find yourself thinking you didn't do something well enough or got something wrong, try identifying what might be the positive in the situation. It is very rare that you get everything wrong and there will be positive aspects even in failure.

Listen to sports coaches talking about their team after a defeat. Most will acknowledge the defeat but they will also identify what went well and will often identify the mistakes as opportunities for improvement. The important thing here is to understand that things do go wrong and we do make mistakes but very rarely is it fatal. Instead, give yourself credit for what you do, remember that you are not perfect and that you can do better next time. A good discipline is to take time out to consider:

- What kinds of thing always make me think negatively?
- What kinds of thing always make me think positively?

- What advice would you give to someone who consistently shows these negative thoughts?
- How could you identify the positives in these situations? (It can be useful to work with others to do this.)

What will I do tomorrow?

At the end of each day, identify one, two or three things that you are very confident you can accomplish the next day. The fewer the better – you need a virtual guarantee of success. The tasks must be achievable.

This operates by reinforcing/applying the old adage, 'success breeds success'. Most people like the sense of winning and it banishes the sense of failure like nothing else can. Once a more positive mindset is achieved you can take on more challenging tasks with the confidence that you can succeed with those too.

Visualization

23

Although described here as a separate technique, there is a close relationship between visualization and other positive thinking techniques.

Most of us don't have to learn how to visualize – we do it all the time. What we have to do is learn how to harness it for our benefit. The challenge lies in the fact that often when we consider a situation in our mind we will visualize it in a negative way. If asked to do a presentation we will imagine it going horribly wrong. We'll fluff our line; we'll lose our place; we'll drop our notes; the audience will ask awkward questions that we fail to answer properly, and so on. Similarly, students visualizing an examination will often imagine arriving in the exam room unprepared; they will look at the exam paper and not understand the questions; they imagine running out of time, etc.

Creating these negative pictures can change you emotionally and these have a negative effect on your mind and body that impacts on the real performance when it arises. But it can work the other way around. Creating positive pictures can have a positive impact on the mind and body.

You can use your mental voice to increase self-belief in your ability to deal with change and deadlines; and to relax, you can use your imagination. Your imagination communicates your mind at the deepest levels and visual imagery is far more potent than words alone. Psychologists will confirm that practising something in your head is as real to your mind as doing it. The human mind doesn't discriminate between the two sets of experiences. Instead of telling yourself that you will be successful, you 'see' yourself being successful. Visualization is like watching a video of yourself.

Visualization is widely used in sports, particularly to support 'anchoring' behaviour. Consider penalty takers in soccer. They will imagine taking penalties before they ever get to a live situation. If they have a picture in their mind of the ball sailing into the net and scoring a goal they will tend to function better when talking a real penalty. Moreover if they see, in their mind's eye, a huge goalkeeper and a small goal, they will approach their task with less confidence than if they can imagine a large goal and a small goalkeeper. This is similarly true for golfers, place kickers in rugby, athletes, tennis players, etc. It's also true for just about everything we do that is moderately challenging.

To be effective with visualization:

- It should be grounded in real life using information from your experiences.
- Focus on the positive feelings you are experiencing within your imagined scenario.
- Any negative thoughts should be pushed away and replaced with positive thoughts or affirmations.

Visualization is believed to encourage activity in the right side of your brain – related to creativity and emotions. It leaves you free to focus on overcoming a fear, achieving insights about an emotional anxiety or focusing on a particular goal you want to pursue.

Useful visualization exercises include 'Imagine a pink elephant' (or any unusual depiction of a normal situation). This exercise simply describes the capability to visualize. Imagine an elephant. Most elephants are uniformly grey. Then imagine it in a different bright colour – say, pink. Develop that in your mind until it is a robust image. Then imagine an even more unlikely or outrageous addition – like adding big yellow spots, putting a hat on the elephant, giving it four tusks instead of two.

Visualizing success

One of the best places for us to rehearse a daunting task, especially an intellectual task, is inside our head. You have at your disposal an environment that you can control, adjust and adapt at will.

Athletes will often use visualization to imagine winning and particularly what it feels like to be a winner. If success breeds success you can start that in your head. Athletes will imagine stepping onto a podium having won a competition – and will be able to sense what that feels like.

Most of us at some time will be asked to do a presentation or address a group of people. It can be formal presentation; it can be a casual address; it can be a wedding speech. Few people find these activities without challenge. However, you can imagine the presentation and even when you imagine something going wrong you can stop the 'tape in your head', rewind and imagine how you can do it better. You can be difficult with yourself, asking the most awkward questions imaginable, knowing that you can envisage how you might respond smoothly and smartly.

Visualize yourself in the situation, behaving, reacting and looking as you would wish to do. Imagine yourself there. What does it mean to you? How do you react? How do others around you respond? How do you feel? What emotions are you experiencing? Try the following exercise.

You have an important presentation coming up.

See yourself there; fill in all the details that you know – the office, the people, right down to the coffee machine in the corner.

The more realistic the visualization the more effective it will be.

Imagine yourself there, looking confident, relaxed, in control, and aware of everything that is going on around you.

See yourself preparing your materials, greeting people, and asking them to take a seat.

As you stand up to begin your presentation hold onto that feeling of mastery and calmness.

See yourself working through your materials, everything in order and according to plan, answering questions as they arise with confidence and authority.

Imagine the questions you might be asked. And imagine providing a ready response.

Visualize the engaged expressions on your colleague's faces as they lean forward slightly to take in everything you are saying…

Now try imagining and writing your own script:

Guided imagery

Guided imagery is extremely useful when in challenging situations that are creating stress and pressure and there is little you can do about it. The principle behind the use of guided imagery is that you can use your imagination to recreate the situation and enjoy a situation that is very relaxing. The more intensely you imagine the situation, the more relaxing the experience will be.

The situation can be real, such as a particularly satisfying experience from your past. It can be imagined – based on a scenario you would like to experience but have not yet done so. The steps are:

- Make yourself comfortable. If a lying-down position would make you go to sleep, opt for a cross-legged position, or sit in a comfortable chair.

- Use diaphragmic deep breathing (see Chapter 24) and close your eyes.

- Once you are in a relaxed state, begin to envision yourself in the midst of the most relaxing environment you can imagine. For some, this would be floating in the cool, clear waters off a tropical beach, where you are waited on 'hand and foot'. For others, this might be sitting by a fire in a secluded snow cabin, deep in the woods, sipping hot cocoa and reading the latest prize-winning novel.

- As you imagine your scene, seek to involve all your senses. Are there any particular smells or sounds? What does it look like? Is there a special feeling emerging? Can you taste the scenario? The more detail you can develop the better.

- Do this for as long as you need to feel relaxed. When you return, you'll feel more calm and refreshed.

An example of a guided imagery scenario is shown in the next box.

'Happy memories' is a particular form of guided imagery. It makes use of the happy events in your past to enable a form of controlled distraction. You can effectively transport yourself, in your mind, to a time when things were going better. Think of a time when you were happy or things went well. Develop it in your mind until you see it in substantial detail and you sense how you felt at that time. Savour it.

Having made yourself comfortable, gradually allow your mind to enter a place that is quite special to you. This place can be real or imaginary; somewhere you have visited on holiday; a beach or woodland; or somewhere you like to visit; somewhere from your dreams. Allow your mind to drift... drift to a pleasant, peaceful place; a place that you know... where you will always feel able to relax... completely; a safe... secure place... where no one... and nothing can ever bother you.

This is your place... your safe place... your haven. It could be outside... a clearing in the woodland; a meadow in the countryside; a secluded beach. Or it may be a room... a room you once had, or still have... or a room you would like to have. It is a place where you feel free to let go... completely... your haven... a haven of tranquillity... unique and special to you.

Really experience this place... notice first the light: is it bright, natural, dim... where is the light coming from: is it sunlight, candle light, lamplight? Notice also the temperature... is it hot, warm, cool... what is its source... can you feel the warmth from the sun, a fire, can you feel a cool breeze? Be aware of the colours that surround you... the shapes... textures... the familiar objects that make this place special.

Begin to see it in all its detail. You can just be there... enjoying the sounds... the smells... the atmosphere... with nobody wanting anything, nobody needing anything, no one demanding anything from you. This is your place... your time... relax.

A psychological context of confidence development

The worlds of confidence development and psychology have huge overlaps. It is the core business of many psychology professionals. The interventions briefly described in this chapter all have something in common: they are techniques that help us control our inner voices. As already mentioned, many of the techniques are drawn from the world of cognitive behavioural therapy. This approach was developed by Aaron Beck. When dealing with his clients he noted that their internal thought processes were complicated and often deeply flawed. They were often more interested in what he thought about them than dealing with the real problem. Basically he became aware that thinking impacts on feeling and feelings impact on thinking. It is easy therefore to get caught up in a serious downward spiral.

Our minds are undoubtedly cluttered with often unwanted thoughts. These negative thoughts often stop us achieving our full potential. It is clear that for many of us our own worst enemy is us. We are quick to point the finger of blame at the 'amorphous them' as the root of our troubles, but with a little insight we can begin to see it is perhaps us. Earlier in the book we talked about attribution errors. We are all naive scientists, trying to make sense of a complex world. However, we can confidently say that our data analysis is deeply flawed. We try to deal with the world on the basis of what we think is happening, not what is really happening. Thoughts are not the truth: they are a subjective representation of reality.

The important lesson in this chapter is to recognize that you can control what goes on in your brain. In fact I often say to our undergraduates it's the only thing we can control. We can influence others, but no more than this. By 'thinking about thinking' we can first recognize the patterns and then tackle them. Basically we are talking to ourselves. We often know what we are going to say – it is after all just us talking to ourselves – but on occasion negative thoughts seem to pop up from nowhere. We need to find out where these are coming from and, more important, learn how to counter them.

It is unclear where these thoughts emerge from. Psychologists have very different perspectives. These range from the psychoanalytic tradition that often refers to the unconscious mind. This, by definition, is not easily accessible. It is a dark recess that may reveal itself through dreams and talking therapies. At the opposite end of the scale it can be argued that the thoughts occur due to inappropriate firing of neurones – a sort of faulty wiring. Whatever the causes – which are beyond the remit of this book – it can be agreed that controlling your thoughts is a positive thing. Mentally tough individuals are better able to do this. Time and time again we find that mentally tough people are better able to face reality. They consistently adopt fewer avoidance strategies and tend to attack the problem straight on. Excitingly we can now begin to explain this. Brain scans show that the reality testing centres in the brains of tougher individuals are more active.

Positive psychology and mental toughness

A philosophy or school of thought that has gained much credibility in recent years is that of positive psychology. We have spent a lot of time trying to ascertain whether or not this is a competing or supportive model.

Positive psychology is most interested in happiness. The work is spearheaded by the excellent Professor Seligman. At a first glance it would appear that happiness is not at the forefront of mental toughness research. However, it is there – just below the surface. Much of this book is devoted to examples of performance enhancement related to mental toughness. It is our core philosophy that mental toughness is about providing every individual with the opportunity to reach his or her full potential.

Seligman and the positive psychology school are right when they say that a great deal of psychology concentrates too much on the negatives of life. We tend to look for problems and then solutions. We do not really focus on the positives. In this chapter we show that this can be done, and should be done.

However, many people are not in a position to count their blessings. Much of the work we have done has been carried out in Hull, a once proud city that now has an unemployment rate that is twice the national rate, and suffers the social issues that go along with it. Most psychological models reflect the environment in which they developed. Ours is no different. We seek positive growth but make no apologies for identifying and trying to repair the holes that society leaves. Happiness is predicated on a secure foundation of resource, health and opportunity.

Wellbeing can be described in two ways. First there is subjective wellbeing, which is about a state called 'happiness' and will often have a material undertone. This is what the positive psychology school appears to focus on. It is often associated with ideas such as avoiding challenge and avoiding putting people at risk. Alternatively, there is psychological wellbeing. This is driven from older traditions of motivation and satisfaction (for example, Maslow and Hertzberg). Here we are concerned with self-actualization and with being a fully functioning person, accepting risk, meeting challenge and understanding that hard work can produce reward and be its own reward. In addition, with any move forward the risk of failure cannot be far away. Rather than use the term 'happiness' we can use a related term – 'contentment'.

This approach is supported by an article in the UK *Sunday Times*. A head hunter described himself as possessing awesome power. He said that he often approached people who appeared to be perfectly happy in their roles. They earned a good salary (say £100,000 a year), had a good package and enjoyed status and authority. All he had to say was, 'I can get you double your present salary, a bigger office and a better car' and he could often create instant unhappiness. But nothing had actually changed for the individual. He or she was instantly dissatisfied with his or her situation. The same

TABLE 23.1 Contentment and happiness compared

Component	Contentment Self-actualization Hard Working Culture	Happiness X Factor Culture
Competence – compared to others	Self-confidence in abilities in being able to express ideas	What you think will make you happy won't always make you happy
Growth	Commitment – determination to achieve	
Self-regulation	Control	
Self-acceptance	Confidence	Hedonic treadmill – often running just to stand still
Positive relationships with others	Interpersonal confidence	
	These are all the components of mental toughness!	

situation that 10 minutes before had provided 'happiness' now produced a state of 'unhappiness'. He pointed out that if the person was truly content and in control of his or her life this couldn't happen most of the time.

It's useful to take a philosophical perspective when looking at these concepts. A philosopher will say that happiness is not a proper goal for humans. Happiness is just an emotion, a transitory feeling, not an adequate purpose for a life. They suggest that it is infantile to expect to feel happy. Your life's work should be something more enduring – like contentment or fulfilment of your potential or self-actualization.

So if we construct a checklist of the components that create lasting well being we can compare and contrast the two ideologies as shown in Table 23.1. The upshot is that we think that you can't make people happier in any meaningful way, but perhaps you can make people more content. Contentment is just as aspirational.

Mental toughness is about opening doors to opportunity and contentment and then having the psychological equipment to go through them.

Relaxation: A physiotherapist's perspective

24

ANGELA CLOUGH, MCSP, MSC, DIPAAPP (SPORT), FSOM

There are many physiotherapeutic approaches to relaxation. This chapter will first focus on the method widely used and taught by physiotherapists: the physiological relaxation technique described by Laura Mitchell (Mitchell, 1977, 1990). Her textbook has been reprinted five times and the latest edition was 1990. It is well-validated, safe and effective. It is the method of relaxation most commonly utilized by physiotherapists (Salt and Kerr, 1997) in the United Kingdom for the management of stress is the physiological relaxation. It is hoped this chapter will see a new audience benefitting from this approach to relaxation. Other techniques will also be described. These techniques all have their place as well. Their main advantage is that they are quicker.

I was fortunate to meet the physiotherapist Laura Mitchell when I was an undergraduate student myself in the early 1980s. Laura was an inspiring teacher. Her approach was well received by those she taught and it has become my personal favourite approach to teaching a versatile method of relaxation to a variety of clients.

The first time I used the approach in a clinical setting, post-graduation, was with some of the first liver transplant patients in Leeds. Patients appreciated their traditional respiratory physiotherapeutic care being enhanced by the Laura Mitchell method of relaxation, reporting a positive response to their wellbeing, and appreciated learning a skill to make them feel less tense and less stressed. Although they were self-reported, subjective comments made by patients, prior to the accepted present-day focus on evidence-based practice, those patients' positive comments have stayed with me as a clinician and now as a university lecturer of some long standing.

Over the years I have successfully used the approach with patients with asthma, chronic pain and low back pain. I have utilized it widely in a sporting context with a variety of top-level athletes and particularly successfully in rugby league players as part of training and enhancement of wellbeing. I teach the approach to all my undergraduate honours degree students as a technique to add to their 'toolkit' in dealing with their own exam stress as well as being a skill for the students to practise and utilize with future clients. Physiotherapy, sports rehabilitation and psychology undergraduate students have benefited from an appreciation of learning the skill of the Laura Mitchell physiological approach to relaxation and incorporating it into their own lives and those of clients they deal with.

Mitchell (1977) stated that the technique brings about postural realignment by reversing stress-related posture, termed as 'the punching position'. This position is commonly adopted whilst sitting slouched working for long periods at a computer. The poor postural position tends to include a' poking chin' posture of the head, a clenched jaw, rounded shoulders, bent elbows on crossed legs. The overall position is very 'flexed', often mimicking the foetal position of a growing baby in the womb. The 'punching position' is thought to increase muscle tension and as a consequence influences the nervous and endocrine system. This releases epinephrine and norepinephrine, which if sustained may enlarge adrenal and lymphatic glands, eventually resulting in physical illness and even being a contributing factor to death.

The brain does not understand the word 'relax'. 'Relax' conveys no definitive information to produce muscle and change in body position. It needs appreciating positions of tension, then to contrast this sensation by appreciating the new position of ease by a series of controlled instructions to muscle groups. Exact, clear orders are required as that is what the human body is used to receiving and acting upon.

Learning the technique

There are six important factors that are key to successful mastery of the Laura Mitchell method of physiological relaxation:

1 The brain must be given a definite 'order' – a clear, descriptive word and action that it recognizes will produce work.

2 The 'order' Mitchell chose to instruct each joint will produce relaxation in the tense group of muscles if the client performs the movement *exactly* as indicated by the words. When instructed to 'Pull your shoulders towards your feet'. The action is 'pull' *not* 'drop'. Only an active voluntary activity will produce the reciprocal relaxation in the muscle group opposite to the 'working' muscle group.

3 When instructed to 'stop', it must mean just that. The client must stop moving the part. It is essential that the therapist does *not*

try to substitute the word 'relax' for 'stop'. Clients understand 'stop moving', so utilize that instruction and correct any misunderstandings early in the mastery of this relaxation method.

4   Clients are instructed to be 'aware' of or to register the feeling of the new position, to focus on this new position of ease. It requires concentration and repetitive practice. Often it is useful to give clients the analogy of learning to play an instrument or driving a car. They require concentration and practice to become a consolidated skill. The Laura Mitchell method of physiological relaxation requires that same dedicated practice to become skilled at it and to reap the benefits from it.

5   Clients must be reminded that they will be training themselves in both *joint* and *skin* consciousness and *not* muscle consciousness as that is the way the human body works. There are *no* nerves that recognize muscle tension connecting with the brain. The client should be made aware of that so that they are educated to not waste time trying to feel it. The client will instead be focusing upon the millions of sensory messages that a conscious brain is constantly receiving from human joints and skin as muscles change their position.

6   It is important to train the conscious brain to discriminate sensations that have always been received but which the client may not have been previously aware of before being told about them and instructed on how to focus upon them.

A systematic approach

It is vital to utilize a systematic approach to ensure effectiveness of the technique. Clients are required to consider:

- if they are working with a reader as a partner, or alone;
- the room;
- the starting positions;
- the order of the instructions;
- the use of additional skills – diaphragmatic breathing, visualization, use of background music.

Working with a reader as a partner

If the client is working with a partner to read out the orders, there are some useful tips to enhance the effectiveness:

- Partner to use a clear but ordinary voice.
- Select the partner carefully; it is essential the partner considers it as important as the client and has an understanding of the reasoning and principles behind the technique.

- Avoid the temptation to add bits.
- Partner to follow the timing of the client.
- Partner to sit as far away as is practicable so as not to interfere with what the client is doing.
- As soon as the orders have been memorized it is advisable to dispense with the use of a reader as a partner.

Working alone

If the client is confident with the principles of the approach he or she may prefer to work alone and to memorize all the orders from the outset, the orders for each body part, or to record it.

The room

It is recommended that the room used is at a comfortably warm temperature. The reason for this is that the human body loses heat as muscles relax. It is not practical to have a room with absolute silence as it would make it impractical to incorporate the approach into busy lifestyles.

The starting positions

The client may choose from three starting positions: A, B or C.

Position A

The client lies on his or her back on a mat or carpeted floor. If this position is comfortable for the client it is probably the best starting position to use. One pillow to support the client's head. Ideally, the legs should be uncrossed and the hands resting either on the client's own tummy or thighs. Some clients find it helpful to have additional pillows: one under the knees, one under each upper arm. Other client may find them unnecessary.

Position B

Client to sit on a firm chair at a table, as an alternative to position A if it is not possible due to either heart or breathing problems. Client to sit well back in the chair for good support for the thighs. It is essential that the feet are supported flat on the floor. Two pillows on the table is normally sufficient but as many pillows as the client wishes may be utilized to raise the height in order to position the arms and head comfortably.

Position C

An additional alternative position that clients with more severe respiratory problems may find useful is sitting upright in a supportive high-back chair with arms on the chair, often favoured by the elderly or infirm. Ideally the back of the chair should be high enough to rest the head against.

FIGURE 24.1 Position A

FIGURE 24.2 Position B

FIGURE 24.3 Position C

The client is advised to sit well back in the chair so the back is supported and the feet are resting on the floor. The arms of the chair support the forearms and the hands, and should ideally be broad and long enough to support outstretched fingers.

The order of the instructions

Orders to the arms

Shoulders. The order is 'Pull your shoulders down towards your feet.'
   Elbows. The order is 'Elbows out and open.'
   This can be done in position A, B or C.

Hands. The order is 'Reach your fingers out...'

Orders to the legs

Hips. The order is, 'Let your feet roll outwards' (this will result in your hips rolling outwards).
   Feet and ankles. The order is 'Push your feet down, away from your face.'

FIGURE 24.4 Shoulders

FIGURE 24.5 Hands, 1

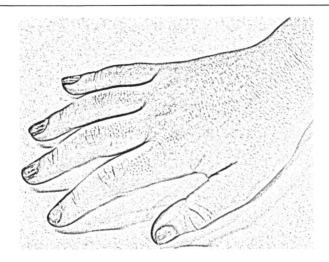

Orders to the body

The order is 'Push your body into the support'.

Orders to the head

The order is 'Push your head into the support'.

Orders to the face

The order is 'Drag your jaw downwards.' If the eyes remain open, add the order 'close your eyes'.

FIGURE 24.6 Hands, 2

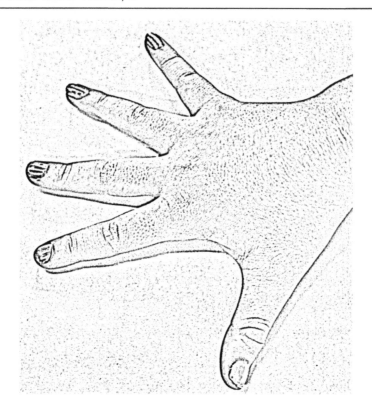

FIGURE 24.7 Hands, 3

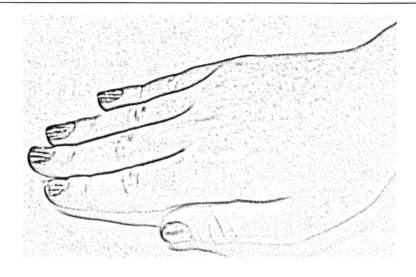

FIGURE 24.8 Hips

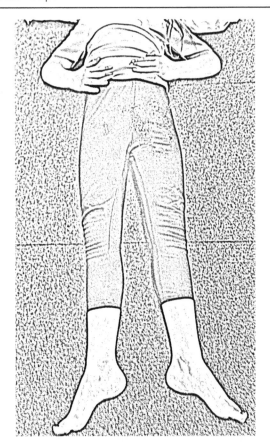

The use of additional skills

Other relaxation strategies can also be extremely helpful and useful in managing stress, tension and anxiety. The relaxation techniques described below can be used anywhere and definitely become easier with practice. Ultimately they help you to cope more effectively with stressors and challenges. It is important that you put relaxation at the centre of your day and utilize the techniques that work for you!

Diaphragmatic breathing

Diaphragmatic breathing, sometimes known as stomach breathing, has a long history. More recently Mitchell (1977, 1990) included breathing techniques to complement the effectiveness of relaxation. Bell and Saltikov (2000) investigated the effectiveness of Mitchell's technique including diaphragmatic breathing compared with diaphragmatic breathing alone and lying supine (on the back). They found that diaphragmatic breathing with and without

FIGURE 24.9 Feet and ankles

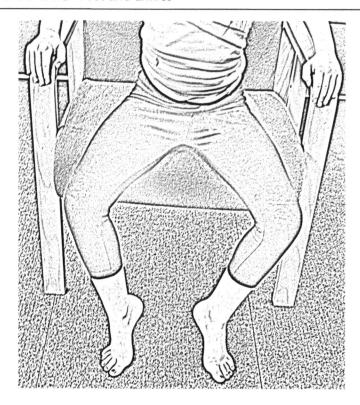

Mitchell's relaxation technique significantly reduced heart rate. Peddicord (1991) suggested that breathing techniques such as diaphragmatic breathing could be used alone for stress reduction and need not be incorporated into a more generalized relaxation technique to elicit the relaxation response.

Diaphragmatic breathing exerts its effects on the cardiovascular system in two ways. One mechanism is due to stimulation of the vagus nerve, resulting in parasympathetic dominance and therefore reduction in heart rate and stress. The second mechanism occurs during the inspiratory stage of diaphragmatic breathing, where increases in thoracic volume result in a flattened diaphragm. This causes an increase in the intra-abdominal pressure and compresses abdominal veins, increasing venous blood flow towards the heart. As a result the improved venous return increases stroke volume causing a reduction in heart rate to maintain cardiac output at an appropriate level.

A quick guide to diaphragm breathing   When new to the technique it is probably best to do it lying down. It is important that your head is fully supported and shoulders relaxed. You may find it comfortable to use two pillows, one under the shoulder blades and a second one in a 'butterfly'

Shortened version of the Laura Mitchell technique

Upper limb

Shoulders

Order – pull your shoulders down toward your feet. *Stop.*

Results – feel your shoulders are now further away from your ears. Your neck may feel more elongated.

Hands

Order – reach out with your fingers and thumb. *Stop.*

Results – appreciate the stretch, elongation and increased space between your fingers during the movement and the heavy position of ease when resting back on the supporting surface.

Lower limb

Hips

Order – turn your hips outward. *Stop.*

Results – feel your thighs roll outward and kneecaps facing outward from the body.

Feet

Order – push your feet away from your face. *Stop.*

Results – feel the new position of ease. Appreciate the heaviness.

Trunk/Head

Trunk

Order – push your back into the supporting surface. *Stop.*

Results – feel the contact of your body on the support.

Head

Order – push your head into the supporting surface. *Stop.*

Results – feel the contact at your head on the supporting pillows.

Overview

Appreciate the supporting surface under the head, back, arms, thighs, calves and heels. Appreciate the new supported position of ease.

Focus on breathing control, on the passive component of breathing out and pause before you breathe in again.

shape to cradle and support the curve of the neck. If it is more comfortable you may also use a pillow under your knees. This takes the stretch of the abdominal muscles.

Place a hand (in a light 'fist') at the end of the sternum (the midline bone that joins the ribs). Gently breathe in through your nose and out through the mouth. Focus on letting the air coming in around the lower ribs, feel your stomach rise gently against your fist. Breathe deeply and regularly.

After practice it is quite easy to modify this technique to other positions so that it may be incorporated into every day. An alternative position is sitting with the shoulders relaxed and forearms supported on a couple of pillows to support the weight of the arms and enable the shoulders to relax.

Controlled breathing

Most of us only use between 10 and 20 per cent of our full breathing capacity. By learning to breathe properly you can begin to feel less fatigued, less overwhelmed by your thoughts and more able to cope with each new challenge. You will also become more optimistic as you learn to cope better:

- When done properly it can relieve anxiety, improve circulation, concentration and digestion and increase energy.
- It is bigger, stronger, deeper and more rhythmic than typical shallow breaths.
- Once you gain control of your breathing in a non-stressful environment, you can more readily call up your relaxation breathing during times of stress.

Breathing exercise

1 Take a deep breath. Exhale fully and completely.
2 Inhale again whilst mentally counting 1 to 4.
3 Hold your breath, and count from 1 to 4.
4 Slowly count from 1 to 8 while exhaling fully.
5 Repeat the sequence four times.

Directed relaxation (sometimes known as self-hypnosis or deep relaxation)

Directed relaxation is the process of directing yourself into a deep state of relaxation and suggestibility. Similar to classical hypnosis, this method allows you to 'programme' your unconscious mind with suggestions to help you experience fewer stress symptoms, sleep better, stop smoking, or to achieve other goals or improvements in your lifestyle.

In this state of relaxation you are fully aware of what is going on, have a focused frame of mind and are in complete control at all times. Directed relaxation increases our 'suggestibility'. Suggestions should be decided upon before you start. They should be short but visual suggestions are most effective – 'see' what you want to achieve. Alternatively you could embed the idea of being relaxed upon hearing or thinking a certain word.

Sarnoff Squeeze

The purpose of the Sarnoff Squeeze is to block the body's production of noradrenalin or epinephrine, the body's fear-producing chemicals in your system. This is a simple preventative tool against feeling nervous, ideally suited before delivering presentations:

1 Sit on a straight-backed chair, keeping your back straight, but not rigid.
2 Lean forward slightly while keeping your back straight.
3 Put your hands together in front of you with your fingertips pointing up and push.
4 Say 'sssss' as if you were a snake or a leak in your car tyre.
5 As you exhale while saying 'ssss', contract those muscles located right where your ribs begin to spread apart.
6 Be aware of the muscle tightness under your ribcage while you exhale (this should feel like tightening a corset).
7 Relax the muscles at the end of your exhalation, and then inhale gently.
8 When you master the Sarnoff Squeeze, you will be able to tighten those muscles at will without having to sit in a chair and actually push your hands against each other.

Ear tap

To release tension in various parts of the body, tap the skin in front, above and behind the ear. This simulates an area rich in acupressure points.

Smile and laugh

Strange as it may seem, smiling and laughing trigger chemicals in your body that make you feel better:

1 Take a moderate breath and smile as you exhale.
2 Feel the corners of your mouth go up and feel the relaxation in your forehead.
3 Repeat 10 times or until you can't help but chuckle.

The role of fitness

The evidence shows physical development and physical challenge can lead to psychological development. Originally demonstrated by a Canadian psychologist called Dienstbier, this was confirmed in some widely publicized work by Dr Peter Clough and colleagues in 2005. Doing things that stretch you physically has a positive impact on an individual's mental toughness. Furthermore it seems that exercise and physical activity that gently stretch you appear to work best for most people. Big stretches can be counterproductive and can achieve the opposite effect.

However, it is also true that the more mentally tough you are the more likely you are to maintain exercise and to challenge yourself physically. To get yourself going you may need to use positive thinking, goal setting and visualization. For some this could be highly structured such as joining a gym or some form of classes such as yoga, swimming or running, or opting to do a sponsored 15-kilometre walk. For others it could be less formal. Good examples include setting targets to walk to the summit of a hill or small mountain, to run a half marathon, to clear the garden of weeds or dig over a patch of ground and replant it, or to redecorate some or all of your home.

The essence here is to do something physical that requires some time and effort to complete and which you will find satisfying when completed. When achieved there is a double bonus: you have done something that develops your feeling of control (you can do it), commitment (you can set targets and achieve them), challenge (you can see challenges as opportunities) and confidence (you can persevere); and your mental toughness enables you to maintain fitness and health more easily. This is a significant factor in enabling you to deal with the stress and pressures of everyday life as well as developing your mental toughness.

The role of diet

There are two sets of considerations here. First, there is some evidence to show that eating a healthier, more balanced diet enables you to maintain the right weight and to achieve better physiological performance. Athletes demonstrate that all the time. It is also true that the more mentally tough you are the more likely you are to be disciplined about what you eat. There is scope for a 'virtuous circle' here. The opposite will also be true. We often see people respond to stress and pressure with comfort eating, which soon has its impact on the physical wellbeing of the individual.

Secondly, there is no such thing as a super food or a particular nutrient that creates mental health and wellbeing, but there is some evidence that combinations of some types of food can promote good mental health. These can be correlated with improved memory, better attentional control and better reasoning abilities – leading to better performance. These appear to include polyunsaturated fats (especially Omega 3), minerals (such as zinc, magnesium and iron) and vitamins (vitamins B, C and E as well as folic acid).

Biofeedback

Biofeedback is a technique in which people are trained to improve their health by using signals from their own bodies. These techniques can be very effective, especially for those people who find it difficult to fully get to grips with the more standard approaches. For example, individuals who are particularly anxious often find it difficult to 'quieten their mind'. The negative thoughts just pop up. Biofeedback allows the individual to concentrate on something external to themselves and thus reduces the 'psychological intensity' of the relaxation programme. In many ways the Laura Mitchell method and biofeedback share a common core: they rely on physiology to drive relaxation.

There are two 'classic' biofeedback approaches: Galvanic Skin Response (GSR) and monitoring brain activity. The most common form of this technological approach uses GSR. This refers to the ability of the skin to conduct electricity. A number of instruments are able to measure this. They pass tiny electrical charges around the body and measure their speed of return. These simple machines can be very useful, especially when working away from the laboratory. The exact mechanism by which GSR works is unclear. McCleary (2007) carried out a review of 60 years of work on GSRs and described three principal theories that purport to account for the phenomenon:

1 Muscular activity – GSR is the direct display of bio-electric changes in muscle.

2 Vascular changes – GSR is the electrical activity attendant on vasodilatation or vasoconstriction.

3 Secretory changes – GSR is the pre-secretory electrical activity of the sweat glands.

He reported that the third explanation was the most likely, but the evidence is not definitive.

A more modern approach is to monitor brain activity directly. Even 10 years ago this would have involved a massive and prohibitive cost. Recent advances in sensor technology allow this approach to be available to everyone.

AQR/Hull University make extensive use of this applied work, especially in their one-to-one sessions. Two different but related technologies are used. The first is Mindball, which is basically a table with a small ball on it. Individuals move the ball by the 'power of their mind'. What this means in reality is that the more relaxed and focused they are the more they can move the ball. With Mindball you can set up a direct competition, allowing individuals to learn how to stay in the zone when under real and tangible pressure. We have recently started using headsets designed to work with computers rather than a physical device. These are much more cost-effective and are a lot easier to transport and use. We have used them in professional sports, the classroom and for managers in industry.

The devices use complex formulae to combine the various waves measured in the brain to produce simple, interpretable output. In general, they rely on four types of wave:

Alpha – awake, non-focused, relaxed.

Beta – alert, focused and problem solving.

Theta – visual imagery and light sleep.

Delta – deep restful sleep.

It is the combination of alpha and beta states that produces the ideal performance state – *relaxed concentration.*

The main advantage of using biofeedback is that it allows us to train more complex states. It's not simply about getting someone to relax or to concentrate. The end goal is to get them to do both at the same time!

Applying directed relaxation

This is a very effective technique but requires a degree of practice to be able to apply it properly and achieve the desired benefits. Basic directed relaxation is applied in five stages, as follows.

1. Preparation

Make sure you won't fall asleep.

Make sure you won't be disturbed and there are no unwelcome background noises.

It is important to write yourself a schedule of when you are going to practise.

Work out and memorize your suggestions.

2. Relaxation

Get your mind to slow down.

Relax your muscles, feel the tension drain out of you.

Progressive muscular relaxation is a good technique to adopt at this stage of self-hypnosis.

Don't rush.

3. Deepening procedures

Don't wait for this to happen, because if you do it won't. It will distract you.

This stage does take practice. Some will find this stage easier than others. Be patient.

Counting down from 100 or the 'swinging watch' techniques can help at this stage.

Don't count out loud.

4. Suggestion application

Suggestions should be worked out and memorized in advance.

Try to crystallize these suggestions into short phrases or a word, such as 'I am calm and relaxed.'

You could engage in a monologue but make sure you use 'I' rather than 'you'.

Image suggestion is most effective – see what you want to achieve.

5. Termination

Don't just open your eyes.

Think to yourself that you are going to be fully alert and awake after you count to three.

When finished don't stand up suddenly. Periods of deep relaxation can lower blood pressure and any sudden movements may cause faintness or dizziness.

Attentional control

25

DR DAVID MARCHANT

Understanding attentional control

If there is one factor that underpins people's ability to perform at their best, whatever their occupation, whatever the situation, it is their ability to focus and control their focus of attention effectively.

Professor Aidan Moran from University College Dublin defines concentration as our capacity to direct our mental effort in the face of distractions. Attentional control is something that is well understood in sports, where most of the important and valuable research has taken place. But it is just as important and valuable in almost every other activity in which people are engaged. Yet it remains, until now, one of the most underdeveloped areas for application in the occupational and educational worlds.

For the athlete the ability to focus (avoid distraction) is vital and many psychological interventions are aimed at allowing him or her to focus better and for longer. Typically, for example in soccer, many individuals and teams emerge as winners because they have managed to maintain concentration until the final whistle, the end of the game. Losers are often those whose concentration wavers as they tire.

Similarly penalty takers in soccer or place kickers in rugby are generally more successful if they can block out unwanted distractions such as the behaviour of opponents, the barracking of the crowd and even the (unhelpful) advice from teammates. They focus their attention, albeit for a short period of time, on the one thing that matters – a good contact between the boot and the ball. Exactly the same applies in work, in play and in education.

It is variously estimated that the average attention span of a young person in the UK at the start of the 21st century may be as short as 7–8 minutes.

The estimates 20 years earlier were in the order of 10–12 minutes. It is hypothesized that the advent of new technology and the speed at which anyone can access information may be a causal factor here.

A study at Exeter University several years ago confirmed what many instinctively understood. When you are interrupted whilst carrying out a piece of mental activity (studying, writing, thinking, etc) or you break off to do something else, when you return the original activity, you do not return at the point you left. You have to retrace your steps to some extent and often redo what you have already done before making fresh progress with that mental activity. In fact each time you stop you run the risk of losing up to 30 per cent of the mental work you have just done!

Given that mental activity is stressful in its own right, this simply adds another level of stressor to an already stress-laden activity. The suggestion therefore is that, if we can improve attention span, we can carry out activities that involve some mental component (including creative work) more effectively, more efficiently and much less stressfully.

In education this would apply to study, revision and essay/dissertation writing. In the workplace this would apply to carrying out intricate work, high-quality work, report writing, preparing for important meetings and conferences, etc. In each of these areas the ability to focus and to do so for as long as possible is a clear advantage and brings significant benefits.

Recent research in the United States shows that it is possible to improve attention span fairly easily to 45 minutes or more and in many cases to two hours. Achieving this makes most mental activity much easier to accomplish. It is suggested that there is a need for a (short) break between sustained periods of focus to provide some opportunity to 'refresh' the mind.

Attentional control and mental toughness

When we consider focus and mental toughness, it is a variable that is intricately linked to each of the main components of mental toughness. Mentally tough people can effectively focus their attention under pressure (challenge), refocus their attention in the face of distraction (control), allocate attention to relevant tasks to achieve success (confidence) and know what their attention should be directed to in line with goal intentions (commitment).

Indeed, research has highlighted that mentally tough individuals are aware of what to focus on, particularly when under pressure. For example, research by Stephen Bull and colleagues from the Sport Psychology Support team for the England and Wales Cricket Board showed that the in-performance confidence of mentally tough individuals was underpinned by a controlled self-focus. That is, these individuals were able to focus on their own needs to ensure that effective performance was supported. Furthermore, these researchers showed that concentration of the mentally tough during the task is characterized by an awareness of the relevant information on which they must focus.

This chapter will initially look to scientific research and findings from sport and exercise psychology to highlight key skills and techniques necessary for optimal focus. In particular, how can we deal with attentional problems such as: not focusing on the right things, being unable to maintain focus, and distractions? Importantly, it is worth noting that research consistently shows that individuals are not necessarily born with the ability to effectively focus, but that these skills are developed over time through experience and training. Then the reader will be introduced to some very accessible and highly effective tools and techniques for improving attentional control.

Practice

Our ability to focus effectively improves with practice, but this is not necessarily a simple relationship. It appears that practising to concentrate may not always facilitate effective concentration. For example, research by Iain Greenlees and colleagues at Chichester University assessed the utility of a concentration exercise commonly used to improve individuals' ability to concentrate.

Male soccer players were randomly allocated to a nine-week training programme or a control group. In the training programme, the soccer players completed a concentration grid exercise at least five times a week. This activity involves scanning a 10-by-10 block grid of two digit numbers ranging from 00 to 99 whilst crossing out as many consecutive numbers in a sequence starting from 00 in one minute. Although this task is commonly used to improve concentration, these researchers showed that training using the concentration grid did not improve ability to concentrate as assessed by various measures (eg, speed and accuracy on a visual search task). This is one of the few studies that has tried to utilize the scientific method to establish the usefulness of concentration interventions. It is clear that the jury is still out.

So, how can practice help with focus? When we practise tasks, whether this is learning a sports skill, driving a car, or mental arithmetic, their attentional demands reduce. That is, the amount of attentional resources we have to allocate to them is less, and we can then allocate these to other things. Think about how hard it was to concentrate on all the steps involved in driving when you were first learning. Then, with practice, these skills became more automatic, and required less of our mental effort or focus.

Such changes have been observed in brain activation research. Research by Dan Landers and colleagues at Arizona State University showed that novice archers changed their brain activation patterns from the start to end of a 15-week training scheme. As these novices improved their skills through practice, so their brain activation patterns more closely resembled those of experienced archers. Specifically, the activation of their left hemisphere increased, which the authors noted reflected changes in attentional allocation.

So, it seems that for us to improve our focus, we must practise those tasks that we are looking to perform.

But, does practice need to be physical or mental? It appears that both are effective. Physically practising something assists in the learning process, which leads to improved automaticity and improved attentional allocation. The focus moves from being on step-by-step components of a task (slow and effortful focus) to the outcome of the task (fast and effective focus). As such, deliberate practice is essential if individuals are to be able to effectively focus their attention on relevant information whilst performing a task. Furthermore, increased expertise allows individuals to make quicker judgements and rely on 'gut-instinct' – an approach that is often effective and does not demand conscious focus.

Practice that closely resembles the task being prepared for assists the individual in dealing with distractions in the environment and in identifying relevant information to focus upon. However, mental practice can also help individuals develop skills and their concentration. Appropriate visualization can help identify what they need to be focusing on when it comes to perform. Visualizing performances or tasks can assist learning, and it provides a situation where control over distraction can be practised. Visualizing a task whilst under pressure from distractions (eg, music or noise) can help develop the ability to focus in the face of such distractions.

Why do routines help?

Rituals and routines are as much part of everyday life as they are part of sport. And research consistently shows that effective pre- and during-task routines help improve concentration during tasks through drawing attention to task-relevant information and away from distractions.

Routines help us to stay organized before and during tasks, without which our attention is free to wander in the run-up to important events or during tasks. Identifying routines for effective task completion is an important skill of the mentally tough individual, as such routines are often highly personalized and specific to the task at hand. Routines become even more important when under pressure or when attentional focus has lapsed.

People often find it difficult to refocus their attention after being distracted or after a break. Developing effective refocusing routines can assist in getting attention back to relevant information. Such refocusing routines involve people identifying what they need to achieve in their next period of activity. Effective routines involve imagery and 'focus-words' that prompt the individual to identify relevant information to focus upon, for which an appreciation of outcomes and goals is important.

The power of goals

Focusing on what you are trying to do, rather than on how you are trying to do it, can help keep attention focused on relevant information.

Research conducted at Edge Hill University (by Dr David Marchant) has shown consistently that when individuals focus their attention onto the outcome of a task they perform better than when they focus their attention onto the specific aspects and/or movements involved with that task. Such benefits have been observed for fine motor skill control (eg, dart throwing) as well as force production and endurance. It seems that when we focus our attention on the step-by-step components of a task, our attentional resources are significantly taken up. This leads to slower processes and more opportunity for error. It can also result in fewer attentional resources being free to process other vital information. Focusing on the outcome of a task is associated with more effective attentional allocation, leaving attention free to process other information that will be vital to success.

In a similar manner, it is difficult to focus our attention if we do not know what our goal is. Setting goals is critical to effectively focusing attention as they influence where we will direct our attention whilst approaching and performing tasks. A goal sets us up for looking for specific information that will support our progress. If an individual starts a day with an effective goal in mind, his or her attention will be focused on information to work on that task. Without an effective goal, attention is free to wander as it is not set to seek specific information and ignore irrelevant information.

Minimizing distractions

During our daily life we face many distractions. In sport and exercise psychology, these have often been discussed as being either internal (eg, self-doubts or anxiety) or external (eg, noise or visual distractions).

Managing distractions is critical to maintaining focus, in particular when life is full of many potential distractions. Research by Terry Orlick and John Partington from the Universities of Ottowa and Carelton demonstrated that an ability to control and reduce distractibility was a critical characteristic of successful Canadian Olympic athletes. In particular, they identified that these athletes had strategies in place for remaining focused in the face of distraction, and to refocus when things hadn't gone well. Success was linked to the ability to stay focused on the task at hand, and not be distracted by unrelated information. Two issues are important to consider here.

First, effort should be made to reduce the opportunity for distraction. Remove distractions from your environment that distract from the task at hand, or remove yourself from distracting environments. Recognize what those distractions are. Secondly, some distractions cannot be removed or are intrinsically linked to the task being carried out, so plan for potential distractions. Being aware of the distractions you will face will help you control them. Plan for how you will deal with them, how you will approach the task, and be organized in your approach to the task to be completed.

Finally, a key strategy for effective focus in the face of distractions is to recognize when one has been distracted. Knowing what distracts you can help you control those distractions. For example, e-mail is a common distraction, and recognizing this allows individuals to develop strategies to control this. Using a personal journal can help identify when we have become distracted on tasks through regular reflection on task progress and experiences.

The use of technology

For many, technology provides many distractions. The internet and e-mail both support and detract from everyday work and tasks through constant availability of information. However, modern technology allows for many opportunities to develop concentration and focus.

Many computer games require constant directed mental focus in the face of distractions, and as such can be used to develop an appreciation of prolonged effective focus in addition to distraction control. They may also provide an opportunity to reset focus after prolonged engagement with attentionally demanding tasks.

Managing stress and fatigue

Research has consistently shown that stress leads to a narrowing of attentional focus.

When we perceive that we are under pressure, we are likely to miss important information. Such pressures can be situational (eg, performing an important task whilst under the scrutiny of others) or cumulative (eg, generally stresses of daily life). For example, research conducted by Tracie Rogers and Dan Landers demonstrated that negative life events experienced by athletes induced a narrowing of attentional focus, which put them at a higher risk of injury.

As such, it is important for us to realize that when people experience significant or enduring stressful events their ability to focus effectively is reduced. Recognizing this and looking to manage and cope with stressors are therefore important skills in being able to focus. It is also necessary to recognize that attention is limited in terms of our ability to focus for extended periods of time. Taking breaks in work allows for attentional resources to recover from fatigue. Forcing ourselves to work through fatigue decreases our ability to focus on relevant information and increases the chances of distraction.

The impact of health and fitness

Our ability to focus effectively is intrinsically linked to our physical health. In particular, research has shown that that being physically fit and active can impact upon concentration in two significant ways.

First, those individuals who are active enough that it impacts upon their fitness have been shown to exhibit beneficial effects on their ability to concentrate and control their attention. Secondly, individual sessions of physical activity have been shown to immediately improve our ability to focus and concentrate.

So, taking a physically active break is an effective technique for helping maintain appropriate focus throughout a prolonged task. Making sure we stay physically fit allows us to develop and maintain our attentional capacity throughout our lifespan.

Nine ways to enhance your focus

1 Practise, practise, practise!

2 Use routines – reduce the cognitive load.

3 Set clear and realistic goals – you need to know what you are doing and when you have finished!

4 Minimize distractions.

5 Control technology – don't let it control you!

6 Manage stress and fatigue. If you're stressed or tired you cannot concentrate for long.

7 Work to stay fit and healthy.

8 Take a break – with a degree of physical activity

9 Utilize the tools and techniques described below on a regular basis.

Some simple tips, tools and techniques that work

One of the challenges for developing attentional control compared to many of the other techniques described elsewhere in this book is that they have to be learnt. Other techniques can be taught. One of the best ways to learn something is to use experiential learning. Do something, experience it and practise it until it becomes embedded.

The Stork Stand

Find a spot away from chairs and other hazardous objects. Begin by standing and putting all your weight on one leg. Raise your arms out to the sides at shoulder level, and gradually raise your free leg. Keep that leg just off the ground. Close your eyes and try to maintain your balance.

For most people this becomes easier if they 'empty their mind'. That is, they don't concentrate on not falling over.

Number Grid

A number grid is shown in Figure 25.1. Described earlier in the chapter, this is a 10 x 10 grid which contains, in random order, the 100 numbers from 00 to 99. Create a few of those with different random orders.

FIGURE 25.1 Number grid

24	43	58	90	49	67	89	86	62	50
3	64	76	84	10	52	27	94	8	77
92	45	53	37	29	17	54	42	19	99
81	00	22	57	31	96	39	12	33	20
25	36	65	88	14	2	78	85	47	87
56	13	6	74	48	23	90	73	98	91
60	41	80	5	11	51	68	38	72	83
97	75	34	79	26	46	82	9	63	16
35	44	21	40	1	69	61	7	55	71
4	30	93	66	59	32	18	70	28	15

Set a start time. Mark off in sequence as many consecutive numbers as possible in 90 seconds starting with the number 00. Clearly the person who is able to concentre on this task will achieve a higher score than one who is distracted. Plot repeated scores on a graph. Repeated practice should produce better results.

Stroop Test

There are many versions of this available on the internet. It typically consists of grids containing words that describe a colour. Each of the words is in a different colour, but only one or typically two of the words are in the same colour as that described by the word. (The Nintendo DS Brain Training Software contains Stroop tests amongst other attentional control exercises.)

You are provided with sight of the grid for a limited period of time. The better your ability to focus the better your ability to identify correctly the words that are in the same colour they describe.

Computer games

Whilst new technology is often cited as a cause of reducing attentional control, many computer games are excellent at developing focus, particularly for long periods of time.

Racing games and 'war games' commonly demand high levels of sustained concentration from the user, and consequently with practice the user can often develop a heightened sense of attentional control. The challenge lies in helping people to reflect on this, to make them aware of what it feels like to focus at this level, to recall how they managed to achieve this and to consider how they might transfer this learning to other activities in their lives.

The internet is also a rich source of attentional control exercises; www.luminosity.com is a particularly good site to visit. Many exercises are free of charge but the best do require a small outlay.

FIGURE 25.2 Bop-It

Games

Many everyday games require a degree of concentration to 'beat' your opponent. Many card games require the ability to focus to recall which cards have been played and therefore which cards remain. Card games such as whist, bridge, rummy, etc are good for developing attentional control.

One of the most successful games for developing attentional control is Bop-It (Figure 25.2). This is an electronic game that requires the player to follow four or five oral instructions quickly. If completed within an acceptable time frame the game barks out the next instruction. The game continues until an instruction is either incorrectly carried out or the instruction is carried out too late. The game then calculates how many instructions have been correctly followed and provides this as the score.

It is almost entirely about the ability to focus. The better one's attentional control the higher the score achieved. It is therefore possible to monitor progress in improving attentional control. Commonly players master the game (it is then possible to switch it into a more difficult mode) and learn what the focus experience feels like. The challenge again lies in reflection – awareness of what it feels like to focus at this level, to recall how one managed to achieve this and to consider how one might transfer this learning to other activities in one's life.

The game is particularly useful in large groups. It is extremely noisy and if several players play this at the same time the potential for distraction is very significant. This challenges the player to focus amidst a wide range of distractions – and most do master this.

Interruptions and distractions

Obstacles and distractions are things you notice when you 'take your eye off the ball'. Learning to sustain attention – to concentrate – is extremely important. Learning to still or park the mind enhances concentration.

Attentional control is essentially about maintaining focus. Failure to do this can affect performance and wellbeing in two important and potentially damaging ways. It impacts on commitment, confidence in your abilities and emotional control.

It's one thing to learn how to avoid being distracted by interruptions but it is also useful to minimize the possibility of distraction. When carrying out

Exercise – Minimizing unwanted interruptions

Think of situations where interruptions can cause problems for you
and the ways in which you can minimize interruptions.

important and valuable work, seek to do it in an environment free from interruption – and free from the prospect of interruption. Being distracted and losing focus can significantly affect performance, behaviour and wellbeing.

Conclusions

Briefly highlighted here are important considerations in understanding and developing effective focus. Ultimately, we must appreciate the limits of our ability to focus, but also how we can train and prepare ourselves to focus more effectively. This can range from simple tasks such as removing opportunities for distraction to more effortful processes of deliberate practice and routine development. However, without such efforts, our attention is free to wander. Focus is not a resource to switch on or off: it is always online.

Goal setting

26

Goal setting is widely recognized as an effective means of motivating individuals to achieve some valuable or important purpose. In this context we are talking primarily about individuals developing the ability to set goals for themselves (and perhaps for others too).

Goal setting theory suggests that establishing clear, measurable, achievable goals is an important step in the process of achieving those goals. Goals provide both direction and intensity.

Much of the pioneering work on goal setting has been carried out by Dr Edwin Locke. He found amongst other things that well-constructed goal setting has the ability to act as a mechanism that motivates the individual towards the goal. Locke and Latham (2002) have found four mechanisms through which goal setting can impact on individual performance. Goals appear to motivate by:

1 focusing attention on activities directly relevant to the goal (and away from activities that are not important for the achievement of the goal);

2 serving as an energizer; interestingly Locke found that the more challenging the goal and the more specific it is, the harder the individual will work towards its attainment;

3 affecting commitment;

4 activating cognitive abilities and strategies that allow people to cope with the prevailing situation.

Locke and Latham (1990) originally confirmed the need to set specific and difficult goals and identified three other factors, which have been variously described as the five goals or moderators of goal setting. To motivate, goals must have:

1 Clarity: setting SMART goals. Clarity focuses the individual on the goal.

2 Challenge: identifying challenging goals that are perceived as difficult but achievable opportunities.

3 Commitment: how important is the ultimate goal? Self-efficacy – a belief in the ability to achieve the goals – is closely related to the concepts of control and confidence in abilities in mental toughness. The extent to which promises are made to self and to others is at the heart of commitment in mental toughness.

4 Feedback: particularly whilst on the journey to the goal. Feedback enables a sense of progress and provides the opportunity to flex or adapt as needed.

5 Task complexity. The more complex the task the more difficult it will be to achieve. This needs to be taken into account in both planning and execution. There is a risk that individuals can take on too much without giving themselves a realistic chance of achieving the task.

Ultimately, understanding how goal setting works and how it can be applied helps the individual to be more effective. Our experience in the full spectrum of applications indicates to us that there are three aspects of goal setting that are important:

1 Setting clear, realistic achievable goals – where the SMART or SMARTER process is a good way of achieving this.

2 Dealing with big goals – how do you eat an elephant?

3 Balancing goals.

Important aspects of goal setting

1. SMART(ER) Goals

Setting goals gives meaning and direction as well as fuel and energy to achieve objectives. For goals to be effective they should be SMARTER: This is a seven-letter acronym that describes the key steps in effective goal setting and is shown in Table 26.1. It is often found in the abbreviated original format SMART, which describes the first five steps. Either is effective.

2. Dealing with big goals – eating the elephant

Sometimes we find that we have to achieve something big or significant. Even if we have the time and resources to do it in relative comfort the goal can appear overwhelming. It can appear to be too big a stretch. The challenge is to take these significant goals and turn them into something that is realistic and achievable.

Question: How do you eat an elephant?
Answer: A slice at a time.

TABLE 26.1 SMARTER goals

Specific	You must be able to define them clearly and concisely. The clearer the goal the more effective it is. 'I want to do well at school' is better replaced with 'I want to get four Grade A passes in my A level exams'. It is useful to be equally clear about the benefit (to you or others) of achieving the goal.
Measurable	You must know when you have achieved success and what success will look like. As Henry Ford is reported to have said, 'If it ain't measured, it doesn't get done.' Measures are usually unambiguous and tangible – they remain in sight.
Achievable	Sufficiently challenging but not impossible. Generally the evidence shows that most people make progress by 'gently' stretching themselves. If you overreach yourself this can diminish motivation and failure can be damaging.
Relevant	It should be relevant to the circumstances and have a real impact.
Time bound	There must be a deadline to work towards. To say 'I'll write that report soon' is very different to 'I will write that report by the last day of the month'.
Exciting	They should inspire enthusiasm and commitment. The benefits and impact should be assessed as worthwhile or valuable. The process (the way the goal is achieved) should also provide a source of inspiration or development, for example, the need to learn a new skill.
Reviewable	There must always be provision for reviewing and re-establishing targets to take account of changing circumstances.

The key to achieving big goals is to break the task down into smaller relevant tasks which when completed are clear steps towards the achievement of the big goal. Not unreasonably these intermediate tasks each have SMART goals attached, which we commonly call 'milestones'.

A useful technique that works well is the 2-4-8 Rule. This simply takes a big goal that has to be achieved at some time in the future (say 8 weeks) and work out what you would need to have achieved by the mid-point (4 weeks) if you are to be on track for the big goal. These milestones should now appear to be more achievable.

Then you repeat the exercise to establish what you have to have done by the mid-point (2 weeks away) of this shorter period to be on track for the mid-point and the end goal. Tasks and goals that are achievable in a 2-week time frame should in most cases be eminently achievable:

- Take a large goal or target, eg write a whole new course on leadership in 8 weeks.
- Work out what you must do by the end of 8 weeks if this is to be achieved.
- Work out what you must do by the end of 4 weeks if this is to be achieved.
- Work out what you must do by the end of 2 weeks if this is to be achieved.
- Work on what you must achieve in the next two weeks, which should now be very accessible. The actions will typically be small actions, which are more easily handled.

Review progress every 4 weeks and roll the targets forward for the next 2, 4 and 8 weeks. Ask someone to monitor your review with you to ensure some form of discipline. At any point you can ask:

- Does the 2-week target appear achievable? Are you more confident that you can achieve this target? Do you fell more in control?
- What might stop you achieving each target – have you planned to deal with it? Are there lead times you need to take into account?
- How confident do you feel that you will now hit the big target?
- How can you explain this to others and gain their commitment?

A psychological perspective on goal setting

Goal setting allows an individual to navigate through a complex world. There are many, many forces acting in many directions. By identifying a path an individual can deal with these stressors more effectively.

Locke *et al* (1981) suggest that goal setting works to improve performance in four distinct ways:

1 it causes the individual to focus;
2 it mobilizes effort;
3 it enhances long-term persistence;
4 it promotes new learning strategies.

Most of the research into goal setting has been focused on how to maximize the technique. Much less attention has been paid to the underpinning psychology. What we can say is:

- Goal setting works better for some people. Certain personalities are drawn to it; others find it limiting and stifling. Everyone can benefit – not everyone wants to.
- It reduces anxiety. By allowing an individual to deal more effectively with competing demands, it reduces anxiety. Anxiety is usually a precursor to poor performance.
- Nearly everybody puts things off. Goals help to alleviate this. The reasons for procrastination are many but they probably have their roots in some other complex psychology. This includes self-handicapping (giving yourself an excuse), fear of failure, low self-esteem and attribution distortions.

It is clear that an individual's wellbeing impacts on goal setting, and is in turn impacted upon. Setting appropriate goals is one of the keys aspects of self-development. It forms the bedrock of coaching. By better understanding the mental toughness of an individual you can help him or her become a more effective goal setter. However, you must always bear in mind that poor goal setting is not necessarily a product of poor technique; it could be a symptom of a more deep-seated issue. Failure to resolve this would certainly impact on the goal setting process.

Research using the MTQ48

27

DR LEE CRUST

Introduction

Something that is really important to the 'mental toughness team' at AQR and Hull University is that the model and its associated interventions are based on a robust research foundation. Information about the psychometric properties of the MTQ48 is presented elsewhere in this book. This chapter provides an accessible overview of some of recent research using the questionnaire. The work cited is in peer reviewed journals – the bedrock of scientific investigations – and is mainly carried out by independent research teams with no affiliation to the test designers. The work reported here is primarily sports related; however the MTQ48 is definitely not a sports-specific measure, rather the sports domain offers the controlled and high pressure environment that is needed to test the model.

It is hoped that this chapter makes cutting edge research more accessible to a wider constituency. The readership of academic papers is very narrow, and for those end-users not employed in an academic institution often incurs significant costs. In reality, over-reliance on academic papers can easily disempower the individuals we are trying to help. It is vital that information about tests is in the public domain, and free of charge. Interested readers are encouraged to download the full manual from http://www.aqr.co.uk/html/top_menu/Psychometrics/Products/Downloads/. It is equally important that the test is made available to researchers who wish to carry out there own independent work. This indeed is the model adopted by the developers of the MTQ48. The instrument has been frequently made available to many independent researchers, producing a rich and meaningful data set.

Since the development of the MTQ48 and the MTQ18 (short version), researchers have been more able to objectively measure and quantify mental toughness, and a steady stream of scientific research has been conducted using these questionnaires. This chapter provides an overview of some of that research. These studies have contributed to a greater understanding of what mental toughness is and how it develops. However, while the MTQ48 has been the most frequently used measure of mental toughness in published research, it is important to acknowledge that other mental toughness questionnaires have been developed and used for research purposes.

Prior to the publication of the MTQ48, some researchers used the Psychological Performance Inventory (PPI; Loehr, 1986) to measure mental toughness. However, the PPI has fallen out of favour as it is based on an out-dated view of what mental toughness is, and doesn't measure key components of mental toughness such as control. More recently, Sheard *et al* (2009) produced a 14-item inventory called the Sports Mental Toughness Questionnaire (SMTQ). The SMTQ has been shown to differentiate between higher and lower level sport performers. Sheard *et al* (2009) provide good evidence of how the SMTQ was developed, but the questionnaire has yet to be fully tested by independent researchers and appears less comprehensive than the MTQ48 (Crust and Swann, 2011). Use of the SMTQ outside of athletic populations would not appear appropriate.

Others such as Gucciardi and colleagues (Gucciardi and Gordon, 2009; Gucciardi *et al*, 2009a) have developed questionnaires designed to measure mental toughness in specific sports (eg, cricket and Australian football) and argue that mental toughness exists differently between sports. This position is somewhat difficult to defend given that research has consistently supported the existence of core components of mental toughness across a wide range of sports (Jones *et al*, 2007; Sheard, 2010). Furthermore, mental toughness would also seem to be relevant in other pressurized performance settings outside of sport (business, military, etc).

Testing the MTQ48

Since its development in 2002, thousands of people have completed the MTQ48, which has allowed the questionnaire to be evaluated using a process termed 'psychometric testing'. Developing sound measures of any psychological construct is a long process that involves evaluation using complex statistical procedures. Among other things, a sound questionnaire should be valid, reliable, and have a clear factor structure (ie, subcomponents). 'Validity' refers to whether the questionnaire is measuring what we think it is measuring, while 'reliability' concerns whether it gives a consistent result regardless of when or in what context it is completed. Establishing validity and reliability is considered to be an important ongoing process, but various forms of testing have thus far provided good support for the MTQ48 (see Clough *et al*, 2002; Crust, 2008). One of the most important aspects of any questionnaire is 'internal consistency', or how well the items on the questionnaire relate to each other. The overall internal consistency of the MTQ48 has repeatedly been found to be excellent (eg, Kaiseler *et al*, 2009).

In developing the MTQ48, Clough *et al* (2002) found that mental toughness consisted of six components or factors:

1 challenge, the extent to which individuals see problems as opportunities for self-development;

2 commitment, which reflects deep involvement with whatever one is doing;

3 emotional control – the ability to keep anxieties in check and not reveal emotions to others;

4 life control, which concerns a belief in being influential and not controlled by others;

5 confidence in abilities, which reflects belief in individual qualities with less dependence on external support; and

6 interpersonal confidence, which is about being assertive and less likely to be intimidated in social contexts.

Since the identification of these factors, independent researchers have tested the factor structure of the MTQ48 using a statistical procedure called 'confirmatory factor analysis'. With a large sample of participants, Horsburgh *et al* (2009) provided support for the factor structure proposed by Clough *et al* (2002). Furthermore, the factors identified closely resemble the core components of mental toughness that have been proposed by other mental toughness researchers (ie, Bull *et al*, 2005; Jones *et al*, 2007). Other approaches have made significant contributions to present understanding (ie, Bull *et al*, 2005; Gucciardi *et al*, 2008; Jones *et al*, 2007), but research using the MTQ48 has undoubtedly helped to increase knowledge by allowing mental toughness to be quantified and measured.

Mental toughness and coping

A number of studies have used the MTQ48 to investigate relationships between mental toughness and the ways in which people cope with stress. In a systematic review of coping in sport, Nicholls and Polman (2007: 18) suggested investigating the 'obvious' relationship between mental toughness and coping. Numerous researchers have previously reported the ability to cope effectively when under pressure as being a key component of mental toughness (Bull *et al*, 2005; Jones *et al*, 2002). In a large study of 677 athletes from a variety of sports and different levels of performance, Nicholls *et al* (2008) found significant relationships between mental toughness and the use of coping strategies. Consistent with expectations, mental toughness was found to be associated with more problem- or approach-coping strategies (ie, reducing or eliminating the stressor) such as mental imagery, effort expenditure, thought control, and logical analysis; but less use of avoidance-coping strategies such as distancing, mental distraction or resignation. This finding suggests mentally tough athletes prefer to tackle problems head-on by actively seeking solutions. However, Nicholls *et al* did not address how stressors were viewed by athletes or the effectiveness of coping strategies in relation to mental toughness.

Building on this work, Kaiseler *et al* (2009) used the MTQ48 and assessed stress appraisal, coping, and coping effectiveness in a study where 482 athletes reported how they coped with a self-selected intense stressor experienced within a two-week period. These researchers reported higher levels of mental toughness to be significantly related to experiencing less stress and more control. This finding was consistent with Nicholls *et al* (2008) as higher mental toughness was associated with more problem-focused coping strategies and less emotion-focused (ie, to regulate emotional distress) coping strategies. The results were the first to offer support to the notion that mentally tough athletes cope more effectively. Mentally tough athletes reported greater coping effectiveness when using problem-focused coping strategies as opposed to emotion-focused coping.

Mental toughness and emotional control/reactivity

Numerous theorists have proposed emotional control to be an important part of being mentally tough (Clough *et al*, 2002; Gucciardi, *et al*, 2008; Jones, *et al*, 2007). While research has found mentally tough athletes to use more problem-focused coping as opposed to emotion-focused strategies, this line of research did not rule out the possibility that participants with higher or lower levels of mental toughness experienced more or less intense emotions. Thus the ability to remain relatively unaffected by competition or adversity (Clough *et al*, 2002) might relate to being less emotional rather than using specific coping strategies to maintain control.

To investigate links to emotionality, Crust (2009) had 112 regular sports participants complete the MTQ48 to measure mental toughness and the Affect Intensity Measure (Larsen, 1984) as a measure of typical responses to emotion-provoking stimuli. Previous research (Larsen *et al*, 1987) had shown individuals with high affect intensity tend to engage in more personalizing (ie, absorbed in personal meaning), generalizing (ie, blowing things out of proportion) and selective abstraction (ie, focus on emotional aspects of events). No relationships were found between affect intensity, total mental toughness and the six sub-scales of the MTQ48. Thus there was no evidence to suggest that being able to remain calm and in control under pressure reflects mentally tough athletes being less emotional. It appears that differences in coping strategies are more likely to explain different reactions of athletes with higher or lower mental toughness when facing challenging or pressure situations. This appears to be good news in terms of developing mental toughness as coping strategies can be learnt.

Mental toughness and performance/levels of achievement

Many sports psychologists have suggested or implied relationships between mental toughness and performance although few have objectively tested these relationships. For example, Jones *et al* (2002; 2007) studied mental toughness by interviewing elite/super-elite athletes, and justify their approach on the basis that mental toughness should be related to successful outcomes. However, other psychologists have cautioned against solely focusing on the elite or super-elite as this can be restrictive and potentially misleading (Crust, 2008; Nicholls *et al,* 2009). While having high levels of mental toughness can be an advantage in sport, numerous other characteristics are likely to impact upon whether athletes are more or less successful (ie, physiological and, anatomical factors).

During initial testing of the MTQ48, Clough *et al* (2002) tested differences in performance between participants with higher or lower levels of mental toughness on a cognitive planning task following manipulated feedback. Those with higher levels of mental toughness were found to perform consistently well regardless of the feedback, while participants with lower levels of mental toughness performed much worse following negative feedback. Crust and Clough (2005) used the MTQ48 and found some support for a significant yet relatively small relationship between total mental toughness and performance in an isometric weight-holding task (pain tolerance). Additionally, the sub-scales of control and confidence, but not challenge and commitment, were associated with greater endurance. This outcome is likely to be due to participants believing in themselves and being able to ignore or block out pain.

Using a relatively small sample (n = 107), Crust and Azadi (2010) found athletes of county standard and above reported significantly higher levels of mental toughness than club or university athletes, although the differences were relatively small. In the business domain, researchers have recently evaluated mental toughness across different levels of management.

Not all studies have found differences in performance or standard to be related to mental toughness. In a study assessing the mental toughness of trainee football players in an English Premier League football academy (using the MTQ18) no significant differences were found between players who were retained by the club, or released at the end of the competitive season (Crust *et al,* 2010). However, it is possible that the rather simplistic research design in this study did not capture the complexities of studying mental toughness within such a dynamic environment; this is one area where interviews with key personnel might be useful. More recently, Nicholls *et al* (2009) tested for differences in mental toughness on the basis of achievement level, gender, age, experience and sport types. Specifically, analyses of a large sample of athletes (n = 677) representing international, national, county, club/university and beginner levels revealed no significant differences in mental toughness between different levels of performer.

On the basis of these findings, and others that have used alternative measures of mental toughness (eg, Golby and Sheard, 2004), Nicholls *et al* (2009) concluded that differences in mental toughness between different levels of athletic achievement are minimal or subtle. Such findings might offer support to the proposal of Crust (2008) who suggested mental toughness might best be considered in relative (making the most of one's abilities) rather than absolute terms. Future mental toughness researchers should also give more attention to non-elite athletes and under-represented samples such as athletes with disabilities. Assessing mental toughness in match officials might also provide a useful comparison with athletic samples.

Nicholls *et al* (2009) found men reported significantly higher levels of mental toughness than women in their sample, and that age and experience predicted higher levels of mental toughness. Gender has previously been little considered in mental toughness research and these findings suggest this aspect is in need of much greater attention by future researchers. More recently, Crust and Keegan (2010) also found gender differences in mental toughness with male athletes reporting significantly higher values. With mental toughness found to be related to age, these results appear to offer support to researchers who found experience was a crucial factor in the development of mental toughness (Connaughton *et al*, 2008).

Mental toughness and psychological skills

Although Clough *et al* (2002) and other researchers (Horsburgh *et al*, 2009; Kaiseler *et al*, 2009; Nicholls *et al*, 2008) consider mental toughness to be a personality trait, different views exist and some suggest it is a mindset (Sheard, 2010). Viewing mental toughness as a mindset suggests that changing the way individuals think through psychological skills training could lead to improvements. Indeed, there is some evidence that mental toughness or at least components of mental toughness can be influenced through a systematic mental skills training intervention (Sheard and Golby, 2006; Gucciardi *et al*, 2009b). In terms of developing mental toughness, other researchers who used qualitative methods (interviews), have proposed a more significant role for environmental influences such as upbringing or competitive rivalries with others (Bull *et al*, 2005).

Beyond the work concerning mental toughness and coping, little is known about the relationship between mental toughness and the use of psychological skills. On the basis of previously reported relationships between mental toughness and performance (Crust and Clough, 2005), the use of mental skills and performance (Gould *et al*, 2002) and evidence to suggest mental skills training can influence mental toughness (Gucciardi *et al*, 2009b; Sheard and Golby, 2006), Crust and Azadi (2010) predicted a positive relationship between use of psychological strategies and mental toughness. Mental toughness (as measured by the MTQ48) and use of a number of psychological performance strategies as measured by the Test of Performance

Strategies (TOPS; Thomas *et al*, 1999) were found to be significantly related. Three performance strategies were found to be significantly and positively related to mental toughness in both practice and competition: relaxation strategies, self-talk and emotional control. The small to moderate correlations found by Crust and Azadi appear similar to those reported for mental toughness and coping (Nicholls *et al*, 2008). Perhaps most noteworthy were relationships between the sub-scales of the MTQ48 and the use of psychological strategies. Specifically, commitment was found to be the sub-scale most frequently related to use of psychological strategies, which the authors speculated could reflect being deeply committed to one's chosen sport and thus seeking out alternative ways of enhancing performance. Despite these findings, it should be noted that the results were based on a relatively small sample, and that the TOPS inventory only measures the frequency with which athletes use psychological strategies and not effectiveness.

Mental toughness and personality

Through studying mental toughness in identical and non-identical twins, Horsburgh *et al* (2009) found that mental toughness is influenced by both genetics and features of the environment, and as such behaves, "in the same manner as virtually every personality trait that has ever been investigated in behavioural genetic study." (p. 104). In establishing significant correlations between the MTQ48 and the so-called big five personality factors (extraversion, openness, agreeableness, conscientiousness, and neuroticism) Horsburgh *et al* suggest that mental toughness is strongly influenced by genetics and as such may not be easy to modify. However, these researchers did contend that aspects of mental toughness that showed least hereditability (ie commitment or control) may be easier to strengthen. Horsburgh *et al* support Clough *et al*'s (2002) view of mentally tough individuals having lower anxiety levels, being sociable, outgoing and competitive.

Other studies using the MTQ48/MTQ18

A number of other studies have used the MTQ48. As would be expected, positive psychological constructs such as optimism have been found to be significantly related to mental toughness (Nicholls *et al*, 2008). While investigating the relationships between mental toughness and sports injury rehabilitation, Levy *et al* (2006) found higher levels of mental toughness (as measured by the MTQ18) were significantly related to more positive threat appraisals, greater pain tolerance, and higher levels of attendance at clinic-based sessions. However, the relationship between mental toughness and injury rehabilitation needs to be further explored as the MTQ18 only provides an overview of total mental toughness.

Crust and Azadi (2009) assessed the leadership preferences of mentally tough athletes using the MTQ48, and the Leadership Scale for Sports (Chelladurai and Saleh, 1980). Higher levels of mental toughness were significantly and positively related to a preference for training and instructive behaviours. This result appears consistent with the view that mentally tough athletes focus on the task at hand (Gucciardi *et al*, 2008; Jones, *et al*, 2007). Marchant *et al* (2009) looked at mental toughness and how it related to managerial level. A total of 522 participants working in UK-based organizations completed demographic information and the MTQ. The analysis revealed that mental toughness ratings were higher in more senior positions, and that mental toughness generally increased with age. This suggests that increased exposure to significant life events may have a positive developmental effect on mental toughness and would suggest that mental toughness can be developed through appropriate training programmes.

Finally, Crust and Keegan (2010) used the MTQ48 to measure mental toughness and attitudes to risk-taking in a diverse group of athletes. Significant and positive correlations were found between mental toughness and attitudes to risk-taking although actual behaviour was not measured. This finding offers some support to previous reports of mentally tough cricketers as being prepared to take calculated risks (Bull *et al*, 2005).

Conclusion

A significant amount of research has been produced using the MTQ48. This instrument appears to be a useful tool in assessing mental toughness in both research and applied settings. The MTQ48 is at present the most frequently used measure of mental toughness in sports research but is equally applicable in other performance settings. The body of evidence from studies using the MTQ48 complements rather than competes with other perspectives and approaches to studying mental toughness. There are some limitations since at present the vast majority of studies employing the MTQ48 have simply examined the correlates of mental toughness. While there are some experimental studies, further experimental work is necessary to understand how thoughts, feelings and behaviours differ between individuals with higher or lower levels of mental toughness. This experimental research programme is currently underway at Hull University and is beginning to produce some very interesting results.

A summary and thoughts about 'what's next?'

28

At the start of the book we described our work for the past 15 years as a journey. It remains just that in many ways. We are very confident that there now exists a concept, and an assessment tool that goes with it, which is extremely valuable in a very wide range of applications. We hope the reader agrees. But we are also acutely aware that the journey continues and there is much more that is exciting, interesting and valuable on the horizon, almost all of which has been provoked by the growing band of people who work with us around the world.

We meet many who say, 'Nice idea... but I need some specific evidence before I'll think of using it in my area.' It can lead to a frustrating 'chicken and the egg' dilemma. It's an understandable position for potential end-users. Fortunately we also meet many who take the time to understand what the model and the measure offer and take the view, 'I have "got" this idea and I am pretty sure I know how I can make it work in my world.' These people have been invaluable to us. Some of them are contributors to this book.

Writing the book has also been extremely valuable for us. Until we took the time to do this we hadn't, for a long time, sat down and reflected on the 'roller-coaster' journey and where it was heading. The process has helped both of us to develop a comprehensive big picture of where we are and where new interests are emerging. Having done this we have been pleasantly surprised by the amount of evidence emerging for mental toughness and its application both in academic research and in practical applications in the world we live in.

In consequence we will bring this chapter of the story to a conclusion by focusing on three themes: the big picture – a global perspective; a psychological perspective – how is this resonating with what is happening elsewhere in psychology and, for the practitioner, what next?

A global perspective

Between us, we now deliver more than 80 presentations a year on mental toughness around the globe. This too is increasing exponentially. We try to make them as participative as possible and encourage attendees to ask questions and contribute to the discussion.

Two questions emerge on almost every occasion: 'Is mental toughness more important now than ever before because life is more stressful now than ever before?' and, 'Are we suggesting that everyone should become mentally tough – what about the mentally sensitive?' These are very good questions because they provoke thinking about mental toughness and where it fits into the scheme of things.

Doug's background as an economist may prove useful here. Economics is all about the allocation of wealth to competing ends (ie, those that need or want it). We mean 'wealth' in the widest sense of the term: the scarce resources all people need to live and prosper. One of the challenges for society is how to grow that wealth to deal with the demands of a growing global population who have little wealth and a desire to raise standards of living from those that have a fair share already. This is apart from dealing with issues like how equitably is this to be done.

Technology may provide part of the solution. The individual and collective response of people is likely to be part of that solution too. This suggests that people will need to respond to stressors, to pressure and to challenge and that some form of resilient and positive response would be more than useful.

In economics there is a useful notion that helps us to take a considered view on such matters. Economists will talk about macro-economics (the big picture) and micro-economics (the specific picture). It is possible to examine the same issues from both perspectives and come to two conclusions that are not necessarily in agreement. The trick is to find solutions to the same issue that make sense at both levels.

The macro picture currently suggests that life will become more challenging. If we look at only India and China, there are 2.5 billion people who have nothing like the standard of living enjoyed in the West but who are now demanding an improvement in their own lives and are creating wealthy economies that will enable them to compete for those scarce resources previously enjoyed in the West. This has to create pressures. In work we need to become more productive and less wasteful; in education we must become more efficient and develop not just well-qualified graduates but people who are ready for life and the world of work; in society we need to examine where there is waste and to help those who are left behind to be confident about their place in society – minimizing the kind of helplessness that manifests itself as worklessness.

Returning to the first of the questions raised above, 'Is mental toughness more important now than ever before because life is more stressful now than ever before?' the answer is yes, no and maybe. It is unlikely that life has been more stressful over the past 50 years than in any time before then. Mortality rates and advances in health would support that. But it must generally be the case that life in previous times was more stressful. That probably led to people learning how to deal with stressors. That is, to survive they developed some degree of mental toughness. It is true that there are different stressors these days but it is likely to be the case that we have generally become less adept at dealing with crises, with stress and with challenge. Will life become more stressful? Probably. Will mental toughness become more important? Maybe it will.

A related development with which we are increasingly engaged is looking at issues previously treated as separate and 'joining the dots' to see a bigger picture. For example, the relationship between education and employment has often been a difficult one, with employers arguing that education systems don't provide them with suitable people and the educationalist arguing that employers don't value the education that is provided.

The common ground that is emerging is that of transition. In Switzerland the use of MTQ48 in a major business school was provoked by a change in its key goals, which added one entitled 'to produce graduates who are fit for the world of work' – not just well-qualified graduates. In Scotland a 2011 project found that FE colleges and employers could collaborate better to achieve the same end – and the key was assessing, understanding and developing mental toughness (in the employers as well as graduates!).

Parenting provides another very good example. It's always been understood to be important but it has been a very complex area. It has implications for education, for developing balanced people who contribute to society, in employability and in developing social cohesion. Each area has attempted to do something without always connecting with others with the same interests in this subject. Mental toughness can provide the common ground where this might be achieved. It cannot be the solution to the whole problem but it might provide an important contribution to making progress. Again, it is reassuring to see interest in this develop and what has surprised us is how often parents call the AQR offices to learn more about what we do.

To summarize this section:

- 'Do we think that mental toughness has value for society and its different components?' We do, and more importantly key players out there increasingly do too.
- 'Do we know how that will shape up?' We have our ideas but it is more important that we engage with practitioners and researchers out there and are guided by them. These are the people who understand the issues best and we see our role as developing people such as managers, coaches, trainers and specialists to work with them to solve problems.

- 'Are we suggesting that everyone should become mentally tough – what about the mentally sensitive?' The straight answer is 'no' although the macro and micro perspectives are also useful here.

From the macro perspective a healthy society is one that contains a rich mix of different people, types, personalities, etc. They all bring something to the party. At a micro level, if we look at individuals there is evidence that the more mentally tough do get more out of life than the mentally sensitive (although the latter can and do lead happy and fulfilling lives).

A fuller response might that there could be a case for shifting the mental toughness of the whole population a little to the right, which is not the same as saying that everyone should become mentally tough. If life generally is to be more challenging then improving our response to that should be beneficial.

As we know, it's not yet clear, when developing mental toughness, to what extent we are actually changing the mental toughness of individuals and to what extent we are simply equipping people with a better set of coping strategies. In practice, the distinction may not matter to the 'person on the street'.

The psychological perspective – where does mental toughness fit into the rest of the picture?

We are working with researchers and students at more than 20 universities and colleges around the world as well carrying out presentations to psychologists and academics. Again we are consistently asked the same or similar questions. 'How does mental toughness fit with other ideas emerging such as positive psychology and emotional intelligence?', 'Where is research on mental toughness heading?', 'The constructs appear in other models; how does mental toughness relate to these?' and so on.

Mental toughness is not and never can be a standalone concept. It is embedded in the beginnings of resilience research and is designed to be complementary to its research relatives. Self-efficacy, self-esteem, locus of control and many other valid and important concepts described in this book have a major role to play in understanding human behaviour.

In psychology a new model does not wipe away its predecessors. It builds on them and tries to add explanatory power. Our aim is to understand why people do what they do and how we can help them to do it better. Mental toughness has a 'new flavour', driven largely by its clear focus and applied origins.

We are always looking out for new connections. One of the major drivers in science is finding that, when asked a question, you answer, 'I don't know.' Nature, and researchers, hates a vacuum. That is how many of the projects have emerged. Of course, what often happens is that identifying an answer to a question simply generates five more questions – which is what research is all about.

From a research perspective there are two psychological drivers when developing our model, tools and techniques. First there is the need to investigate the linkages with other psychological, sociological and cultural perspectives. Secondly, there is the need to continue to try and validate our approach and to extend the validation process itself.

Looking at linkages, the two most high-profile ones are arguably with positive psychology and emotional intelligence. The positive psychology movement is predicated on the notion that the psychology profession has concentrated too much on the negatives. There is undoubtedly a case to answer here. Psychologists do appear to look for problems, then label them! However, we feel that you can't ignore the negatives. Many people do have significant challenges to deal with. Our work does not deal with people with psychological illness and those dealing with life's major problems, but rather focuses on how they deal with everyday, but non-trivial, problems.

Labelling this as 'not positive' depends on your perspective. We do not feel that stress, challenge and problem solving are necessarily a negative. Is stress bad? Obviously chronic stressors are, but many people find a 'buzz' from dealing with stressful situations, as long as they have the right tools. The challenge of earning a living, making a difference, feeding the family, is what gets people out of bed each day – often with a spring in their step even though the day will be challenging.

Burn-out is terrible, but so is brown-out

Brown-out is the feeling associated with slowly 'rusting away', being stuck in a mundane rut. When training we often pose the following hypothetical question. Imagine that, instead of the job you are doing now, which is interesting and requires real effort to do it well, you were offered a job stacking shelves in a supermarket. This would pay what you get now, without the need to take work home or work long hours at times. Who would take it? No one ever has.

Stress is both something that needs to be controlled and something that attracts people to it. Our approach is somewhat akin to the warning most of us got from our parents – you can't have any pudding unless you eat your vegetables. In our case the vegetables are the everyday problems and challenges we all face. The 'pudding' is life's good bit – the things that drive wellbeing. By dealing with the problems, we can develop our coping skills in the same way that eating vegetables provides vitamins and other essential nutrients.

In our work we have focused more on contentment than happiness. Happiness is more transient and ephemeral in nature. It can be materialistic and acquisitive. Contentment is about self-actualization – facing risk and facing challenge. Problems cannot be ignored, but they can be the root of growth.

The second burgeoning link is between mental toughness and emotional intelligence. What we can say for certain is that this link is not an obvious or straightforward one. Mentally tough individuals appear to experience the same affect intensity, but deal with it a different way. In other words it's not that they don't understand feelings – this understanding must be the core of any definition of emotional intelligence – but they might not act on them. Very recent work seems to show not only are mentally tough individuals not lower in emotional intelligence, they may indeed be higher.

It can be the case that many mentally tough individuals may underestimate the importance of the emotional world – but that is not the same as saying they don't understand it. When coaching high scorers we often discuss that they might bruise others by not fully understanding the needs of more-sensitive people. However, very sensitive individuals have a similar view, but reversed. They feel that feelings should be the dominant element in any interpersonal interaction. Neither ignoring feelings, nor allowing feelings to be the dominant force seems to be a sensible way forward. As always, it's shades of grey.

Finally in this section we would like to make a few brief comments on the validation process of the MTQ48. The well-proven validation model, relating to internal and external validity, is the core foundation of establishing the usefulness and credibility of a model or measurement instrument. We will continue to do this work. However, with advances in technology it is now possible to cheaply and effectively monitor what is going on 'inside' a person. We no longer have to rely solely on the subjective. The subjective viewpoint is always important; after all, as mentioned elsewhere in this book much of behaviour is driven by attributions. It's not 'what is' but rather 'what we think and feel is' happening that truly drives behaviour. Coupling this personal perspective with objective data provides a much more comprehensive picture of what is happening.

Our recent work relating to genetics and brain structure has been described in this book. The investigations are at an early stage, but already they are beginning to uncover some interesting facts. There is clearly a genetic component to mental toughness. This genetic component may be reflected in differential brain functioning. The findings relating to the greater activity in the 'reality-testing' parts of the brain are very thought-provoking. They complement the research papers showing that mentally tough individuals are more likely to adopt an active coping approach to the world.

Our model of mental toughness appears to be valid. Traditional psychometric and statistical analyses show this. The genetic and brain structure evidence allow a whole new level of validation to take place. We would expect to see these differences and we do!

Finally, the practitioner's needs – product development

There are three things that practitioners need: good products, good training and support materials, especially case studies. The emergence of a strong body of practitioners who understand the model and how to use it effectively is important to us. The more people use it well the more widely and more quickly the model and the measure will be adopted.

Products – the questionnaires

The MTQ48 was developed and launched in January 2003 and has served us very well. The design has stood the test of time and has proved popular. Like everyone and everything else it needs to evolve, especially if we are to meet most needs of most users. There is and will be a commitment to this activity.

Some development has taken place in translating the measure into more than 10 languages. That will continue. The reading age of the questionnaire and the reports was set originally at 11 years of age. We have introduced a bubble text option for those who do not understand the items. Hovering over an item can generate a small window with a short explanatory note. This is proving popular in some situations.

At the same time, although the core questionnaire has remained essentially unchanged, the expert report text database has changed. There are no versions with text specifically relevant for general occupational application, application with sports persons and application for those in secondary education. As demand arises, and there is an economic case for so doing, this will also continue.

The questionnaire has now been completed tens of thousands of times. These data are captured and together with other work we are at a stage where we will, in the next two or three years, begin to look at improving and developing the measure. Options under consideration are to create two basic formats – one for general application (which may be slightly longer than the current 48 items) and an abbreviated version for frequent use in schools and with young people. A more fundamental development being considered is the creation of a short (12–18 item) version for use in junior schools (age 8–10). There is a steadily growing demand for this as educationalists grasp its application in transition, especially from junior school to secondary school, where the transition can be very marked.

Training for users

There are two core sets of programmes available. One is for those who wish to administer and use the questionnaires and is principally focused on assessment and feedback. The other is for those who wish to be involved in mental toughness development work. Both are supported with workbooks and materials.

The programmes are currently being reviewed and in all cases extended. As research emerges and case studies appear this has added to the content of the programmes.

Development of support materials

This is possibly the most important area for development. Those engaged in the use of mental toughness as a concept, or indeed the measure, tend to look for two things: case studies and research.

There is a huge volume of case studies and research papers (many published in peer reviewed journals). These are important to practitioners as forms of evidence for the application of mental toughness as well as sources of inspiration for particular applications in which the practitioner is interested. They are also an important and valuable support and addition to this book. AQR makes these routinely available through its website.

However, the volume is growing so quickly that it can be overwhelming to the casual visitor to the site. There is a major commitment to:

- Structure, catalogue and organize the case study and research database.
- Develop processes that make the material more accessible to those interested in it – including creating abstracts and using IT to automatically issue updates to registered practitioners so that they are kept up to date.
- Encourage the development of case studies and research. Bona fide research is supported. This includes the formation of special interest groups.

Support materials include any form of materials that help the practitioner explain or apply the model. However, for most this means access to interventions and exercises. As with the case studies, there is a commitment now to:

- Catalogue and make available exercises and interventions useful for the practitioner. This includes collating over 100 exercises currently in use.
- Lead the development of new and engaging exercises and interventions – particularly in the development of attentional control.
- Support development groups, particularly those interested in specific applications.

What we currently have works well. Like the world we have described above, we can't and won't stand still: we can do it better still.

> It is not the strongest of the species that survive, or the most intelligent, but the one most responsive to change. (Charles Darwin)

What are we really saying about sensitive people?

We strongly suspect that lack of toughness is one of the key reasons why many people fail to reach their potential. It is clearly linked to physical and psychological health and wellbeing. The cost to the individual is potentially huge; the cost to society of under-achievement is perhaps beyond measure.

We can show that mentally tough individuals can function better in the world as it is today; this does not mean they are 'right'. Sensitive individuals have much to offer, however they seem seldom to be in a position to offer it. We find it hard to think of a senior politician who is not tough. Similarly, most leaders in business and sport are mentally tough. Those in charge set the parameters. This is often not done with malicious intent; rather most of us find it difficult to see the world from other perspectives.

It is important that the more sensitive amongst us are supported and listened to. It is hoped that by providing a toolkit of toughness interventions we can help this process. These are not designed to necessarily change the 'core person' but allow them to prosper in a potentially hostile environment.

True diversity is predicated on a) understanding yourself, b) respecting yourself, c) understanding others, and d) respecting others. We hope that understanding your mental toughness allows, in some small way, for this mutual respect to flourish.

Ultimately our presentation of mental toughness is emerging as a concept, an approach and a measure that achieves two goals which are not always seen as mutually compatible. These are helping individuals, groups and society to improve performance (to create that wealth we need for growth) whilst at the same time indicating how wellbeing can be enhanced through the same approach.

REFERENCES

Ackerman, P L (2011) *Cognitive Fatigue: Multidisciplinary perspectives on current research and future applications,* American Psychological Association, Washington, DC

AQR (2005) *MTQ48 Technical Manual,* AQR Ltd, Chester

Astrand, P and Rodahl, K (1986) *Textbook of Work Physiology,* McGraw-Hill, New York, p 238

Averill, J R (1973) Personal control over aversive stimuli and its relationship to stress, *Psychological Bulletin,* 80, 286–303

Bandura, A (1977) Self-efficacy: Towards a unifying theory of behavioural change, *Psychological Review,* 84, 191–215

Bandura, A (1986) *Social Foundations of Thought and Action: A social cognitive theory,* Prentice Hall, Englewood Cliffs, NJ

Bandura, A (1997) *Self-efficacy: The exercise of control,* Freeman, New York

Bandura, A (1997) *Self-efficacy in Changing Societies,* Cambridge University Press, Cambridge

Bell, J and Saltikov, J A (2000) Mitchell's Relaxation Technique: Is it effective?, *Physiotherapy,* 86, 473–8

Bloom, B S (ed) (1985) *Developing Talent in Young People,* Ballantine, New York

Borg, G (1978) Subjective aspects of physical and mental load, *Ergonomics,* 21 (3), 215–20

Borg, M G and Riding, G (1993) Occupational stress in British educational settings: A review, *Educational Psychology,* 10 (2), 103–26

Bourgeois, A E, Meyers, M C and LeUnes, A (2009) The sport inventory for pain: Empirical and confirmatory factorial validity, *Journal of Sport Behavior,* 32, 19–35

Boyce, C J, Wood, A M and Brown, D A (2010) The dark side of conscientiousness: Conscientious people experience greater drops in life satisfaction following unemployment, *Journal of Research in Personality,* 44, 535–39

Brennan, S (1998) Mental toughness wins out, *Christian Science Monitor,* 90 (173)

Bresser, F and Wilson, C (2010) in (ed) J Passmore, *Excellence in Coaching: The industry guide,* Kogan Page, London, pp 9–26

Brewer, J and Davis, J (1995) Applied psychology of rugby league, *Sports Medicine,* 13, 129–35

Bull, S, Shambrook, C, James, W and Brooks, J (2005) Towards an understanding of mental toughness in elite English cricketers, *Journal of Applied Sport Psychology,* 17, 209–27

Burger, J M and Cooper, H M (1979) The desirability of control, *Motivation and Emotion,* 3, 381–93

Butler, R J (1989) Psychological preparation of Olympic boxers, in (eds) J Kremer and W Crawford, *The Psychology of Sport: Theory and practice,* British Psychological Association, Leicester, pp 78–84

Butler, R J and Hardy, L (1992) The performance profile: Theory and application, *The Sport Psychologist,* 6, 253–64

Cannon, W B (1929) Organization for physiological homeostasis, *Physiological Review,* 9, 399–431

Chelladurai, P and Saleh, S (1980) Dimensions of leader behavior in sports: Development of a leadership scale, *Journal of Sport Psychology,* 2, 34–45

CIPD (2007) *Helping People Learn: Overview and update* (online), Chartered Institute of Personnel and Development, London

Clark, E H (1980) An analysis of occupational stress factors as perceived by public school teachers, *Dissertation Abstracts International,* 41, 10

Clough, P, Earle, K and Sewell, D (2002) Mental toughness: the concept and its measurement, in (ed) I Cockerill, *Solutions in Sport Psychology,* Thomson, London, pp 32–43

Clough, P J, Earle, K and Earle, F (2005) Can training 'toughen you up'? An experimental approach to training evaluation, *BPS Division of Occupational Psychology: Annual Conference Published Proceedings,* 131–2

Clough, P, Earl, K and Strycharczyk, D (2008) Developing resilience through coaching, in (ed) J Passmore, *Psychometrics in Coaching,* Kogan Page, London

Clough, P J, Newton, S, Bruen, P, Earle, F, Earle, K, Benuzzi, F, Gardini, S, Huber, A, Lui, F and Venneri, A (2010) Mental toughness and brain structure, Poster presented at the 16th Annual Meeting of the Organisation for Human Brain Mapping, June 6–10, Barcelona

Cohen, J (1988) *Statistical Power Analysis for the Behavioural Sciences,* 2nd edn, Erlbaum, Hillsdale, NJ

Connaughton, D, Wadey, R, Hanton, S and Jones, G (2008) The development and maintenance of mental toughness: perceptions of elite performers, *Journal of Sport Sciences,* 26, 83–95

Contrada, R J, Dimsdale, J, Levy, L and Weiss, T (1991) Effects of isoproterenol on T-wave amplitude and heart rate: A dose-response study, *Psychophysiology* 28, 458–62

Coulter, T, Mallett, C and Gucciardi, D (2010) Understanding mental toughness in Australian soccer: Perceptions of players, parents and coaches, *Journal of Sports Sciences,* 28, 699–716

Cox, E, Bachkirova, T and Clutterbuck, D (eds) (2010) *The Complete Handbook of Coaching,* Sage, London

Cox, R H (1998) *Sport Psychology: Concepts and applications,* McGraw-Hill, Boston, MA

Coyne, I J, Clough, P J, Alexander, T and Clemment, G (2006) Workplace bullying the role of mental toughness, in *British Psychological Society, Division of Occupational Psychology, Annual Conference Book of Proceedings,* BPS, London, pp 107–10

Crust, L (2008) A review and conceptual re-examination of mental toughness: Implications for future researchers, *Personality and Individual Differences,* 45, 576–83

Crust, L (2009) The relationship between mental toughness and affect intensity, *Personality and Individual Differences,* 47, 959–63

Crust, L and Azadi, K (2009) Leadership preferences of mentally tough athletes, *Personality and Individual Differences,* 47, 326–30

Crust, L and Azadi, K (2010) Mental toughness and athletes' use of psychological strategies, *European Journal of Sport Science,* 10, 43–51

Crust, L and Clough, P J (2005) Relationship between mental toughness and physical endurance, *Perceptual and Motor Skills,* 100, 192–4

Crust, L and Clough, P J (2011) Developing mental toughness: from research to practice, *Journal of Sport Psychology in Action*, **2** (1), 21–32

Crust, L and Keegan, R (2010) Mental toughness and attitudes to risk-taking, *Personality and Individual Differences*, 49,164–8

Crust, L and Swann, C (2011) Comparing two measures of mental toughness, *Personality and Individual Differences*, 50, 217–21

Crust, L, Nesti, M and Littlewood, M (2010) A cross-sectional analysis of mental toughness in a professional football academy, *Athletic Insight Journal*, 2, 165–74

Csikszentmihalyi, M (1990) *Flow: The psychology of optimal experience*, Harper and Row, New York

Curtis Management Group (1998) *Motivation Lombardi Style*, Celebrating Excellence Publishing, Lombard, IL, p 20

Dale, G A and Wrisberg, C A (1996) The use of a performance profiling technique in a team setting: getting the athletes and coaches on the 'same page', *The Sport Psychologist*, 10, 261–77

deCharms, R and Carpenter, V (1968) Measuring motivation in culturally disadvantaged school children, in (eds) H J Klausmeirer and G T O'Hearn, *Research and Development Toward the Improvement of Education*, Educational Research Services, Madison, WI

de Haan, E (2008) *Relational Coaching: Journeys towards mastering one-to-one learning*, Wiley, Chichester

Deloitte Foundation (2007) *Employability Skills: Supporting young people*, Deloitte and Touche, London

Dembkowski, S, Eldridge, F and Hunter, I (2006) *The Seven Steps of Effective Executive Coaching*, Thorogood, London

Dienstbier, R A (1989) Arousal and physiological toughness: Implications for mental and physical health, *Psychological Review*, **96** (1), 84–100

Dienstbier, R A (1991) Behavioral correlates of sympathoadrenal reactivity: The toughness model, *Medicine and Science in Sports and Exercise*, **23** (7), 846–52

Downey, M (2003) *Effective Coaching*, Cengage Learning, Florence, KY

Dyer, J G and McGuinness, T M (1996) Resilience: analysis of the concept, *Archives of Psychiatric Nursing*, **X** (5) (October), 276–82

Earle, F (2004) The construct of psychological fatigue: a psychometric and experimental analysis, Unpublished PhD dissertation, University of Hull

Easterbrook, J A (1959) The effect of emotion on cue utilization and the organisation of behaviour, *Psychological Review*, 66, 183–201

Ellis, A (1980) Rational-emotive therapy and cognitive behavior therapy: Similarities and differences, *Cognitive Therapy & Research*, 4, 325–40

Evers, W J, Brouwers, A and Tomic, W (2006) A Quasi-experimental study on management coaching effectiveness, *Consulting Psychology Journal: Practice and Research*, **58** (3), 174–82

Eysenck, H J (1967) *The Biological Basis of Personality*, Thomas, Springfield, IL

Fazey, J and Hardy, L (1988) *The Inverted U-hypothesis: A catastrophe for sport psychology?*, British Association of Sports Sciences Monograph No 1, The National Coaching Foundation, Leeds

Ferrari, J R and Tice, D M (2000) Procrastination as a self-handicap for men and women: A task-avoidance strategy in a laboratory setting, *Journal of Research in Personality*, 34, 73–83

Frankenhaeuser, M (1971) Behavior and circulating catecholamines, *Brain Research*, 31 (August 20), 241–62

Funk, F C (1992) Hardiness: A review of theory and research, *Health Psychology,* **11** (5), 335–45

Galluci, N T (2008) *Sport Psychology: Performance enhancement, performance inhibition, individuals and teams,* Psychology Press, New York

Glaser, B and Strauss, A (1967) *The Discovery of Grounded Theory,* Aldine, Chicago, IL

Golby, J and Sheard, M (2004) Mental toughness and hardiness at different levels of rugby league, *Personality and Individual Differences,* 37, 933–42

Golby, J and Sheard, M (2006) The relationship between genotype and positive psychological development in national-level swimmers, *European Psychologist,* 11, 143–8

Golby, J, Sheard, M and Lavallee, D (2003) A cognitive behavioural analysis of mental toughness in national rugby league football teams, *Perceptual and Motor Skills,* 96, 455–62

Goleman, D J (1996) *Emotional Intelligence: Why it can matter more than IQ,* Bantam Books, New York

Gould, D, Dieffenbach, K and Moffett, A (2002) Psychological talent and its development in Olympic champions, *Journal of Applied Sport Psychology,* 14, 177–210

Grant, A M (2009) *Workplace, Executive and Life Coaching: An annotated bibliography from the behavioural science and business literature,* Coaching Psychology Unit, University of Sydney, Australia

Green, L S, Oades, L and Grant, A M (2006) Cognitive-behavioral, solution focused life coaching: Enhancing goal striving, wellbeing, and hope, *Journal of Positive Psychology,* **1** (3), 142–9

Green, L S, Grant, A M and Rynsaardt, J (2007) Evidence-based life coaching for senior high school students: Building hardiness and hope, *International Coaching Psychology Review,* **2** (1), 24–32

Gucciardi, D and Gordon, S (2009) Development and preliminary validation of the Cricket Mental Toughness Inventory (CMTI), *Journal of Sports Sciences,* 27, 1293–1310

Gucciardi, D, Gordon, S and Dimmock, J (2008) Towards an understanding of mental toughness in Australian football, *Journal of Applied Sport Psychology,* 20, 261–81

Gucciardi, D, Gordon, S and Dimmock, J A (2009a) Development and preliminary validation of a mental toughness inventory for Australian football, *Psychology of Sport and Exercise,* 10, 201–9

Gucciardi, D, Gordon, S and Dimmock, J (2009b) Evaluation of a mental toughness training programme for youth-aged Australian footballer: 1 A quantitative analysis, *Journal of Applied Sport Psychology,* 21, 307–23

Hackman, J R and Oldham, G R (1976) Motivation through the design of work: Test the theory, *Organisational Behaviour and Human Performance,* 16, 250–79

Hanin, Y L (1980) *A Study of Anxiety in Sports,* Movement, Ithaca, NY

Hanin, Y L (1986) *State and Trait Anxiety Research on Sports in the USSR,* Hemisphere, Washington, DC

Hanin, Y L (1997) Emotions and athletic performance: Individual zones of optimal functioning, *European Yearbook of Sport Psychology,* 1, 29–72

Hardy, L and Parfitt, G (1991) A catastrophe model of anxiety and performance, *British Journal of Psychology,* 82, 163–78

Hardy, L, Parfitt, G and Pates, J (1994) Performance catastrophes in sport: A test of the hystereris hypothesis, *Journal of Sport Sciences,* 12, 327–34

Hawkins, P and Smith, N (2006) *Coaching, Mentoring and Organizational Consultancy*, Open University, Maidenhead

Heider, F (1944) Social perception and phenomenological causality, *Psychological Review*, 51, 358–74

Heider, F (1958) *The Psychology of Interpersonal Relations*, Wiley, New York

Hiroto, D S and Seligman, M E P (1975) Generality of learned helplessness in man, *Journal of Personality and Social Psychology*, 31, 311–27

HMIe (2009) *Analysis of HMIe Reviews of Quality and Standards in Scotland's Colleges: Academic years 2004/05 to 2007/08*, Scottish Funding Council, Edinburgh

HMIe (2011) *Adam Smith College, A report by HM Inspectors on behalf of the Scottish Further Education Funding Council*, Her Majesty's Inspectorate of Education, Livingstone

Hockey, G R J (1993) Cognitive-energetical control mechanisms in the management of work demands and psychological health, in (eds) A D Baddeley and L Weiskrantz, *Attention, Selection, Awareness and Control: A tribute to Donald Broadbent*, Oxford University Press, Oxford, pp 328–45

Hockey, G R J (1997) Compensatory control in the regulation of human performance under stress and high workload: a cognitive-energetical framework, *Biological Psychology*, 45, 73–93

Holahan, C J and Moos, R H (1990) Life stressors, resistance factors, and improved psychological functioning: An extension of the stress resistance paradigm, *Journal of Personality and Social Psychology*, 58, 909–17

Holloway, S D (1988) Concepts of ability and effort in Japan and the United States, *Review of Educational Research*, 58 (3), 327–45

Holman, D (2005) Employee wellbeing in call centres, *Human Resource Management Journal*, 12, 35–50

Horsburgh, V, Schermer, J, Veselka, L and Vernon, P (2009) A behavioral genetic study of mental toughness and personality, *Personality and Individual Differences*, 46, 100–105

Houlihan, M (2004) Tensions and variations in call centre management strategies, *Human Resource Management Journal*, 12, 67–85

HSE (2003) *Wellbeing in Call Centres*, HSE, London

Hull, C L (1943) *Principles of Behaviour*, Appleton-Century-Crofts, New York

Hull, C L (1951) *Essentials of Behaviour*, Appleton-Century-Crofts, New York

Jackson, R and Watkin, C (2004) The resilience inventory: Seven essential skills for overcoming life's obstacles and determining happiness, *Selection and Development Review*, 20 (6), 13–17

Jackson, S A (1992) Athletes in flow: A qualitative investigation of flow states in elite figure skaters, *Journal of Applied Sport Psychology*, 4, 161–80

Jackson, S A (1995) Factors influencing the occurrence of flow state in elite athletes, *Journal of Applied Sport Psychology*, 7, 138–66

Jackson, S A (1996) Toward a conceptual understanding of the flow experience in elite athletes, *Research Quarterly for Exercise and Sport*, 67, 76–90

Jackson, S A and Marsh, H W (1996) Development and validation of a scale to measure optimal experience: The flow state scale, *Journal of Sport and Exercise Psychology*, 18, 17–35

Jones, C M (1982) Mental toughness, *World Bowls*, 30–31

Jones, G (1993) The role of performance profiling in cognitive behaviour interventions in sport, *The Sport Psychologist*, 7, 160–72

Jones, G and Hanton, S (1996) Interpretation of competitive anxiety symptoms and goal attainment expectancies, *Journal of Sport and Exercise Psychology*, 18, 144–57

Jones, G and Hanton, S (2001) Pre-competitive feeling states and directional anxiety interpretations, *Journal of Sports Sciences*, 19, 385–95

Jones, G, Hanton, S and Connaughton, D (2002) What is this thing called mental toughness? An investigation of elite sport performers, *Journal of Applied Sport Psychology*, 14, 205–18

Jones, G, Hanton, S and Connaughton, D (2007) A framework of mental toughness in the world's best performers, *The Sport Psychologist*, 21, 243–64

Kaiseler, M, Polman, R and Nicholls, A (2009) Mental toughness, stress, stress appraisal, coping and coping effectiveness in sport, *Personality and Individual Differences*, 47, 728–33

Karasek, R A (1979) Job demands, job decision latitude, and mental strain: implications for job redesign, *Administrative Science Quarterly*, 24, 288–308

Kline, N (1999) *Time to Think*, Cassell, London

Kobasa, S C (1979) Stressful life events, personality, and health: an inquiry into hardiness, *Journal of Personality and Social Psychology*, 37 (1), 1–11

Kobasa, S C, Maddi, S R and Kahn, S (1982) Hardiness and health: A prospective study, *Journal of Personality and Social Psychology*, 42, 168–77

Kobasa, S C, Maddi, S R, Puccetti, M C and Zola, M A (1985) Effectiveness of hardiness, exercise, and social support as resources against illness, *Journal of Psychosomatic Research*, 29, 525–33

Larsen, R (1984) Theory and measurement of affect intensity as an individual difference characteristic, *Dissertation Abstracts International*, 5, 2297B (University microfilms No 84-22112)

Larsen, R, Diener, E and Cropanzano, R (1987) Cognitive operations associated with individual differences in affect intensity, *Journal of Personality and Social Psychology*, 53, 767–74

Lazarus, R S (1966) *Psychological Stress and the Coping Process*, McGraw-Hill, New York

Lazarus, R S (1968) Emotions and adaptation: Conceptual and empirical relations, in (ed) W J Arnold, *Nebraska Symposium on Motivation*, 16, pp 175–266, University of Nebraska Press, Lincoln

Lazarus, R S (1991) From psychological stress to the emotions: A history of changing outlooks, *Annual Review of Psychology*, 44, 1–21

Lazarus, R S (1993) Coping theory and research: Past, present, and future, *Psychosomatic Medicine*, 55, 234–47

Lazarus, R S and Cohen, F (1973) Active coping processes, coping dispositions, and recovery from surgery, *Psychosomatic Medicine*, 35, 375–89

Lazarus, R S and Cohen, J B (1977) Environment stress, in (eds) L Altman and J F Wohlwill, *Human Behavior and the Environment: Current theory and research*, Vol 2, Plenum, New York, pp 89–127

Lazarus, R S and Folkman, S (1984) *Stress Appraisal and Coping*, Springer, New York

Lazarus, R S and Folkman, S (1987) Transactional theory and research on emotions and coping, *European Journal of Personality*, 1, 141–70

Lazarus, R S and Launier, R (1978) Stress related transactions between person and environment, in (eds) L A Pervin and M Lewis, *Perspectives in International Psychology*, Plenum, New York, pp 287–327

Levy, A, Polman, R, Clough, P, Marchant, D and Earle, K (2006) Mental toughness as a determinant of beliefs, pain, and adherence in sport injury rehabilitation, *Journal of Sports Rehabilitation,* 15, 246–54

Locke, E A (1968) Towards a theory of task motivation and incentives, *Organisational Behaviour and Human Performance,* 3, 157–89

Locke, E A and Latham, G P (1990) *A Theory of Goal Setting and Task Performance,* Prentice Hall, Englewood Cliffs, NJ

Locke, E A and Latham, G P (2002) Building a practically useful theory of goal setting and task motivation: A 35-year odyssey, *American Psychologist,* 57, 701–17

Locke, E A, Shaw, K N, Saari, L M and Latham, G P (1981) Goal setting and task performance (1969–1980), *Psychological Bulletin,* 96, 125–52

Loehr, J E (1982) *Achieving Athletic Excellence: Mental toughness training for sport,* Forum Publishing Company, pp 58–70

Loehr, J E (1986) *Mental Toughness Training for Sports,* Stephen Greene Press, Lexington, MA

Loehr, J E (1995) *The New Toughness Training for Sports: Achieving athletic excellence,* Plume Publishers, New York:

Luthans, F, Avey, J B and Patera J L (2008) Experimental analysis of a web-based training intervention to develop positive psychological capital, *The Academy of Management Learning and Education,* 7, 209–21

McCleary, R A (2007) The nature of Galvanic Skin Response, *Psychological Bulletin,* 47 (2), 97–117

McClelland, D C (1962) Business drive and national achievement, *Harvard Business Review,* July–August, 99–112

McCrae, R R and Costa, P T, Jr (1987) Validation of the five-factor model of personality across instruments and observers, *Journal of Personality and Social Psychology,* 52, 81–90

Maddi, S R (1987) Hardiness training at Illinois Bell Telephone, in (ed) J P Opatz, *Health Promotion Evaluation,* National Wellness Institute, Stevens Point, WI, pp 101–5

Maddi, S R (1991) The personality construct of hardiness, Unpublished manuscript University of California, Irvine

Maddi, S R (2004) Hardiness: An operationalization of existential courage, *Journal of Humanistic Psychology,* 44 (3), 279–98

Maddi, S R and Hess, M J (1992) Personality hardiness and success in basketball, *International Journal of Sport Psychology,* 23, 360–68

Maddi, S R and Khoshaba, D M (2001) *Personal Views Survey,* 3rd edn, rev, The Hardiness Institute, Newport Beach, CA

Maddi, S R, Hoover, M and Kobasa, S C (1982) Alienation and exploratory behaviour, *Journal of Personality and Social Psychology,* 42 (5), 884–90

Maddi, S R, Kahn, S and Maddi, K L (1998) The effectiveness of hardiness training, *Consulting Psychology Journal: Practice and Research,* 50, 78–86

Marchant, D, Polman, R, Clough, P, Jackson, J, Levy, A and Nicholls, A (2009) Mental toughness: Managerial and age differences, *Journal of Managerial Psychology,* 24, 428–37

Martens, R, Vealey, R S and Burton, D (1990) *Competitive Anxiety in Sport,* Human Kinetics, Champaign, IL

Maslach, C (1976) Burned-out, *Human Behavior,* 5 (9), 16–22

Mento, A J, Steele, R P and Karren, R J (1987) A meta-analytic study of the effects of goal setting on task performance: 1966–1984, *Organizational Behaviour and Human Decision Processes,* 39, 52–83

Middleton, S C, Marsh, H W, Martin, A J, Richards, G E, Savis, J, Perry, C and Brown, R (2004) The Psychological Performance Inventory: Is the mental toughness test tough enough?, *International Journal of Sport Psychology*, 35, 91–108

Miller, W R and Seligman, M E P (1975) Depression and learned helplessness in man, *Journal of Abnormal Psychology*, 84, 228–38

Mitchell, L (1977) *Simple Relaxation. The Mitchell method for easing tension*, Butler and Tanner, London

Mitchell, L (1990) *Simple Relaxation. The Mitchell method for easing tension*, new edn, John Murray, London

Moss, G E (1973) *Illness, Immunity, and Social Interaction*, Wiley, New York

Murray, H A (1938) *Explorations in Personality*, Oxford University Press, New York

Muscio, B (1921) Is a fatigue test possible?, *British Journal of Psychology*, 12, 13–46

Nesti, M (2004) *Existential Psychology and Sport: Theory and application*, Routledge, London

Nesti, M (2010) *Psychology in Football*, Routledge, London

Nicholls, A and Polman, R (2007) Coping in sport: A systematic review, *Journal of Sport Sciences*, 25, 11–31

Nicholls, A, Polman, R, Levy, A and Backhouse, S (2008) Mental toughness, optimism, and coping among athletes, *Personality and Individual Differences*, 44, 1182–92

Nicholls, A, Polman, R, Levy, A and Backhouse, S (2009) Mental toughness in sport: Achievement level, gender, age, experience, and sport type differences, *Personality and Individual Differences*, 47, 73–5

Palmer, S and Whybrow, A (eds) (2007) *Handbook of Coaching Psychology: A guide for practitioners*, Routledge, London

Passmore, J (ed) (2008) *Psychometrics in Coaching*, Kogan Page, London

Passmore, J (ed) (2010) *Excellence in Coaching: The industry guide*, 2nd edn, Kogan Page, London

Peddicord, K (1991) Strategies for promoting stress reduction and relaxation, *Nursing Clinics in North America*, 26, 867–74

Peterson, C and Barrett, L C (1987) Explanatory style and academic performance among university freshmen, *Journal of Personality and Social Psychology*, 53, 603–7

Rhodewalt, F and Aguostsdottir, S (1984) On the relationship of hardiness to the Type A behavior pattern: Perception of life events versus coping with life events, *Journal of Research in Personality*, 18, 212–23

Rogers, C (1957) The necessary and sufficient conditions of therapeutic personality change, *Journal of Consulting Clinical Psychology*, 21 (2), 95–103

Rotter, J B (1966) Generalised expectancies for internal versus external control of reinforcement, *Psychological Monographs: General and Applied*, 80 (1), all of No. 609

Rush, M C, Schoel, W A and Barnard, S M (1995) Psychological resiliency in the public sector: hardiness and pressure for change, *Journal of Vocational Behavior*, 46, 17–39

Rutter, M (1985) Resilience in the face of adversity: Protective factors and resistance in psychiatric disorder, *British Journal of Psychiatry*, 147 (1), 598–611

Salt, V L and Kerr, K M (1997) Mitchell's Simple Physiological Relaxation and Jacobson's Progressive Relaxation Techniques: A comparison, *Physiotherapy*, 83, (4), 200–207

Schwarz, R S (1975) Another look at immunologic surveillance, *New England Journal of Medicine*, 293, 181–4

Seligman, M E P (1969) For helplessness: Can we immunize the weak?, *Psychology Today*, June, 42–5

Seligman, M E P (1972) Learned helplessness, *Annual Review of Medicine*, 23, 407–12

Seligman, M E P (1973) Fall into helplessness, *Psychology Today*, 7, 43–8

Seligman, M E P (1974) Depression and learned helplessness, in (eds) R J Friedman and M M Katz, *The Psychology of Depression: Contemporary theory and research*, Winston-Wiley, New York

Seligman, M E P (1975) *Helplessness*, Freeman, San Francisco, CA

Seligman, M E P and Beagley, G (1975) Learned helplessness in the rat, *Journal of Comparative and Physiological Psychology*, 88, 534–41

Seligman, M E P and Groves, D (1970) Non-transient learned helplessness, *Psychonomic Science*, 19, 191–2

Seligman, M E P, Maier, S F and Solomon, R L (1971) Consequences of unpredictable and uncontrollable trauma, in (ed) F R Brush, *Aversive Conditioning and Learning*, Academic Press, New York

Selye, H (1936) A syndrome produced by diverse agents, *Nature*, 138 (32), 112–31

Selye, H (1950) *Stress*, Acta, Montreal

Selye, H (1976) *The Stress of Life*, 2nd edn, McGraw-Hill, New York

Selye, H (1983) The stress concept: Past, present, and future, in (ed) C L Cooper, *Stress Research*, Wiley, New York, pp 1–20

Sheard, M (2009, 2010) *Mental Toughness: The mindset behind sporting achievement*, Routledge, London

Sheard, M and Golby, J (2006) Effect of psychological skills training program on swimming performance and positive psychological development, *International Journal of Sport and Exercise Psychology*, 2, 7–24

Sheard, M, Golby, J and Van Wersch, A (2009) Progress towards construct validation of the Sports Mental Toughness Questionnaire (SMTQ), *European Journal of Psychological Assessment*, 25, 186–93

Sloman, M (2007) *The Changing World of the Trainer: Emerging good practice*, Elsevier, Oxford

Spence, G and Grant, A M (2007) Professional and peer life coaching and the enhancement of goal striving and well-being: An exploratory study, *Journal of Positive Psychology*, 2 (3), 185–94

Spence, J T and Helmreich, R L (1983) Achievement-related motives and behaviours, in (ed) J T Spence, *Achievement and Achievement Motives: Psychological and sociological approaches*, W H Freeman, San Francisco, CA, pp 7–74

SPICe (2010) *Widening Access to Higher Education: Policy in Scotland*, Scottish Parliament Information Centre, Edinburgh

Spielberger, C D (1983) *Manual for the State Trait Anxiety Inventory*, Consulting Psychologists Press, Palo Alto, CA

Strycharczyk, D and Brause, J (2010) *The Coaching Workbook: Using the GROW model with mental toughness*, AQR Ltd, Chester

Taylor, A H and May, S (1996) Threat and coping appraisal as determinants of compliance with sports injury rehabilitation: an application of protection motivation theory, *Journal of Sports Science*, 14, 472–82

Tenenbaum, G (1984) A note on the measurement and relationships of physiological and psychological components of anxiety, *International Journal of Sport Psychology*, 15, 88–97

Thelwell, R, Weston, N and Greenlees, I (2005) Defining and understanding mental toughness within soccer, *Journal of Applied Sport Psychology*, 17, 326–32

Thelwell, R, Such, B, Weston, N, Such, J and Greenlees, I (2010) Developing mental toughness: Perceptions of elite female gymnasts, *International Journal of Sport and Exercise Psychology*, 8, 170–88

Thomas, P, Murphy, S and Hardy, L (1999) Test of performance strategies: Development and preliminary validation of a comprehensive measure of athletes' psychological skills, *Journal of Sports Sciences*, 17, 697–711

Thompson, W C and Wendt, J C (1995) Contribution of hardiness and school climate to alienation experienced by student teachers, *Journal of Educational Research*, 88, 269–74

Thomson, B (2009) *Don't Just Do Something, Sit There*, Chandos, Oxford

Thomson, C (2003) Further education in Scotland, in (eds) T K G Bryce and W M Humes, *Scottish Education*, Edinburgh University Press, Edinburgh

Topf, M (1989) Personality hardiness, occupational stress, and burnout in critical care nurses, *Research in Nursing and Health*, 12, 179–86

UKCES (2010) *Towards Ambition 2020: Skills, jobs, growth for Scotland*, United Kingdom Commission on Employment and Skills, London

Van Yperen, N (2009) Why some make it and others do not: Identifying psychological factors that predict career success in professional adult soccer, *The Sport Psychologist*, 23, 317–29

Wallace, C (2000) The sacrificial HR strategy in call centres, *International Journal of Service Industry Management*, 11, 174–84

Weatherley, C (2006) The Critical Skills Programme: Rising above critical levels, *CPD Update Bulletin*, September (http://www teachingexpertise com/articles/critical-skills-programme-risingabove-critical-levels-643)

Weiner, B (1972) *Theories of Motivation: From mechanics to cognition*, Markham, Chicago, IL

Weiss, J M, Glazer, H I, Pohorecky, L A, Brick, J and Miller, N B (1975) Effects of chronic exposure to stressors on avoidance-escape behavior and on brain norepinephrine, *Psychosomatic Medicine*, 37, 153–60

Westman, M (1990) The relationship between stress and performance: The moderating effect of hardiness, *Human Performance*, 3, 141–55

Whitmore, J (2002) *Coaching for Performance*, 3rd edn, Nicholas Brealey, London

Wickens, C D (1986) The effects of control dynamics on performance, in (eds) K R Boff, L Kaufman and J P Thomas, *Handbook of Perception and Performance* (Vol II), Wiley, New York, pp 39–60

Williams, R M (1988) The US Open character test: Good strokes help but the most individualistic of sports is ultimately a mental game, *Psychology Today*, 22, 60–62

Williams, J M and Krane, V (1993) Psychological characteristics of peak performance, in (ed) J M Williams, *Applied Sport Psychology*, 2nd edn, Mayfield, Palo Alto, CA, pp 137–47

Wiseman, R (2003) *The Luck Factor*, Random House, London

Yerkes, R M and Dodson, J D (1908) The relationship of strength of stimulus to rapidity of habit formation, *Journal of Comparative Neurology and Psychology*, 18, 459–82

Index